P9-APX-730

This card summarizes the most important stuff about DOS, for your handy quick reference. Keep this card by your computer, right next to the bowl of pretzels.

Facts Everyone Assumes You Know

▼ The *DOS prompt* looks like C> or C:\>.

▼ To start a program, you type the program's name and press Enter.

▼ If you make a mistake while typing, use the Backspace key to correct the mistake.

▼ To use DOS commands, you type them and press Enter.

What's in a Name?

DOS file names have two parts, the file name (up to 8 characters) and the optional extension (up to 3 characters). The two are separated by a period, as in JUNK.DOC or TRASH.WK1.

File names can't contain spaces. They also can't contain any of these: . " / \ [ ] : * | < > + = ; , ?

Directory Assistance

The root directory symbol is a backslash (\ ). C:\ indicates the root directory of drive C.

The root directory of drive C probably contains one or more other directories (called *subdirectories*). Subdirectories have names preceded by a backslash, like \DOCS. A subdirectory can, in turn, have its own subdirectories. \DOCS\HATEMAIL is a subdirectory of \DOCS. Subdirectory names never end in backslashes.

▼ To change to a subdirectory, type **CD** followed by a space and the subdirectory name. Then press Enter.

▼ To go back to the root directory, type **CD** and press Enter.

▼ A *path name* is a file name that includes the file's subdirectory location (as in \DOCS\HATEMAIL\JUNK.DOC). Note that you have to put a backslash before the file's name (\JUNK.DOC).

▼ A *filespec* tells all about a file's location, including disk and name (as in C:\DOCS\HATEMAIL\JUNK.DOC).

Go Wild

The ? wild card matches any *single* character.

The * wild card matches any character.

. (star-dot-star) matches any file name.

Key into This

To...	Press this...
Cancel a DOS command	Ctrl-C or Ctrl-Break
Pause a long directory list	Ctrl-S or Pause
Print the screen	Prt Scrn
Turn the printer on/off	Ctrl-P

File It Yourself

To...	Type this...
Copy a file to drive A	COPY *yourfile* A:
Copy all DOC files to drive A	COPY *.DOC A:
Delete a file	DEL *yourfile*
Delete all BAK files	DEL *.BAK
Delete all files (caution!)	DEL *.*
Display a directory list by page	DIR /p
Display a directory list	DIR
Display a file's contents	TYPE *yourfile*
Display a wide directory list	DIR /w
Duplicate a file	COPY *yourfile newfile*
Move a file (DOS 6 only) to A:	MOVE *yourfile* A:
Rename a file	REN *yourfile newfile*

Rescue Squad

To...	Type this...
Undelete a file	UNDELETE
Unformat a disk in drive A	UNFORMAT A:
Get help on a DOS command	HELP *command name*
Find a file	DIR *yourfile* /s

When DOS Talks Back

When DOS says...	Do this...
Bad command or file name	Check your spelling and try again, or change to the directory that contains the file.
File not found	DOS can't find a file by that name. Check your spelling and try again.
Non-system disk or disk error	Take the disk out of drive A and press Ctrl-Alt-Del.
Not ready reading Drive A [or B]	Put a disk in the drive, close the latch, and press R for Retry.
Too many parameters	You probably added a space to the command. Check and type again.

The 5 Biggest No-Nos

▼ Don't delete C:\CONFIG.SYS or C:\AUTOEXEC.BAT.

▼ Don't take a disk out of the drive when the light's on.

▼ Don't exit programs by just switching off the power.

▼ Don't leave a disk in drive A when you shut off your system.

▼ Don't type **FORMAT C:**.

I HATE

DOS

Bryan Pfaffenberger

Shoe ®&©, 1993*, Tribune Media Services, Inc. All Rights Reserved.

I Hate DOS

Copyright © 1993 by Que® Corporation

All rights reserved. Printed in the United States of America. No part of this book may be used or reproduced in any form or by any means, or stored in a database or retrieval system, without prior written permission of the publisher except in the case of brief quotations embodied in critical articles and reviews. Making copies of any part of this book for any purpose other than your own personal use is a violation of United States copyright laws. For information, address Que Corporation, 11711 N. College Ave., Carmel, IN 46032.

Library of Congress Catalog No.: 93-83386

ISBN: 1-56529-215-4

This book is sold *as is*, without warranty of any kind, either express or implied, respecting the contents of this book, including but not limited to implied warranties for the book's quality, performance, merchantability, or fitness for any particular purpose. Neither Que Corporation nor its dealers or distributors shall be liable to the purchaser or any other person or entity with respect to any liability, loss, or damage caused or alleged to have been caused directly or indirectly by this book.

95 94 93   6 5 4 3 2 1

Interpretation of the printing code: the rightmost double-digit number is the year of the book's printing; the rightmost single-digit number, the number of the book's printing. For example, a printing code of 93-1 shows that the first printing of the book occurred in 1993.

Screen reproductions in this book were created using Collage Plus from Inner Media, Inc., Hollis, NH.

Cover illustration by Jeff MacNelly.

I Hate DOS is based on DOS Version 6.

Publisher: Lloyd J. Short

Associate Publisher: Rick Ranucci

Publishing Plan Manager: Thomas H. Bennett

Operations Manager: Sheila Cunningham

Dedication

For Julia

I HATE DOS!

Credits

Title Manager:
Shelley O'Hara

Production Editor:
Cindy Morrow

Editor:
Barbara K. Koenig

Technical Editor:
Henry Wasserman

Book Designer:
Scott Cook

Novice Reviewer:
Stacey Beheler

Editorial Assistants:
Julia Blount
Sandra Naito

Production Team:

Claudia Bell
Jodie Cantwell
Brook Farling
Heather Kaufman
Bob LaRoche

Joy Dean Lee
Jay Lesandrini
Caroline Roop
Linda Seifert
Phil Worthington

Composed in *Goudy* and *MCPdigital* by Que Corporation.

About the Author

Bryan Pfaffenberger, called "Hamburger," "Cheeseburger," and other injurious things during painful years at school, at last found obscurity as a sincere, mild-mannered, and bumbling professor at a small Midwestern liberal arts college. But this peaceful existence was rudely interrupted after his 1981 purchase of a Kaypro computer, which occasioned a new round of ridicule. After spending a few months learning how to format a disk, Bryan declared to his astonished friends, family, and colleagues, "If *I* can figure this out, anyone can."

Since then, Bryan has written more than 35 books that translate computer mumbo-jumbo into plain English. An example: his best-selling *Que's Computer User's Dictionary*, with more than 250,000 copies in print.

Bryan knows that computers can help people work better, smarter, and faster, but they can also be a pain in the you-know-what. Worse, most computer books throw all the facts at you, as if you had to know *everything*. Isn't that sick?

Que's *I Hate...* books reflect Bryan's philosophy: "Computer books should teach only what you need to know. They should tell you what parts of the program are pointless and forgettable. And they shouldn't ask you to plow through 200 pages of tutorials just so that you can learn how to print a document."

Bryan's writing style gets right to the point, with an informal and humorous approach. With *I Hate DOS* as your guide, you may not wind up loving DOS—but you'll know how to fake it.

Acknowledgments

Rick Ranucci and Shelley O'Hara deserve a lot of credit for their creative contributions to this book's concept, as well as for their support and encouragement at every step—there wouldn't be an *I Hate DOS*, or its companion volumes, without their leadership, humor, intelligence, good taste (special thanks here), and vision. I would also like to thank my agent, Bill Gladstone, for handling the business stuff so I could sit around and think up Top Ten lists unperturbed by things like the movie rights to this book (any action there yet, Bill?). Thanks are due, too, to Que's fantastic editorial team (Cindy Morrow and Barbara Koenig) for the usual top-notch job, to Scott Cook for the design, to Jeff MacNelly for the cool cartoons, and to everyone at Que who has worked so hard to bring this book to fruition.

Trademarks

All terms mentioned in this book that are known to be trademarks or service marks have been appropriately capitalized. Que cannot attest to the accuracy of this information. Use of a term in this book should not be regarded as affecting the validity of any trademark or service mark.

DOS and Microsoft Windows are registered trademarks of Microsoft Corporation.

IBM is a registered trademark of International Business Machines, Inc.

WordPerfect is a registered trademark of WordPerfect Corporation.

Contents at a Glance

I Fake It Til' You Make It

II The Bluffer's Guide to File Management

III The Bluffer's Guide to Hardware

IV The Bluffer's Guide to Software

V Data Loss Anonymous

VI Quick and Dirty Dozens

Table of Contents

Introduction   **1**

    Some Assumptions about You 2
    What Is "DOS"? 2
    How to Use This Book 3
    About This Book's Icons 3
    How This Book Is Organized 4
        Section One: Fake It 'Til You Make It 5
        Section Two: The Bluffer's Guide to File Management 5
        Section Three: The Bluffer's Guide to Hardware 5
        Section Four: The Bluffer's Guide to Software 6
        Section Five: Data Loss Anonymous 6
        Section Six: Quick & Dirty Dozens 6

I Fake It Til' You Make It   **7**

  1 The Very Basics   **9**

    Turning On the Computer 10
    What You See but Might Not Get 12
    Running a Program 14
        I've Got Those Error Message Blues 16
        You May Need to "Change Directories" 16
    The DIR Command 18
    Making a Graceful Exit 21
    Killing the Computer 22
    Restarting the Computer 23

I HATE DOS!

2 More Basics   25

Inserting Disks 26
Changing Drives 28
And Which Version Are *You* Using? 30
Clearing the Screen of Inflammatory or
 Embarrassing Messages 30
DOS Syntax 31
More Command Information 32
Help! 33
Display a Single File Name 33
File Names: The Curse of DOS 34
Displaying a Set of Files 37
Using Wild Cards with DIR 38
Repeating Commands 38
Abandoning and Canceling Commands 39

3 Managing Files the Hard Way   41

Peeking at a File's Contents 42
Technical Babble about Path Names 44
Deleting a File 45
Deleting a Group of Files 47
Recovering from an Accidental Deletion 48
Making a Copy of a File 50
Copying a File to a Different Drive or Directory 51
Copying a Group of Files 52
Moving Files 52
 Moving Files If You Don't Have DOS 6 52
 Using DOS 6 to Move Files 53
Renaming Files 55

4 Managing Files the Easy Way   57

Taking a Look at the DOS Shell 58
Displaying Files on a Floppy Disk 61
Listing Directories 61

Displaying Files 63
Selecting Files 64
    The Mouse Method 64
    The Keyboard Method 64
Peeking at a File's Contents 65
Deleting Files 66
Copying and Moving Files by Using
    the Keyboard 68
    Copying Files by Using the Keyboard 68
    Moving Files by Using the Keyboard 69
Copying and Moving Files by Using the Mouse 70
    Copying Files by Using the Mouse 71
    Moving Files by Using the Mouse 71
Renaming Files 73
Quitting the DOS Shell 73

II The Bluffer's Guide to File Management   75

5 Managing Disks   77

Floppy Disks vs. Hard Disks 78
Buying Floppies 79
    Floppy Disk Basics 79
    Density and Capacity (Fraternal Twins) 80
    The Floppy Disk Match Up 81
    Buying Disks 82
Inserting and Removing Floppy Disks 82
Don't Mess with This Disk 84
Which Drive Is Which? 85
Formatting Floppies 86
Making an Exact Copy of a Floppy Disk 89
Is the Disk Full? 90
Is the Disk OK? 91
    Physical Problems 91
    Logical Problems 92

6 Hard Disk Housekeeping   93

Why Directories, Anyway? 94
The Famous Directory Tree 95
More on Path Names 96
Viewing the Tree Structure 97
Timesaving Tricks for Changing Directories 99
Making Directories 100
Removing Directories If You Don't Have DOS 6 101
Removing Directories with DOS 6 103
Tips on Hard Disk Organization 104

7 On the Trail of the Missing File   105

Don't Panic—Yet 106
Hunting for the File When You Know the Name 108
    I'm Sure I Know the Name 108
    I Thought I Knew the Name 108
    Maybe I Don't Know the Name 109
    Decoding the Commands 109
Alphabetizing Directory Output 110
The Ultimate DIR Command 111
When All Else Fails 112

8 More Disk Space! Faster Performance!   115

Squeezing More Space Out of Your Disk 117
    Running DoubleSpace 118
Using a Compressed Hard Disk 120
Squeezing a Floppy 121
Using a Compressed Floppy 122
Spiffing Up Your Hard Disk's Performance 123

9 Backing Up Is So Very Hard to Do   127

What to Back Up? 128
Why Using COPY Just Isn't Good Enough 130

Backing Up Using Older Versions of DOS 130
What to Back Up 131
   Backing Up All Files on Your Whole Hard Disk 132
   Backing Up Just Your Data Files 132
   Backing Up Only Files That Have Changed 134
   Starting Over Again 136
Backing Up Using DOS 6 136
   The Compatibility Test (Matchmaking) 136
   Backing Up All Files 138
   Backing Up the Files You've Created or Changed 140
   Starting over Again (DOS 6) 142
Using the Backup Disks 142

10 A Virus Ate My Computer!   143

Dealing with the Virus Scare 144
Get a Checkup 145
Monitoring Your System for Suspicious Activity 147

III The Bluffer's Guide to Hardware   149

11 Handy Guide to Hardware Obsolescence   151

What's "Hardware"? 153
You Say I'm Using a Clone? 153
The Parts of a Typical System 155
   The Parts of the System You Can See 155
   The Parts of the System You Can't See 156
A Quick Guide to All That "80286, 80386, 80486"
   Chatter 157
Timing Clock Speed 160
Disk Drives 162
Ports o' Call 164

12 More Than You Ever Wanted to Know about Memory (RAM)   167

What's Memory For, Anyway? 168
The Art and Lore of Measuring Memory 170
How Much Memory Do You Need? 173
Conventional Memory 174
How Much Conventional Memory Do You Have? 175
And Just What Is This "Extended Memory" Thing? 176
Do You Have Any Extended Memory? 177
     DOS 5 Memory Stats 177
     DOS 6 Memory Stats 178
What about Expanded Memory? 179
And What Is This "Upper Memory Area" Thing? 180
Yet Another Type of Memory 181
OK, OK, I'll Look at the Map 181
The *Angst* of Memory Configuration 183
Memory Magic with DOS 6 184

13 Monitors   187

The Monitor and the Adapter 188
Adapters Demystified 190
Monitors Demystified 192
What Is This Resolution Number All About? 194
Monitor Size 195
Monochrome or Color? 195
And What Adapter Do You Have? 198
What Are Those Funny Knobs? 199
Cleaning the Screen 199
The Heartbreak of Phosphor Burn-In 200
The Wacky World of Display Modes 200

14 The Keyboard   203

Why the Funny Keys? 204
Those Highly Irritating Toggle Keys 206

That Cranky Caps Lock Key 207
The Numskull Num Lock Key 207
The Innocent Scroll Lock Key 208
Decoding Those Keys with the Funny Arrows 208
More and More Keys 209
Hot Keyboard Tricks with DOS 211
The Madness and Mystery of DOS Editing Keys 211
Play It Again, Sam 212
One by One 212
What to Do If You Hear a Beep while Typing Really Fast . . 213
What's That Funny Numb Feeling? 213

15 The Printer   215

Types of Printers 216
Serial and Parallel Printers 217
Printer Names 218
Making the Connection Physically 219
Connecting a Serial Printer 220
The Joy and Anguish of Printer Fonts 221
Test Your Printer 223
Why You Shouldn't Bother Printing with DOS 225
Program to Printer 226
The Pain and Heartbreak of Printing Problems 227

IV The Bluffer's Guide to Software   229

16 Software   231

Application? What's That? 232
System Software and Utilities 233
What the Heck is a DOS Application Program? 233

What Is This Windows Thing? 234
   The Windows and DOS Relationship
     (Friend or foe?) 235
   Do I Have Windows? 236
The Big Three 237
   Word Processing Programs (The Village Wordsmith) . . . 238
   Spreadsheet Programs (I've got your number) 239
   Database Programs 241
Beyond the Big Three 242
What's This "Shareware" Stuff? 245

17 Installing and Running Programs   **247**

"Will It Run on My Computer?" 248
   What I Have 249
   What I Need 250
What's in the Box? 252
Installation 254
Starting the Program 257
Learning New Software 258
Should You Upgrade? 259
Running Two or More Programs
   at the Same Time 260

18 Modifying Those Awful System Files   **263**

CONFIG.SYS and AUTOEXEC.BAT
   in the Real World 264
Starting EDIT 265
Opening the File 266
Adding a Line 267
Editing an Existing Line 267
Saving Your Changes and Quitting EDIT 268
When Do the Changes Take Effect? 269
Some Cool Changes 270

V Data Loss Anonymous 271

19 Fear and Loathing at the DOS Prompt 273

"It Won't Start!" 274
"It Started, But I See An Error Message" 275
"The Power Just Went Off!" 278
"My Program Won't Start!" 279
"The Time and Date Are Wrong!" 279
"It Won't Let Me Copy the File!" 281
"My File's Gone!" 282
"Why Can't I Delete This File?" 283
"I Just Reformatted My Floppy Disk!" 284
"I Just Reformatted My Hard Disk!" 285
"This Floppy Isn't Working!" 285
"The Computer Won't Respond" 286
"My Printer Won't Print!" 288
"I Can't Access My Hard Disk!" 288
"I Have to Restore Data!" 289
"My Files Are Gone!" 290
When to Throw in the Towel 292

20 Deciphering DOS Error Messages 295

Access denied 296
Bad command or file name 297
Bad or missing command interpreter 297
Disk boot failure 297
Disk error reading (or writing) Drive X 298
Duplicate file name or file not found 298
Error reading (or writing) fixed disk 299
File allocation table bad Drive X 299
File cannot be copied onto itself 300
File creation error 300

General failure reading (or writing) Drive X.
  Abort, Retry, Fail? 300
Insufficient disk space 301
Invalid directory 301
Invalid drive specification 302
Invalid file name or file not found 302
Invalid media, track 0 bad or unusable 303
Invalid number of parameters, Invalid parameter 303
Invalid path, not directory, or dir not empty 303
Invalid switch 304
Non-system disk or disk error 304
Not ready reading Drive X 305
Read fault error reading (or writing) Drive X 305
Sector not found error reading (or writing) Drive X
  or Seek error reading (or writing) Drive X 307
Syntax Error 307
Too many parameters 307
Unable to create directory 308
Write-protect error writing Drive X; Abort, Retry, Fail? 308

VI Quick & Dirty Dozens   309

Quick & Dirty Dozens   311

12 Basic Facts about Computers That Everyone
  Assumes You Know 312
12 Minor But Embarrassing
  Beginner's Boo-Boos 316
12 Good Things You Should Always Do 321
12 Naughty Things You Should Never Do 325
12 Acronyms People Expect You to Know 330
12 Darned Good Reasons to Upgrade to DOS 6 334

Index   339

Introduction

"Oh no! Not again!"

"This computer won't do what I want!"

"I *hate* DOS!"

"Aaargh!"

Sound familiar? Welcome to the club. If you hate DOS, but you have to use it, you've come to the right place. This book begins with a simple, dangerous, and irreverent premise: DOS isn't worth learning if that means spending days or weeks being dragged through agonizing, painful tutorials. So this book doesn't "teach" DOS. It just provides useful information that you can use when you need it.

I Hate DOS cuts out all the excess technoweenie fluff. It doesn't try to turn you into a computer-loving nerd. It just boils DOS down to the stuff you really need—the stuff that gets you into the computer, lets you do your work, and tells you what to do when those irritating error messages appear, like `File not found`.

Some Assumptions about You

You have a personal computer, or you've been stuck with one at work. Someone has already set it up for you, and turned you loose after hitting you with a few unintelligible do's and don'ts.

You have more important things to do than spend the next six months taking computer lessons. You're not really nuts about computers. You're certainly not in love with DOS. You don't want to be bored to death by irrelevant technical junk. You don't want to have to "learn" stuff, chapter-by-chapter, in a process that goes on for weeks. You don't want to have to memorize anything. You just want to be able to look stuff up, when the need arises.

What Is "DOS"?

DOS stands for Disk Operating System. This sounds fancy, but it's basically just a grunt-level, exposed-pipes, bald-light bulb, warehouse-type program that controls various parts of the computer system.

DOS is more of a barrier or a necessary evil than something worth learning for its own sake. It doesn't help you get your work done. You can't type a letter or balance your checkbook with DOS. It's necessary for what we technoweenies call *system maintenance*—all those housekeeping tasks like deleting unwanted files or formatting disks—that just have to

be done. (The good fairy, alas, won't do it for you.) Ideally, you get enough DOS under your belt to do these tasks, and then you get on to actually accomplishing something with your computer.

DOS comes in different versions, each of which has its own, pet number (such as Version 3.2). You can use this book with any version of DOS, although some sections talk about features introduced with Version 5 and Version 6. Version 6 is the latest and greatest version of DOS.

How to Use This Book

This book isn't designed to be read from cover-to-cover. Relax. You're not in for a three-week ordeal. There won't be a test.

You just look up the stuff you need. Each chapter is self-contained, with lots of cross-references to other chapters, should the need arise.

When you're supposed to type something, what you type appears in bold or on a line by itself. Like this: **HERE'S WHAT YOU TYPE**. Or like this:

HERE'S WHAT YOU TYPE

After you type the command, you press Enter.

About This Book's Icons

Flip through the book. Do you notice those pictures in the margins? These pictures—called *icons*—signal you to the type of information contained next to the icon. If you're not interested in this type of information, skip it. Here's what the icons mean:

TIP

This icon alerts you to shortcuts, tricks, and time-savers.

EXPERTS ONLY

This icon flags skippable technical stuff that I couldn't resist including. I am, after all, a nerd, although I now understand, after a painful process of self-examination, that most of the rest of the world does not share my enthusiasm for technology.

CAUTION

Warning! Danger! This icon warns you about those pitfalls and traps to avoid.

BUZZWORDS

This icon warns you that you're about to learn technospeak—some nifty word or phrase like *byte* or *bit* or *blip* or *blurp*.

This icon identifies sections about the latest, neatest version of DOS—DOS 6. These sections are only for people who have this version. If you don't have Version 6, there's still plenty of information for you in this book.

How This Book Is Organized

You don't have to read all this book's chapters in order or anything like that. Just turn to the stuff you need. Here's an overview:

Section One: Fake It 'Til You Make It

This section contains the very basics of DOS. But it also contains most of the information you'll need on a day-to-day basis. You learn how to turn on the computer and run programs, how to insert disks and type DOS commands, how to copy and delete files, how to use the DOS Shell, and a host of other basic information you'll need immediately.

Section Two: The Bluffer's Guide to File Management

In this section, you learn how to keep your system humming. You learn hard disk housekeeping. You learn how to go on a Sacred Quest for a missing file. You learn how to double your hard disk's capacity, as well as to keep the disk's performance at the top level. The section even explains the all-important concepts of backing up data and checking for computer viruses. All in all, you learn tons of necessary information about how to keep your whole system happy and productive.

Section Three: The Bluffer's Guide to Hardware

This section covers the basics of your PC system hardware, the actual physical part of the system that you can see, touch, kick, or punch. You learn about the computer system unit and some of the weird stuff inside, what computer memory is and why you need it, and all about the monitor (the screen), the keyboard, and the printer.

Section Four: The Bluffer's Guide to Software

This section covers the basics of software, those programs that make your computer do interesting—possibly useful—things. You learn about application programs, like word processing programs, that (unlike DOS) actually help you *create* something. You also learn about installing programs, getting them to run on your computer, and editing weirdly named DOS configuration files. This section teaches you how to use DOS as the *backbone* for using your computer—which is the whole purpose of DOS.

Section Five: Data Loss Anonymous

Here's where you turn when something goes wrong—and when you're talking about DOS and PCs, that's pretty often. You learn about a variety of DOS and system disasters, ranging from mild to devastating. This section also covers all the latest comebacks for those insulting DOS error messages.

Section Six: Quick & Dirty Dozens

This part of the book provides some useful, additional information that you can look at whenever you'd like. Included are basic facts about the computers that no one ever explains to beginners, some minor but embarrassing boo-boos beginners typically make, naughty things you shouldn't ever do, good things you should always do, assorted acronyms people expect you to know, and some very good reasons to upgrade to the latest version of DOS.

PART I

Fake It 'Til You Make It

Includes:

1: The Very Basics

2: More Basics

3: Managing Files the Hard Way

4: Managing Files the Easy Way

CHAPTER 1

The Very Basics
(Turn On, Tune In)

IN A NUTSHELL

- ▼ Start the computer
- ▼ Tell what's on-screen
- ▼ Run a program
- ▼ Determine what to do if the program doesn't start
- ▼ Determine what's on a disk
- ▼ Exit a program
- ▼ Kill the computer
- ▼ Restart the computer

TIP

Your local DOS technoweenie is a very, very important person for you. At times, you'll need help that's beyond this book's level, and a good computer nerd—preferably sporting a propeller-head beanie—will be indispensable. Some DOS stuff, like configuring your system, needs to be done by people with intermediate or advanced DOS skills. Locate your friendly, neighborhood DOS wizard and begin a long-term project of ingratiating yourself.

Turning On the Computer

(Why they hide the switch)

The big moment is here: it's you and the PC. Where's the switch?

If you're lucky, your system is hooked up to a power strip—an electrical strip with several outlets. (You have to buy the power strip; it doesn't come with the computer.) If so, it's pretty easy to turn on the system: just flip the switch on the power strip. If there's no power switch, you'll have to hunt down the switches for each component. Start with the computer (the box thing) and monitor (the TV thing).

Look for a big red switch on the back of the computer. Some system designers place the switch on the back panel where (1) you fear you'll be electrocuted if you stick your finger in the wrong hole, and (2) you may jar loose some of the data cables, resulting in (even more) bizarre system behavior. As you tenderly but blindly explore the back panel looking for the switch, be careful to avoid the cables, power cords, and the large, poisonous bugs and snakes that creep back there seeking warmth and darkness.

EXPERTS ONLY

Skip this unless you enjoy getting mad at computer designers

It would be nice if the computer's On/Off switch had helpful On and Off labels. But this would be too simple. Instead, the switch is usually labeled O and 1. O, incidentally, stands for Off, while 1 stands for On. Why? O and 1 are the two numbers used in the binary number system—the number system that the computer uses. Computer designers want you to appreciate these numbers. They want you to fall in love with the same techie, nerdy stuff that they love.

Monitor switches are even harder to find. Look on the front, back, right side, left side, bottom, and top of the monitor. After that, kick it.

Checklist

▼ If you found both switches, you'll know it. The computer hums, buzzes, clicks, and whirs. These are happy noises. A great deal of information also flashes past on the screen, much faster than you can read it. Ignore it.

▼ If nothing happens, make sure all the stuff is plugged in.

▼ If you see the message, `Non-System disk or disk error. Replace and strike any key when ready`, there's probably a disk in the floppy disk drive. Look for one or two slots in the computer's front panel. There may be one, two, or even three. The little slots (for 3.5-inch disks) have buttons. Push them. The big slots (for 5.25-inch disks) have latches. If one of the latches covers the slot, move the latch so that it doesn't. Then press any key that suits your fancy.

continues

▼ If you see any other message, such as `Bad or Missing Command Interpreter` or some other arcane notation, get your local computer guru to help you.

What You See but Might Not Get

Most readers see the following on-screen:

    C>

DOS PROMPT

C> is called the DOS prompt. It's called a *prompt* because DOS is telling you, "We've finished all of our business inside the computer, here. What *do* you want to do?" You're supposed to type something, and then press Enter, to make things happen.

The DOS prompt might look like this:

    C:\>

Lots of other things can happen after you start a computer:

▼ Your prompt might say something like `Hi, Sweetie`. You can change the prompt to say anything you like. More on this in Chapter 18.

▼ You might see Microsoft Windows. If you do, you'll have to hate Windows too, so get yourself a copy of Que's *I Hate Windows*. But you'll still need to hate DOS, so keep this book.

▼ You might see a menu, which tells you which key to press to start a program. This is good. You are lucky. Just press the indicated key to start the program you want to run.

▼ You might see the DOS Shell (you'll know it if you do, because there's a bar across the top of the screen that says—you guessed it—`MS-DOS Shell`). To exit, press F3.

▼ Another, more welcome possibility: Your program might start all by itself. If so, skip to the section, "Making a Graceful Exit."

"I HATE THIS!"

"My mouse isn't working!"

Your computer system may be equipped with a mouse, a little soap-sized thing that you can move around on the tabletop. Some DOS applications use the mouse, but the DOS prompt doesn't. If you move the mouse while the DOS prompt is visible, nothing good happens. On the plus side, though, nothing bad happens.

Running a Program

(The rocket launch)

You've started your computer, and you see the DOS prompt. So what do you do now? Run a program. (Computer people don't agree on what this should be called. You may hear the terms *start*, which is simple enough, but you may run into *launch* or even *invoke*. Personally, I like the term *launch*, because it sounds as if you have done something big and exciting like launch a spacecraft.)

Here's how to start a program: type the program's name and press Enter. It doesn't matter whether you use uppercase or lowercase letters. For example, to start Lotus 1-2-3, you type

123

and press Enter. (Pressing Enter confirms what you've typed, and sends it to the computer's brain.) The Enter key is usually the biggest key on the keyboard, so it's hard to miss. It's where the Return key would be on a typewriter.

Checklist

▼ What if you make a typing mistake? Before you press Enter, you can correct the mistake by pressing the Backspace key. (Look for the Backspace key above the big Enter key. Sometimes the Backspace key isn't labeled Backspace, but instead has a left arrow on it.) Pressing Backspace rubs out what you've typed—one character at a time—so that you can correct the error by retyping.

▼ What if you don't know what to type? Sometimes you type the name of the program, as in **WORD** (for Microsoft Word for DOS) or **123**. More often, though, you type initials, as in **WP** (WordPerfect) or **Q** (Quattro Pro). To find out what to type in order to start your program, ask other users, call technical support, experiment with different possibilities, or as a last resort, check the program's manual. Or see the section, "The DIR Command," later in this chapter.

Top Ten Reasons for Calling Technical Support Hotline

10. Manual further away than telephone; prefer to let fingers do the walking

9. Manual too hard to read; not interesting like *National Enquirer*

8. Don't have manual for "borrowed" copy of program

7. Unable to start program

6. Unable to exit program

5. Unable to quit using program

4. Error beep too loud; audible by coworkers

3. Heard moaning sound from disk drive after installing program

2. Lonely; "just wanted to chat"

1. Apology demanded for insulting error message

I've Got Those Error Message Blues

You typed your program's name or initials and you pressed Enter. And what do you get for following instructions? Something like this:

```
Bad command or file name
```

If you get this message, there are several possible causes. Start with this one: you may have typed the program name or initials wrong. Make sure that you know *exactly* what to type, and then try again.

If you still get the message, you probably need to switch to the program's directory, as explained in the next section.

You May Need to "Change Directories"

You may have to activate the program's directory before you can start the program.

BUZZWORDS

DIRECTORY and SUBDIRECTORY

A *directory* is a section of your disk that has been set aside to store a group of related files, such as the WordPerfect program and your WordPerfect files. Another term for *directory* is *subdirectory*—for practical purposes, they mean the same thing. Also, you can have directories within directories.

To activate your program's directory, you need to know the name of the directory. Ask the person who set up the computer. If no one's around who can help, you can use the DIR command, as explained in the next section.

After you know the name of the directory, you use the CD command (short for "Change Directory") to activate the directory that contains the program you want to start. Suppose that you want to start Word-Perfect 5.1, and you learn that this program is in the WP51 directory. Here's what you type:

CD \WP51

Then press Enter. Note a couple of things here. First, there's a space between the CD part and the \WP51 part. You don't have to type the space. Second, that funny mark is a backslash. Don't leave that out. It tells DOS, "The letters that follow are a directory name."

Your computer may have been set up so that the DOS prompt shows the name of the directory that's currently active, so your prompt might look like this:

C:\WP51>

But if no one has set up your system to do this, it might just look like the following:

C>

You are in the WP51 directory no matter what the prompt says. And you should be able to start your program now.

Checklist

▼ If you see the message `Invalid directory`, make sure that you've typed the directory name correctly, and try again. Don't leave out the backslash!

▼ If your prompt doesn't show the name of the current directory, you can modify your system so that it does. See Chapter 18 for the thrilling details.

EXPERTS ONLY

Amaze your coworkers with a stunning display of technical virtuosity

To get DOS to show the name of the current directory, type the following at the DOS prompt:

    PROMPT pg

Then press Enter. Make sure that you leave a space between the PROMPT part and the pg part. This change lasts until you switch off the computer or restart it, as explained later in this chapter.

The DIR Command

When you don't know the name of a program or a directory and can't find out easily any other way, use the DIR command. DIR is one of the DOS commands that you'll use frequently. It lists for you the files and directories that are in the current directory.

BUZZWORDS

FILE

A collection of related stuff, such as a program or some work you've done, like a report or letter. Files are stored on disk, and every file has a name, like ESSAY.DOC.

To see what's on a disk, type **DIR** and press Enter. You'll see something like this on-screen:

```
Volume in drive C is HOT_STUFF
Volume Serial Number is 0D57-15
Directory of C:\

COMMAND      COM 4785            11-11-91        5:00a
CONFIG       SYS 1536            07-04-92        5:36p
MOUSE        SYS 30733           03-10-92       11:36a
AUTOEXEC     BAT 1876            05-09-92        8.31p
WP51               <DIR> 05-09-92        8:37p
LOTUS              <DIR> 07-30-92       12:19p
```

Don't worry about most of the stuff you're seeing here. You can learn more about it later, if you want. For now, just notice that this command lists the names of the files and directories that are found in the currently active directory. You can tell that something in the list is a directory because <DIR> appears after the name. This listing shows two directories: WP51 and LOTUS.

When you first turn on the computer, the root directory is usually the current directory.

BUZZWORDS

ROOT DIRECTORY

The top-level directory on a disk. Think of the root directory as if it were a country that contains lots of states (other directories).

TIP

If you want to see a list of subdirectories only, type **DIR *.** and press Enter.

EXPERTS ONLY

An impressive DOS command that will leave your detractors in disarray

If your disk has a lot of files, the names will go by faster than the human eye can read them. This whizbang display is intentional. Humans were never intended to use the computer system. But you can slow the display using an especially cunning DOS command. Instead of typing **DIR**, type

DIR /p

and press Enter. This command has three parts: DIR, followed by a space and the switch (/), followed by another space and p. After you type this command, you see one screen of file names at a time. To see the next screen, just press any old key you want.

Suppose that you're trying to hunt down a program's name or initials so that you can start it. You know that the program is stored in the \123 directory. So you switch to this directory by typing the following command:

CD \123

Then press Enter. \123 is now the current directory. Now type

DIR

and press Enter. You see the files stored in the \123 directory.

Look in the program's directory for a file that has .EXE at the end of its name (like 123.EXE). To start the program, you type the part of the name that comes before the period.

Making a Graceful Exit

Let's assume all has gone well and that you've started your program successfully. The question now arises: how to get out?

CAUTION

> Don't quit a program by just switching off the computer, tempting though it may be. It's much better to exit the program and return to the DOS prompt. There's less risk of losing your work or screwing things up.

It would be nice if all programs gave you the same way to exit. Naturally, they don't. This was decided at a conference titled "Let's Make Things as Difficult as Possible for Our Users," held in the dawning years of the computer industry.

To exit, try one of the following:

▼ If the program has a bar across the top of the screen with names of menus like File and Edit, you can probably exit by holding down the Alt key (one of those funny extra keys on the keyboard) and pressing F. This command opens the File menu. Tap the down-arrow key until you highlight the command that gets you out of the program—Exit, Quit, Die, and so on. If you don't see such a bar, press F10 and see whether one appears.

▼ In Lotus 1-2-3, press the slash key (/) and then tap the right-arrow key until you move the highlight to the command called Quit. Then press Enter.

▼ Some programs give you a list of keys you can press to do various things. Usually, this list is at the bottom of the screen. In one program, the list says `F3=Quit`. If you press F3, you exit the program.

▼ If the program is called WordPerfect, press F7 and press Y when asked whether you're really serious about leaving the program. No other program uses this key to exit, though, which is one of WordPerfect's most beloved little peculiarities.

Killing the Computer

Now that you've exited your program gracefully and returned to the DOS prompt, you may want to turn off your computer. Actually, you may have wanted to kill your computer earlier, but there is a time and place for everything. To kill your computer, remove any floppy disks you may have inserted, and then flip off the power switch.

EXPERTS ONLY

On or off: That is the question

The computer camp is divided over whether it's best to leave a computer on or off all the time.

Every time you shut down your computer, it is off. In order to work with it again, you must switch it on. The sudden flow of current through all those little computer chips is stressful. In fact, the life of your computer may be measured by how many times you turn it on, not how long you leave it on. If you use a computer every day, you might want to leave it on all the time.

On the other hand, while the computer is on, there's a possibility that something damaging can happen. Lightning can send power surges through your power lines and turn your computer's brain to jelly, for instance. So some prefer to turn the computer off. Also, leaving the computer turned on wastes electricity.

CAUTION

It's OK (and probably wise) to leave a frequently used computer on all the time, but turn off the monitor. If you leave the monitor on, you'll get burn-through—a permanent image left on-screen by whatever is left on-screen for a prolonged period (such as the DOS prompt). You might have noticed burn-through on automatic teller machines where the Welcome screen seems to appear as a ghost image on-screen no matter what screen you are viewing.

Another way to avoid burn-through is to use a screen-saver program. These programs blank the screen after a set period—say, 10 or 15 minutes—in which you haven't typed anything or moved the mouse.

Restarting the Computer

You may want to restart your system—to take it back to that magic moment when its memory is cleared and DOS is loaded for a new, fresh computing session. You can do so without switching the power off and on, which decreases your computer's life span. To do so, hold down the Ctrl and Alt keys and press Del. Alternatively, press your computer's Reset button—if your computer has one. (If it does, you'll find it on the computer's front panel.)

When should you restart your system? These are some of the pertinent times:

▼ When a software installation program instructs you to do so. Installation programs change your computer's setup, and the new setup won't take place until you restart.

I HATE DOS!

▼ If your system hangs or freezes (something has gone haywire so that the computer no longer responds to your keyboard input). Be sure that your computer really is frozen. Some operations can take a minute or two to finish, so it appears that your computer is hanging, when really it's just working more slowly than you expected. If any light on the computer is flashing, the computer is still busy. If you hear any computer-related noises, it's probably still working. Go have a cup of coffee and come back. If the system's still comatose, restart it.

CAUTION

When you restart your system, you lose any work that you haven't yet saved. Use Ctrl-Alt-Del only as a last-ditch measure, after you've exhausted all other possibilities—including getting your local computer guru to help. And be sure to remove any floppy disks before you restart. (If a disk is left in the drive, you'll probably get an error message when you restart.)

CHAPTER 2

More Basics

(Mysteries of the C> Prompt Revealed)

IN A NUTSHELL

- ▼ Insert a disk into a disk drive
- ▼ Change drives
- ▼ Determine what version you're using
- ▼ Clear the screen
- ▼ Learn to speak DOS
- ▼ Get help
- ▼ Display files
- ▼ Use DOS switches
- ▼ Repeat a command
- ▼ Make sense of DOS file names
- ▼ Use DOS wild cards
- ▼ Cancel a command

Inserting Disks

Your computer has at least two, and maybe three, disk drives. The one you've been working with, drive C, is the *hard disk drive*. The additional drive or drives are *floppy disk drives*.

BUZZWORDS

DISK DRIVE

A place where you store files. There are two types of disk drives: floppy and hard.

Floppy disk drives hold floppy disks (makes sense). Floppy disks are like VCR tapes or audio tapes. They store information and are portable. There are two kinds of floppy disks: big (flimsy 5.25-inch disks) and little (hard 3.5-inch disks).

Hard disks are usually built into your computer and are nonremovable. They have a lot more space than floppy disks. You store most of your programs and documents on a hard disks. The terms *hard disk*, *hard drive*, and *hard disk drive* are often used interchangeably. The terms essentially mean the same thing.

Checklist

▼ Like the hard disk (drive C), the floppy disk drives have names. If you have just one floppy disk drive, it's drive A. If you have two floppy disk drives, the one on top is probably drive A, while the one on the bottom is probably drive B. The "probably" part is necessary because some computer designers like to mix things up just to keep users on their toes.

▼ To insert a disk, hold it so that the label's up. If you're inserting a big disk (5.25-inch), close the drive door latch after inserting the disk. If you're inserting a little disk (3.5-inch), just push it in until it clicks into place.

"I HATE THIS!"

Take out that disk!

Don't leave a disk in drive A when you shut off your computer. When DOS starts, it always looks for startup files (files that it needs to get started). First it checks drive A; then it checks drive C. Chances are the disk in drive A doesn't have the necessary files, so you see the message Non-System disk or disk error. To clear the message and get DOS running, remove the disk from drive A and press any key.

CAUTION

Don't insert or remove a floppy disk from the disk drive while the drive light is on. This light warns you that the drive is trying to do something. If you move the disk while this light is lit, you could scramble the information on the disk.

CAUTION

If you're using a big (5.25-inch) disk, don't let the surface of the disk get dirty. Spilling or smearing anything greasy, powdery, or sticky on the disk's naked surface could make the disk completely unusable.

Top Ten Substances Found on Surface of Ruined Floppy Disks
10. Thumb grease
9. Coffee
8. Coke
7. Hair spray
6. Potato chip grease
5. Hostess Twinkie cream
4. Tears
3. Milk of magnesia/chocolate (tie)
2. Oatmeal
1. Chapstick

Changing Drives

Only one drive can be current (active) at a time. When a disk drive is *current*, DOS assumes that this is the drive you want to do things to. For example, if you type **DIR** while drive C is current, DOS lists for you all the files and directories on drive C. If you want to look at something on another drive, you need to make that drive current.

To make a drive current, just type the drive letter, type a colon, and press Enter. To make drive A current, for example, insert the disk, type

   A:

and press Enter. The prompt then shows the current drive:

   A:\>

To get back to drive C, you type

   C:

and press Enter.

"I HATE THIS!"

I'm not ready!

When you activate drive A, you may see this message:

```
Not ready reading drive A
Abort, Retry, Fail?
```

What's wrong? There's no disk in the drive, or the drive door isn't latched. DOS cannot look at floppy drives unless there is a disk in them. Insert a disk into the drive, close the latch, and press R to retry the command. It doesn't matter whether you type an uppercase or lowercase R.

Another message you might see is

```
General failure reading drive A
Abort, Retry, Fail?
```

This means that the disk is not formatted or ready for use. The mystery of formatting is revealed in Chapter 5.

And Which Version Are You Using?

It's inevitable that someone some time will ask you "What version of DOS do you have?" Tech support people are big on knowing your version of DOS. Also, when you buy new programs, you need to know the version of DOS because some programs only run with certain versions of DOS. To find out what version you're using, type the following:

VER

Then press Enter. You'll see something like this:

```
MS-DOS Version 6.00
```

This book covers Version 6—the most recent version of DOS. Most of the information in this book pertains to all versions. Look for the Most Recent Version icon for information that pertains to just DOS 6.0 features.

Clearing the Screen of Inflammatory or Embarrassing Messages

Sometimes you will try the same command over and over, and the results of your efforts (`Bad command or file name`) will be clearly displayed on-screen for everyone to see. To cover up any on-screen gibberish, type this simple command:

CLS

Then press Enter.

DOS Syntax

(Who does what to whom?)

As you've probably noticed, to use the computer effectively, you've got to talk the DOS talk. Basically, that means learning the *syntax* (sentence structure) of a foreign language. (And we all know how enjoyable and productive that year of Spanish was in high school. "Hello Juan. How are you? I am fine. How are you? I am fine.")

With DOS, you have to learn which things go first, and which things go second. DOS is a very picky grammarian.

The easiest DOS commands, like VER and CLS, have a simple sentence structure. It is the same one your boss uses:

DO THIS

Other commands employ a slightly more complex sentence structure:

DO THIS to THAT

For instance, sometimes you will tell DOS to do a DIR to drive A. Try putting this exciting knowledge to work! Put a disk in drive A. If you're not already at drive C (c:\> is displayed on-screen when you are at drive C), change to drive C by typing:

C:

Then press Enter. Now type

DIR A:

and press Enter. This command means "Do the DIR command on drive A." After you press Enter, you see a listing of the files and directories on the disk in drive A.

More Command Information

(Taking the switch to DOS)

Some DOS commands have options, called *switches* because you can turn them on or off as you want. You indicate a switch by typing a forward slash (/) followed by the letter that turns the switch on. You can use switches, for example, to display a directory list in different ways.

BUZZWORDS

DIRECTORY LIST

The information that appears on-screen when you use the DIR command. The directory list shows the files and directories that are contained within the current directory.

For example, try the following on a lengthy directory list. Don't forget to leave a space before the slash:

DIR /p

This switch displays the files one screen at a time. Now try this:

DIR /w

This switch displays the files in columns on-screen so that many more file names are visible at once. Now you can get confused on just one screen, instead of several.

Sort a directory with this command:

DIR /on

This switch sorts the directory list in alphabetical order by file name.

Help!

If you're using DOS 6, you can take advantage of a much-improved Help feature. To get help on any DOS command, type **HELP** followed by the command. For example, if you type

>   HELP DIR

and press Enter, you see MS-DOS Help with a screen full of information about the DIR command.

Use the Page Down and Page Up keys to page through the help information. When you're finished, hold down the Alt key and type **FX**.

Display a Single File Name

DIR is probably the handiest of commands. You use DIR when you're trying to answer the perennial questions, "What's on a disk?" or "Is my file in this directory?"

Often, there are zillions of files on a disk or in a directory. You can limit the number of files DIR displays so that the listing is easier to read.

Suppose that you're looking for the WordPerfect file (WP.EXE). You type the following:

>   DIR WP.EXE

This command tells DOS to display the file name WP.EXE. If the file's in the current directory, you see a directory list with just one file, like this:

```
Volume in drive C is HOT_STUFF
Volume Serial Number is 1A2B-5E72
Directory of C:\WP51

WP   EXE      127653      12-21-89      8:24a
```

If the file isn't in the current directory, you see the following message (another all-time favorite among DOS users):

```
File not found
```

Checklist

▼ If the file isn't found, you might need to change to the directory that contains the file. If the hard disk is a house and a directory is a room, DOS can look for files only in the current room. Chapter 1 covers how to change directories.

▼ If the file isn't found and you're a poor typist, try the command again and be sure that you typed the name correctly.

▼ If you still can't find the file, try wild cards, as described in the section "Displaying a Set of Files."

File Names: The Curse of DOS

Everything on your computer—hard disk or floppy disk—is stored in a file. And every file has a name. Some of the files are already on the disk—for instance, program files. Some files are created when you use a program. When you type and save a memo, it is stored in a file.

Least popular among many of DOS's inadequacies is its eight-letter limit on file names, plus other rules and regulations and penalties.

BUZZWORDS

PROGRAM FILE

A type of file that contains instructions rather than data. For instance, a word processing program file would contain instructions that enable you to run the program. Any documents you create in the program are stored in a separate file, and this file contains data rather than program instructions. Note that synonyms for *program* include *application*, *software*, and any combination of the two (such as *software application*).

Checklist

▼ File names consist of two parts: a first name and a last name. You use a period to separate the two names.

▼ The file must have a first name, but it doesn't need a last name.

▼ The first name can have up to eight characters, but it doesn't have to use all eight. The last name can have up to three characters, but it doesn't have to use all three.

▼ You can use the last name, called an *extension*, to show how files are related (just like your last name connects you to your family members). You might have .DOC files for document files and .WKS files for worksheet files.

continues

▼ Programs always have an .EXE, .COM, or .BAT extension.

▼ Stick to using letters and numbers in your file names. Except for that period between the first and last name, avoid punctuation.

▼ You can't use spaces in a DOS file name, but some users like to fake it by typing an underscore instead of a space (SHUT_UP.DOS).

▼ DOS users who are in the know let their applications assign extensions automatically. Some applications are bossy and prefer that you let them assign the extension.

▼ A commonly used extension for text files is .TXT. A text file contains nothing but the standard DOS keyboard characters, without any of the gibberish that programs add to your files.

▼ Another commonly-used extension is .BAK. Files with this extension usually contain backed-up data.

EXPERTS ONLY

Dear Bryan: I'm curious. Which characters can I use in a DOS file name?

Glad you asked. You can't use spaces, periods, commas, backslashes, or periods within the file name. (You must use a period, though, to separate the file name from the extension.) You can use: underscore (__), caret (^), dollar sign ($), tilde (~), exclamation point (!), number sign (#), percent sign (%), ampersand (&), hyphen (-), curly braces ({}), at sign (@), single quote ('), apostrophe ('), and parentheses (()).

Displaying a Set of Files

(Those wacky wild cards)

In poker, the deuce usually is a wild card; it can stand for any other card. If you have three queens, for example, you would want the deuce to stand for a queen.

You can use wild cards the same way in DOS: to match characters in a file name. Doing so enables you to group files together. You can type commands that say, in effect, "Show me all the files that have the extension DOC."

You can use two wild cards in DOS: ? and *. The ? matches any single character. The * matches any number of characters. Here are some examples:

▼ The wild card expression LETTER?.DOC will group all of the following: LETTER1.DOC, LETTER2.DOC, LETTER3.DOC, and so on, up to LETTER9.DOC. But it won't include LETTER10.DOC in the group. That's because the ? wild card only stands for one character.

▼ The wild card expression LET*.DOC will group all the files just mentioned. That's because the * wild card stands for any number of characters.

▼ The wild card expression LETTER.* will group LETTER.DOC, LETTER.TXT, and LETTER.BAK.

▼ The wild card expression ???.??? finds any files with a three-letter file name and a three-letter extension (such as SIN.DOC, FUN.TXT, or TOI.JON).

▼ The wild card expression *.* (pronounced "star-dot-star") stands for all files.

Using Wild Cards with DIR

And now back to the perennial "Where's my file?" question. Suppose that you're hunting for a document file and you aren't sure of its name. You look in WordPerfect's directory, and there are zillions of files. However, suppose that you are clever and have given all your documents the extension .DOC. If you type

>   DIR *.DOC

and press Enter, DOS limits the disk directory to just those files with the extension .DOC. You can then more easily read this list and find the file you want.

Repeating Commands

(Once is not enough)

When you type a DOS command and press Enter, DOS puts the command into a little tiny part of its memory. You can retrieve your last command from this memory by pressing the F3 key.

Why would you want to do this? Suppose that you're back to the timeless hunt, looking on floppy disk after floppy disk for that missing file. You put a disk into the drive, and type **DIR A:**—and, of course, the file is not there. You take out the disk, replace it with another one, press F3 to recall your last command (DIR A:) and press Enter. You've saved yourself a little typing.

Abandoning and Canceling Commands

(Oops! I take that back)

Suppose that you've just typed a lengthy DOS command. Looking at the command, you decide it's just not what you want. If you want to make a little change, you can press Backspace to delete characters to the left and then retype the command. If you want to entirely forget the command, press Esc. DOS enters a backslash after you press Esc, but it also starts a new line, where you can start typing a fresh, new command without worrying about deleting the old one.

If you're already given the command, you can still cancel it. To do so, hold down the Ctrl key and press C (uppercase or lowercase). Alternatively, you can hold down the Ctrl key and press Break. (The Break key is hard to find because the key's name is usually printed on the side of the Pause key.) Most commands are too quick to catch, though.

Managing Files the Hard Way
(More Command-Line Adventures)

IN A NUTSHELL

▼ Look at the con-
  tents of a file
▼ Delete a file
▼ Delete lots of files
▼ Undelete files you
  shouldn't have deleted
▼ Make a copy of a file
▼ Copy a file to a differ-
  ent drive or directory
▼ Copy a group of files
▼ Move files
▼ Rename files

 n this chapter, you learn how to manage files from the DOS prompt, with those good old, clunky DOS commands. The next chapter covers file management the easy way: with the DOS Shell.

Should you skip this chapter? Not necessarily. Often, it's a lot easier to type a quick DOS command rather than to start the DOS Shell. And if you're using an older version of DOS (Version 2, 3, or 4), you have to use DOS commands because the DOS Shell isn't included in these versions.

Peeking at a File's Contents

When hunting for a file, you may not be able to tell by the cryptic name whether you've got the file you want. The TYPE command lets you take a little peek at the file's contents.

To peek at a file's contents, type **TYPE** followed by a space and the name of the file, as in this example:

TYPE POEM1.DOC

Then press Enter.

Checklist

▼ If you created the file by using an application such as WordPerfect or Lotus 1-2-3, don't count on seeing your document the way it last looked on-screen. DOS can display only *text*. It can't display formatting changes such as bold, italic, and so on. You may see lots of ridiculous-looking symbols, such as happy faces, staves, knives, Greek symbols, and card suits (clubs, hearts, and so on). You're looking into the internal world of computer information, a world of happy warriors and gamblers who speak Greek. The file might

contain enough recognizable text that you can tell whether you've indeed found the document that you want.

▼ If the file doesn't exist in the current directory, you see the `File not found` message. Remember that the file might exist in another directory. You can change directories and try again, or type the path name, as explained in the next section.

▼ If you hear a beep when DOS displays the file, the file contains funny computer stuff in addition to text. Don't worry; you haven't hurt the file or your computer. To stop the display, press Ctrl-Break.

EXPERTS ONLY

Awe your coworkers with this impressive trick

When you use TYPE to display a document, the text whizzes by like directories do after you use DIR. To display just one page at a time, use the MORE command, as in this example:

TYPE POEM1.DOC | MORE

Note that there's a space before and after that funny vertical bar character, which you can get by holding down the Shift key and pressing the Backslash key. This command displays your document one page at a time. You press any key to continue.

Technical Babble about Path Names

When you type a command, DOS assumes that you want the command carried out in the current drive or directory. If the current directory is C:\DOCS, for example, that's what DOS uses when you tell it to do something.

But what if you want something done on another drive or directory? You can change drives or directories so that the one you want to affect becomes the current drive or directory. Simple enough. Or you can add path information. This information tells DOS which path to follow on the great mythical hunt for a file.

Here's an example. Suppose the current directory is \NOVELS, and you want to peek at a file called POEM1.DOC that's in the directory called \POEMS. You type the following:

    TYPE \POEMS\POEM1.DOC

Note that there's a space after TYPE, but no other spaces. There's a backslash before and after the directory name (POEMS).

You can also add drive names to the file name, as in this example:

    TYPE A:\OLDJUNK\VAPID.DOC

This command tells DOS, "Let me peek at the file called VAPID.DOC that's on the directory called OLDJUNK, which you'll find on the disk in drive A."

▼ When you type a file name that includes the drive and directory information as well as the name of the file, you've typed a *filespec*. You'll use filespecs a lot when you use DOS's file-management commands, such as COPY, DEL, and RENAME.

▼ Remember, no spaces within a filespec.

▼ You can create directories within directories. Suppose, for example, that you create a directory called \TEDIOUS within the directory \TASKS. A filespec for a file called JUNK.DOC in the \TEDIOUS directory would look like this: C:\TASKS\TEDIOUS\JUNK.DOC. (If you're curious, Chapter 6 explains how to create directories.)

▼ See Chapter 6 for more about directories and path names.

BUZZWORDS

FILESPEC

A file name that includes all the information DOS needs to figure out where the file's located, including its drive and directory location.

Deleting a File

Disks fill up all too quickly. When you're sure you no longer need an old file that contains one of your documents, delete it. (Then, according to Murphy's Law, you will immediately need that file.)

CAUTION

Don't delete any files associated with a program, even ones that look like they're not all that special. Many programs won't run unless dozens or even hundreds of innocent-looking, but vital, files are present.

TIP

If you are unsure whether you'll need a file, copy it to a floppy disk. Then delete the file from the hard disk. (The corollary to the previous Murphy's Law states that making a backup of files assures that the files will never again be needed.)

To delete a file, you use the DEL command. Type the command, a space, and then the file name:

DEL STICKIT.DOC

Checklist

▼ If the file isn't in the current drive or directory, you have to add the drive and path information so that you've typed a complete filespec—for instance, **DEL A:\MEMOS\STICKIT.DOC**.

▼ When you use DEL, it does its thing without giving you any confirmation, which is a little disturbing. You'd think you'd see a message such as

```
Uh-oh. You just deleted a file. I hope you were
sure that you didn't need it.
```

But there's nothing. Zip. The file's gone, and that's that.

▼ If you would like a second chance to think through the deletion, use the /p switch, like this:

DEL STICKIT.DOC /p

When you see the message, `Delete (Y/N)?`, press Y to confirm the deletion, or N to forget the whole thing and leave the file undisturbed.

Deleting a Group of Files

You can use the DOS wild cards to delete more than one file at a time. But beware. This command can really wipe out a lot of files, and if you haven't thought through what you're doing, you could lose a lot of your data! Here are some examples:

DEL *.YOU This command deletes every file that has the extension YOU, such as LOVE.YOU, HATE.YOU, and DANG.YOU. As you can imagine, a command like this one can cause a lot of grief. What if one of those DOC files contains the Great American Novel?

DEL POEM.* This command deletes any file named POEM, no matter what the extension. (POEM.DOC, POEM.TXT, and POEM.BAD will all fall prey.)

DEL *.* This command deletes all files in the current directory.

I HATE DOS!

CAUTION

If you type **DEL *.***, you're doing something pretty drastic—deleting all the files in the current directory. After you press Enter, you'll see a message asking you to confirm the deletion. Press Y to proceed or N to cancel the command, and press Enter. Be careful!

EXPERTS ONLY

Computer fun for the hopelessly paranoid

Just written something you wouldn't *ever* want anyone to see? Thought better of it? Too sensitive? Served its purpose? Well, did you delete it? Think you're safe now? You're not. When you delete a file, DOS just removes the *name* of the file from a little table it keeps on disk. All of the data is still there. A knowledgeable hacker (DOS' equivalent of a safe cracker) can recover this data in a matter of minutes. In fact, next you will learn how to recover deleted data yourself. If you insist on writing confidential and sensitive material on the computer, get a special program that completely obliterates files. (Norton Utilities has a program called WIPEFILE that works well.)

Recovering from an Accidental Deletion

Sooner or later, you will accidentally delete a very, very precious file—one that would take hours, days, or even weeks of work to re-create. You will regret ever having used the computer. Chin up. You may be able to recover the deleted files. The key lies in the UNDELETE command.

There's one catch to the happy news about UNDELETE: You must be using Version 5 of DOS or later.

To undelete a file, type the command, a space, and then the file name you want to undelete:

UNDELETE PRECIOUS.DOC

A great deal of nonsense appears on-screen. Ignore it. If, at the end, you see `File successfully undeleted`, great.

▼ You might see the file name like this:

`?RECIOUS.DOC`

DOS then prompts you, `Undelete (Y/N)?` Press Y. Then type the first character of the file name—which DOS has managed to lose. (Everything else in the file should be OK.)

▼ If DOS can't undelete the file, you see a message such as `The data contained in the first cluster of this directory has been overwritten or corrupted`.

▼ Undelete the file right away. If you delay, DOS may overwrite the file with new data, and then it's gone for good.

▼ If you can't remember the name of the file, type **UNDELETE** and press Enter. DOS will go through each file that has been deleted. Press any key or press N until the file you want to delete is listed. Then press Y. You are prompted for the first character of the file name. Type it, and the file is undeleted.

Making a Copy of a File

Copying comes in handy when you want to give a file to someone else to use or when you want to keep an extra copy for yourself. It's easy to copy a file. Suppose that you want to make a copy of the first chapter of your path-breaking first novel, NOVEL01.DOC. You type the following:

COPY NOVEL01.DOC NOVEL01.BAK

This command creates a copy of the file NOVEL01.DOC and names it NOVEL01.BAK. The copy of the file is located within the same directory as the original.

Checklist

▼ You list two file names when you use the COPY command. The first file is the source file—the one you're copying from. The second file is the copy (also called the *destination*, just to make things a little more obscure).

▼ There's a space after COPY, and after the first file name—nowhere else.

▼ When you name the copy, you must follow DOS regulations about valid file names. (Chapter 2 explains all the DOS rules for naming files.)

▼ If you don't include drive or path information in the filespecs, DOS makes the copy in the same directory.

▼ If you do include the drive and path information and you are copying to another directory, you don't have to type the file name. DOS will use the same file name.

▼ When DOS finishes copying the file, you see a message, such as
`1 file(s) copied.`

Copying a File to a Different Drive or Directory

Most of the time, people copy files to a different disk drive. Why? Two words: backup security. If a disk goes bad, you lose all the files on it—including copies you've made to the same disk. It's a good idea to make lots of copies of very important files. Place them on two or three floppy disks that you keep in separate places. That way, when your 72-oz. Big Gulp of Coke gushes out over your desk, there's a chance that at least one copy will escape the flood.

To copy a file to another drive or directory, include filespec information in the destination file name, as in this example:

COPY NOVEL01.DOC A:NOVEL01.BAK

This command tells DOS, "Make a copy of the file NOVEL01.DOC, name the copy NOVEL01.BAK, and store it on the disk in drive A."

Checklist

▼ When you copy a file to a different drive or directory, you can use the same file name. However, it's a good idea to use a different one, so that you don't lose track of which one is the original and which is the copy.

▼ To copy a file that isn't in the current directory, include the filespec stuff in the first file name (the source file), as in this example:

COPY C:\DOCS\NOVEL01.DOC A:NOVEL01.BAK

Copying a Group of Files

You can use DOS wild cards to copy a group of files. The following command copies all the files in the C:\DOCS directory to drive A:

COPY C:\DOCS*.* A:

The following command copies only the files with the name NOVEL01 (NOVEL01.DOC, NOVEL01.BAK, NOVEL01.BAD) to drive A:

COPY NOVEL01.* A:

The following command copies all the files with the extension *.YOU (including LOVE.YOU, HATE.YOU, and DANG.YOU) to drive A:

COPY *.YOU

Moving Files

Sometimes it's nice to move files—change their current residence from one disk or directory to another. DOS versions prior to Version 6 don't have a MOVE command that lets you move files in one step. However, you can move files by copying them to the new location and then deleting them from the old location. DOS 6 comes with a cool new MOVE command that lets you do the whole thing in one fell swoop. (Incidentally, DOS users have been clamoring for this command for years.)

Moving Files If You Don't Have DOS 6

To move a file, you copy the file to the new place and then delete it from the old place. To complete these tasks, you use the commands

discussed earlier in this chapter. Here's how you would move all the *.DOC files in a directory to a floppy disk:

1. Type **COPY *.DOC A:**.

This command makes a copy of all the DOC files and puts the copy on the floppy disk in drive A.

2. Type **DELETE *.DOC**.

This command deletes the DOC files from the current directory.

CAUTION

Before you delete the files from the old location, check the new location to make sure that all the files were copied!

Using DOS 6 to Move Files

VERSION 6

The new DOS 6 MOVE command copies the file and deletes the original—all in one maneuver. To move the file JUNK.DOC to drive A, you use this command and press Enter:

MOVE JUNK.DOC A:

When DOS moves the file, you see a message that looks like this:

```
c:\junk.doc => a:\junk doc [ok]
```

The [ok] indicates that the file was successfully moved to its new home and deleted from its original residence.

"I HATE THIS!"

"It says there's no such file or directory!"

The new MOVE command also has a unique, new error message: Cannot move file *such-and-such* - No such file or directory. From this, you can see that Microsoft hasn't lost its touch; error messages, even in the snazzy new DOS 6, are still ambiguous, maddening, and frustrating. This one means that you typed something wrong—the file name, the directory, or both. Shake your fist at the computer, check your typing, and try again.

To move all the .DOC files in a directory to a floppy disk in drive A, you use this command and press Enter:

MOVE *.DOC A:

DOS moves the files to the floppy disk, which frees up all kinds of room on your hard disk.

TIP

You can use the MOVE command, or its pre-DOS 6 equivalents (COPY and DEL), to archive files. To *archive* a file means to move it to a floppy disk. This maneuver frees up room on your hard disk, which is good. And it keeps a copy of the file—which is also good. (A recent amendment to Murphy's Law states that three minutes after you delete a file from your disk, you'll need the file.)

Renaming Files

After you get used to the 8-character limit on file names, you may decide to rename some files. LETTER, MEMO, and REPORT aren't going to cut it when you have several hundred letters, memos, and reports. To rename files, DOS provides the appropriately named RENAME command. The following command renames JUNK.DOC with the new name PRECIOUS.DOC:

REN JUNK.DOC PRECIOUS.DOC

Checklist

▼ Note that the old name comes first, followed by the new name, with a space between the two names.

▼ For those who prefer to use full names to nicknames, you can type **RENAME** instead of **REN**.

▼ REN isn't a way of getting around DOS's file name restrictions. The new name must also obey the rules.

Top Ten Ways to Make DOS More Fun

10. Create secret codes to disguise tasteless jokes in file names

9. Use UNDELETE to find any files someone thought he'd better get rid of

8. Figure out ways to use the keyboard to make sideways funny faces, like :) (happy) and :((sad)

continues

Top Ten Ways to Make DOS More Fun Continued

7. Make list of computer terms that sound dirty but aren't ("insert a floppy"; "press the F6 key")

6. Set DOS manuals on fence for target practice with .45 sidearm

5. Give prize at office for "Most Destructive DOS Command"

4. Fold, spindle, and mutilate old DOS disks to "let off steam"

3. Use PROMPT command to add message that speaks to your innermost fantasies, such as "What is thy next command, Your Eminence?"

2. Try to imagine how on earth Bill Gates got rich manufacturing this DOS stuff

1. Try to imagine what you'd do with Bill Gates' money

CHAPTER 4

Managing Files the Easy Way

IN A NUTSHELL

- ▼ Start the DOS Shell
- ▼ Display files on a floppy disk
- ▼ Change drives
- ▼ Change directories
- ▼ Select the files you want to do things to
- ▼ Peek at a file's contents
- ▼ Delete files
- ▼ Copy and move files by using the keyboard
- ▼ Copy and move files by using the mouse
- ▼ Rename files
- ▼ Quit the DOS Shell

There's an easy way to manage files with DOS: you use a nice, friendly application called the DOS Shell. If you have a mouse, you can completely avoid having to type those awful DOS commands. Granted, the DOS Shell isn't all sweetness and light, but it is easier to use than the DOS prompt.

The DOS Shell has lots of features, but this chapter resists the gnawing temptation to drown you in them. This chapter covers just the absolute, fundamental, can't-live-without procedures that you'll use in the DOS Shell. It doesn't go into the basics of file management because those are covered elsewhere in the book. Basically, this chapter is a no-frills look at the DOS Shell.

If you are not interested in the Shell, skip this chapter and go to the next.

The DOS Shell you meet in this chapter comes with Version 6 of DOS. If you're using Version 5, the features work the same way—sort of—but the screen looks a little different. If you're not using Version 5, you're stuck with those clunky commands discussed in Chapter 3.

Taking a Look at the DOS Shell

(Warm up your mouse)

To start the DOS Shell, just type this at the DOS prompt:

DOSSHELL

Don't forget to type two S's! Now press Enter. The program gathers important, complex facts about your hard disk, and your whole screen fills up with information.

Directory Tree window   Files List

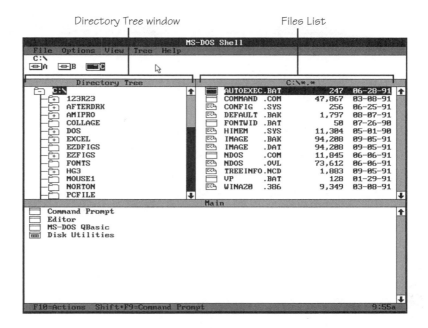

▼ At the top of the screen, below the bar that reads MS-DOS Shell, you see the names of menus. (You'll learn how to use these menus in a minute.)

▼ Below the menu bar you see the name of the current directory, probably C:\, which is the root directory of your hard disk.

▼ Below are the drive letters, which tell you the disk drives that are available on your computer. The current drive is highlighted.

▼ Below this information, you see three boxes called *windows*. In the Directory Tree window, you see the names of all the directories on your hard disk. A plus sign within the brackets means that the directory contains more directories.

continues

59

▼ To the right, you see the Files List. This list shows all the files of the current directory. The current directory is highlighted in the Directory Tree window.

▼ The bottom window is called Main and contains all sorts of techie things you don't need to know about now. Ignore this window for now.

▼ If you want to bone up on directories and what they do, flip to Chapter 1 ("You May Need to Change Directories") or Chapter 3 ("Technical Babble about Path Names").

EXPERTS ONLY

Picture this: Making the DOS Shell cute

The DOS Shell is an example of a major revolution in software design: the graphical user interface (GUI). GUI, incidentally, is pronounced "gooey." This major revolution was brought about by one of the most brilliant insights of the late twentieth century: You can convey information with pictures as well as words.

"Wait," you're probably saying, "I don't see any pictures." True. Right now the DOS Shell is showing a certain kind of display—the type of display the program uses unless you give it strict instructions to the contrary. To see all the cute little pictures, hold down the Alt key, press O, and then press D; you now see the Screen Display Mode box. Now press the down-arrow key until you highlight one of the Graphics options (try the 25 lines, Low Resolution option first); then press Enter. The screen goes blank, and then you see the Graphics display, with cool little pictures of the disk drives, directories, and documents. (The screen in this chapter shows the DOS Shell looking pretty.)

Displaying Files on a Floppy Disk

To display files on a floppy disk, insert a disk into the drive and move the mouse around on the desk so that the pointer is on the [A:] or [B:] at the top of the screen; then click the left button. Or hold down the Ctrl key, and press A (drive A) or B (drive B). DOS displays the files on that disk.

Change back to drive C by clicking on [C:] or pressing Ctrl-C.

"I HATE THIS!"

That darned warning box!

If you didn't put a disk into the drive, you get a stern box with the word WARNING! in large, black letters at the top. This subtle reminder indicates that you forgot to put a disk into the drive. Put a disk into the drive and press Enter. The box will disappear.

CAUTION

If you remove a disk from one of the floppy disk drives and insert another disk, the DOS Shell doesn't automatically update the Directory Tree or Files List for that drive. To refresh the list, press F5.

Listing Directories

(The directory in the directory in the directory)

Think of directories as folders. You can store directories inside directories inside directories, and so on (...and you'll tell two friends, and they'll

tell two friends, and so on and so on). When you start the DOS Shell, the Directory Tree window only shows the top-level directories in the root (main) directory. You can't see any directories that are hiding inside other directories.

The DOS Shell does let you know whether the top-level directories contain any other directories. If the folder that appears next to the directory name has a plus sign (+), there are nested directories within the directory.

BUZZWORDS

NESTED DIRECTORY

A *nested directory* is a directory that is inside another directory. If you have the directory RAP inside the directory MUSIC, RAP is a nested directory.

Checklist

▼ To see the nested directories, click on the plus sign. The listing opens (*expands*, in DOS talk) to show the next level of directories. The folder now shows a minus sign.

▼ To hide nested directories (called *collapsing a directory*), click on the minus sign.

BUZZWORDS

CLICK

Often you are told to click on an item. This has nothing to do with snapping your fingers. Instead, it means to slide the mouse on your desk so that the mouse pointer is over an on-screen item. Then press the left mouse button once. So if you are told to "click on the folder," you would move the mouse pointer to the folder and click the mouse button once. Easy enough.

Displaying Files

Take a look at the DOS Shell. The highlighted directory in the Directory Tree window (on the left) controls the file display in the File List (on the right). You might want to display files in another directory. No problem. You can use either the mouse or the keyboard to display files in another directory. (If you only have a keyboard, you can't try the mouse techniques. You're catching on!)

Here's what you do if you have a keyboard:

1. Press Tab until you see a dark color or shade on the Directory Tree window title bar.

2. Use the up- and down-arrow keys to move the highlight to the directory you want. Voilá! The directory's files appear in the Files List window.

If you're using a mouse, move the pointer to the name of the directory and click the left mouse button.

Checklist

▼ If the list of directories in the Directory Tree window is so long that you don't see the directory you want, use the mouse to click on the little down arrow on the right border of the Tree Directory window. (If you go too far down the list, click on the little up arrow or press the down-arrow key on the keyboard.)

▼ If you don't see the directory that you want listed, the directory might be *nested* within another directory. You need to expand the listing; look at the preceding section to learn how to expand a listing.

Selecting Files

(Identifying the victims)

To do something to a file, you first *select* the file. A selected file appears in a different color (if you are lucky enough to have a color monitor) or in reverse video. You can select more than one file, which lets you do things to lots of files at once.

The Mouse Method

To select a file by using the mouse, click on the file.

Checklist

▼ To select a group of files in a row, click on the first file. Then press and hold down the Shift key and click on the last file.

▼ To select files that are not in a row, click on the first file you want to select. Then press and hold down the Ctrl key and click on the second file.

▼ To select all files, click on File in the menu bar; then click on Select All.

▼ To deselect all files, click on File; then click on Deselect.

The Keyboard Method

If you're using the keyboard, selecting files is a bit more difficult than if you're using a mouse. Switch to the Add mode by holding down the

Shift key and pressing F8. You see the message ADD at the bottom left of the screen. Now press Tab to move to the Files List window. Use the up- or down-arrow keys to highlight a file name. To select the file, press the space bar. The file is highlighted.

Checklist

▼ If you highlighted the wrong file, press space bar again. The highlight disappears.

▼ To highlight a bunch of files in a row, select the first file. Then press and hold down Shift, use the arrow key to move to the last file, and press the space bar.

▼ To highlight all the files in the directory, choose Select All from the File menu. To choose this option, hold down the Alt key and press F (upper- or lowercase; it doesn't matter). Let go of the Alt key, and press S.

▼ To deselect all the files in the window, choose Deselect All from the File menu (press Alt-F, and then press L).

Peeking at a File's Contents

(Seeing is believing)

Got the right file? Before you do dire things to it, have a peek at its contents. You can't hurt or change the file by doing this, so there's nothing to lose.

To view the file's contents, highlight the file and press F9.

▼ When you use the DOS Shell to view your documents, you see lots of funny characters and symbols that weren't in your file when you created it. *Please remain calm.* Nothing bad has happened to your document. Your application program put these funny symbols and characters there to handle stuff like formatting.

▼ If you see five rows of bizarre numbers, press F9 to switch to the text display.

▼ Use the Page Up and Page Down keys to view the file's contents.

▼ When you're finished peeking at your file, press Esc.

Deleting Files

After you have selected one or more files, it's easy to do things to them, like deleting, copying, tickling, tasting, or moving them. In this section, you learn how to delete files that you no longer need. (Of course, you will inevitably need them once you delete them, but that's beside the point.) Here's how:

1. Select the file or files you want to delete.

2. Press Del.

After you press Del, you see a Confirmation box. The computer suspects that you are about to do something foolish, and is asking, "Are you nuts?"

3. If you're really serious about going on, press Enter to choose Yes. If not, just press Esc. (If you're using a mouse, you can just click on Yes or Cancel.)

Checklist

▼ If you selected more than one file, you see a Confirmation box for each file. Choose Yes to delete the file, No to skip this file and continue, or Cancel to give up the whole idea.

▼ If you deleted the wrong file, use Undelete immediately, as described in Chapter 3. Undeleting a file with the DOS Shell is even more confusing than using the DOS prompt.

CAUTION

If you don't see a box warning you that you're about to delete a file, you or someone else turned off the Confirmation option. You should leave this on so that you don't delete valuable files accidentally. To turn on Confirmation, hold down the Alt key and press O to open the Options menu; then type C to choose Confirmation. Use the arrow keys to place the cursor within the brackets next to Confirm on Delete, and press the space bar to place an X in this box. Use the same technique to place X's between the other brackets, too—if necessary—and press Enter to confirm your choices.

Copying and Moving Files by Using the Keyboard

If you have a mouse, skip this section; copying and moving files is much easier, more satisfying, and totally cosmic with the mouse. If you're still reading this part, you obviously don't have a mouse. My condolences. You'll have to type those wicked, awful path names.

Copying Files by Using the Keyboard

Here's how you make a copy of a file:

1. Select the file or files you want to copy.

2. Press F8.

You see the Copy File box.

3. In the To box, type the drive name and path name where you want to put the copy. For example, to copy the files to a disk in drive A, you type **A:** (don't forget the colon). To copy the files to a different directory on the same disk, you type the full path name of the directory (like **C:\DOCS\LETTERS**). Then press Enter.

TIP

If you're curious about path names, flip back to the section "Technical Babble about Path Names" in Chapter 3.

"I HATE THIS!"

Hey! That's *my* name!

If a file with the same name is in the disk or directory to which you're copying the file, you see a warning box that asks you for confirmation. Unless you're sure you know what you're doing, press Esc or click Cancel to cancel the operation. Why? Sometimes people unthinkingly give two different files the same name. If you proceed, you might overwrite a file that contains different data and if you do that, not even Undelete can get it back for you.

Moving Files by Using the Keyboard

The DOS Shell lets you move a file to another drive or a different directory. Here's how:

1. Select the file or files you want to move.

2. Press F7.

You see the Move File box.

3. In the To box, type the drive name and path name of where you want to move the file to. For example, to move the files to a different directory on the same disk, type the full path name of the directory (like **C:\DOCS\MEMOS**).

CAUTION

Remember that when you move files, DOS deletes the original.

I HATE DOS!

EXPERTS ONLY

Two, two, two windows in one

You can display two drives at once—one on the top, and one on the bottom—which makes it easier to keep track of what you're doing when you're copying or moving files.

To display two Directory Trees and Files Lists, hold down the Alt key and press V to open the View menu; then press D to select the Dual File Lists option. Highlight one of the lists, and then either press the Ctrl key (Ctrl-A or Ctrl-B), or use the mouse to click the drive letter ([A:] or [B:]). This displays the Directory Tree and Files List for one of your floppy drives. Now you can copy and move files from both the hard drive and a floppy drive, and you'll be able to see on-screen exactly what you're doing.

Copying and Moving Files by Using the Mouse

You copy files with the mouse by using something called *drag and drop*, which is what the cat does when it brings those dead things in. First you need to know how to *drag* using the mouse. Hold down the mouse button and, while you're still holding down the button, move the mouse across the surface of the desk. That's *dragging*. Then let go of the mouse button. That's *dropping*. Generally, you drag the mouse to move (*drag*) something on-screen.

Copying Files by Using the Mouse

This is how you use drag and drop to copy files:

1. Select one or more files in the Files List window.

2. Move the mouse pointer to the selected file's name or names. Press and hold down the Ctrl key and click and hold down the mouse button. Then drag to the drive to which you want to copy the files (for example, [A:] or [B:]). You can also drag to another directory in the Directory Tree window.

3. When you reach the drive or directory that you want to copy the files to, let go of the Ctrl key and the mouse button.

After you release the mouse button, you see a Confirmation dialog box. The computer demands to know whether you are really serious.

4. If so, click Yes. If not, click No.

Moving Files by Using the Mouse

To move files by using drag and drop, use nearly the same set of steps:

1. Select one or more files in the Files List window.

2. Move the pointer to the selected file's name or names. Click and hold down the mouse button, and then drag to the drive that you want to copy the files to (for example, [A:] or [B:]). You can also drag to another directory in the Directory Tree window.

3. When you reach the drive or directory to which you want to copy the files, release the mouse button and the Alt key.

After you let go of the mouse button, you see a Confirmation dialog box. The computer demands to know whether you are really serious.

4. If so, click Yes. If not, click No.

Top Ten Pet Peeves of Computer Mice

10. Getting choked by the cord

9. Being dragged through spilled Pepsi

8. Ridicule over your name. Mouse? Ha. Ha. Ha.

7. Often left hanging off the desk by your tail

6. Getting filthy cat hair in your mechanism

5. Keyboard feels that it can bully you because of your size

4. Underbelly burn from kid rubbing you back and forth at breakneck speed over the mouse pad

3. That cup of hot coffee teetering precariously close to you

2. When owner doesn't wash his hands first. Lord knows where they've been.

1. Used as makeshift football for impromptu family scrimmage

Renaming Files

If you don't pay close attention to file names, you may end up with file names such as LETTER1, LETTER2, LETTER3, LETTER4. Pretty soon—when you're frantically searching for the letter to the IRS—you'll realize that this isn't the best naming scheme. Fortunately, DOS is forgiving. You aren't stuck with a file name; you can rename a file. Here's how:

1. In the File List window, select the file you want to rename.

2. Hold down the Alt key and press F to display the File menu; then press N to choose the Rename option. (If you're using a mouse, click on File and then click on Rename.)

You see the Rename File box.

3. Type the new name in the space next to New Name, and then press Enter (or click OK) to confirm your choice.

"I HATE THIS!"

Denied!

If you chose a name that's already in use by another file, you see the helpful message, **Access denied**. Press Esc to give up the whole idea, or press the down-arrow key and then press Enter to try again with a new name.

Quitting the DOS Shell

To quit the DOS Shell, press Alt-F4. Easy enough.

PART II

The Bluffer's Guide to File Management

Includes:

5: Managing Disks

6: Hard Disk Housekeeping

7: On the Trail of the Missing File

8: More Disk Space! Faster Performance!

9: Backing Up Is So Very Hard to Do

10: A Virus Ate My Computer!

CHAPTER 5

Managing Disks

IN A NUTSHELL

- ▼ Understand the difference between floppy and hard disks
- ▼ Buy the right floppy disks for your computer
- ▼ Insert and remove floppy disks
- ▼ Protect the disk from being erased
- ▼ Figure out which drive is which
- ▼ Format floppy disks
- ▼ Make an exact copy of a disk
- ▼ Determine whether a disk is full
- ▼ Determine whether there's a problem with your disk

This chapter quickly covers the basics of using disks, whether floppy or hard. You don't need to learn all the technical details about disks; you just need to learn a few key tasks, as covered here.

Floppy Disks vs. Hard Disks

(The battle of the century)

There are two kinds of disks: floppy and hard. Both disks serve the same purpose: they are used to store information (your files or programs). The computer reads information from the disk, and writes information to the disk. This process is similar to a tape recorder. The player reads what's on the tape and then plays it. It also can write information on the tape. Disks work the same way.

A *floppy disk* is small (either 3.5 inches or 5.25 inches) and portable. You can take a floppy disk with you. The 5.25-inch disk is floppy (flexible). The 3.5-inch disk is covered with a hard plastic case, but it is still considered a floppy disk.

A hard disk is a nonremovable drive; that is, you can't take it with you. You can't see the hard disk because it is inside the system unit (the box thing). A hard disk can store much, much more information than a floppy disk. And it's faster.

TIP

> Remember that the important thing about hard disks isn't that they're hard—it's that they're big, fast, and non-removable. The important thing about floppy disks is that you can remove them from the drive.

Buying Floppies

Earlier computers didn't have a hard disk. You had to store all your information on floppy disks. And you had to run programs from a floppy disk. You spent the majority of your time doing the floppy shuffle—inserting and removing disks.

Most computers now have a hard disk as standard equipment. Still you use floppy disks when you install new programs and back up your data. You can also use them when you want to exchange files with someone.

Floppy Disk Basics

You have to decode a lot of technical information in order to understand the different types of floppy disks. Here are the basics:

▼ Disks come in two sizes, little (3.5 inches) and big (5.25 inches).

▼ Floppy disks are misnamed because they aren't really floppy—especially the 3.5-inch disks.

▼ Of the two, bigger isn't necessarily better. Big disks are vulnerable to damage because of a big, open area that lets the drive mechanism contact the surface of the disk. Little disks have a cunning aluminum door that slides shut when you remove the disk from the drive. If you have a choice, use 3.5-inch floppy disks; they're more durable and they can store more information.

▼ These days, all computers come with double-sided (DS) drives, which can use both sides of the disk—much like you can use both sides of an audio tape. (Earlier computers used only one side of the disk.) The disks you buy still have the abbreviation DS on the box. Ignore the DS; it doesn't mean anything of value.

79

I HATE DOS!

▼ Both kinds of disk, little and big, come in two storage capacities. (The next section reveals horribly fascinating statistics about capacities.)

▼ You can't use disks without formatting them. *Formatting* is a process in which the disk drive lays down a pattern on the disk's surface—a pattern that is needed for recording and reading data. This process is something like painting lines on a parking lot so that you know where to park cars. Formatting is covered later in this chapter.

Density and Capacity (Fraternal Twins)

Not only do disks come in different sizes; they also come in different densities.

Density refers to the recording method (*how* DOS crams the information on a disk). There are two densities: double density and high density. Density is related to capacity—how much information can be stored on a disk. Double-density disks (DD) cannot store as much information as high-density disks (HD).

Capacity refers to the *amount* of data you can store and is measured in kilobytes or megabytes.

HUH?

BUZZWORDS

BYTE, KILOBYTE, and MEGABYTE

A byte equals about one typed character. A kilobyte (abbreviated KB or K) equals around 1,000 bytes. A megabyte (abbreviated MB or M) equals around 1,000,000 bytes.

The Floppy Disk Match Up

Now that you know the different sizes and capacities, you have to match the right disk with the right drive. It's easy to figure out the size: you can't put a 5.25-inch disk in a 3.5-inch hole (unless you fold it, maybe).

It's more difficult to pick the right *capacity*. The trick is to find out the capacity of your drive. Remember that the drive has to be able to read the disk.

The easiest way to find the capacity is to ask the store where you bought your computer.

If you're using DOS 6, you can use a neat command called MSD (short for *Microsoft System Diagnostics*) to find out what drives you're using. Just type **MSD** at the DOS prompt. You'll see a screen with lots of big buttons. Press D to see a screen listing all the drives in your system. For each drive, MSD lists the disk size (5.25-inch or 3.5-inch) and capacity (such as 360K, 720K, 1.2MB, or 1.44MB). To exit, just press F3.

If you're not sure still, ask someone for help.

After you find out what kind of drive you have, use this table to figure out what disk you need:

You have this drive:	Buy these disks:
3.5-inch, 720K	3.5-inch DS, DD
3.5-inch 1.44MB	3.5-inch DS, HD
3.5-inch, 2.8MB	3.5-inch, DS, extended capacity

continues

You have this drive:	Buy these disks:
5.25-inch, 360K	5.25-inch, DS, DD
5.25-inch, 1.2MB	5.25-inch DS, HD

K=Kilobyte   MB=Megabyte   DS=Double sided (not important)
DD=Double density (stores less)   HD=High density (stores more)

Buying Disks

OK. You know what kind of disks you need. Now there are some tips on how to buy disks successfully:

▼ Buy formatted disks, if you can. You can format disks yourself, if you must, but this process is tedious; formatting a whole box of disks might take a half hour—maybe longer. Look for disks labeled *Formatted - IBM*. The IBM part is referring to the IBM formatting standard; you can use these disks even if your computer wasn't made by IBM.

▼ You can save a little money by buying generic, no-name disks, but the disks might contain flaws. For reliable backups, choose disks from established, brand-name companies such as Verbatim, Memorex, 3M, or Maxell.

Inserting and Removing Floppy Disks

You've probably had some experience inserting and removing floppies already, so you know there's only one way you can look like a goof doing

it: inserting it the wrong way. Here's the trick: Make sure the label is facing up and is toward you.

Checklist

▼ If you're inserting a big (5.25-inch) disk, make sure that the drive door is unlatched. After you insert the disk, close the latch.

▼ Make sure that there isn't already a disk in the drive. Remove the disk before you insert another one.

▼ If you're inserting a little (3.5-inch) disk, there's no latch. Just push the disk into the drive until it clicks into place. The drive button (which is just below the door) pops out when a disk is inserted.

▼ To remove a big (5.25-inch) disk, release the latch. The disk should pop out. If it doesn't, there's a space that lets you put two fingers in far enough to grab it.

▼ To remove a small (3.5-inch) disk, just press the button under the drive door. The disk pops out.

CAUTION

Don't force a disk into a drive. If it won't go in easily, there may be another disk in the drive, or you might be inserting the disk upside down or backward. Also, don't insert or remove disks when the little light is on. If you do, you could scramble the information on the disk.

EXPERTS ONLY

An impressive trick known only to true computer geniuses
What's this disk? Is it double or high-density? This question is pretty easy to answer for 3.5-inch disks because the manufacturers helpfully stamp HD on a corner of the disk. But what about 5.25-inch disks? Here's how to tell. Those old, obsolete double-density (360K) disks have a reinforcement ring about 1/8 inch wide around the hole in the center of the disk. The spiffy, new, modern 1.2MB disks don't.

Don't Mess with This Disk

Both kinds of floppy disks can be *write-protected*, which means you can prevent the computer from erasing what's on the disk or adding any new information to it. The computer can still read the information that's on the disk; it just can't alter the disk in any way. For this reason, you might want to write-protect a floppy disk that contains valuable data that you don't want to alter accidentally. Also, you should write-protect original program disks.

To write-protect a 5.25-inch disk, you use the little tabs that come with the disks. Wrap the tab over the notch so that half of the tab covers the notch on one side and half of the tab covers the notch on the other side. To unprotect the drive, remove the label. If you use all the tabs to wrap Christmas presents, you can use Scotch tape instead.

To write-protect a 3.5-inch disk, turn the disk over and find the little write-protect slider, which is on the upper-left corner on the back of the disk. When you move it up to uncover the hole, the disk is write-protected. To unprotect the disk, move it down to cover up the hole again.

"I HATE THIS!"

Error message, error message

If you've write-protected a disk and try to save data on it, DOS gives you its `Write-protect error` message. Just remove the disk, unprotect the disk, and try again.

Which Drive Is Which?

Floppy drives look like mail slots on the front of your computer. If you have only one floppy drive, it's drive A. If you have two floppy drives, one is drive A, and the other is drive B. The first floppy drive in your system, probably the top one if you have two, is drive A and the bottom is drive B.

You can't see the hard disk; it's inside the system unit. Your hard disk is drive C.

EXPERTS ONLY

On a network?

If you use a computer that's connected to a network, you'll find a network drive, which looks just like a hard disk from your viewpoint as you use DOS. It's probably called drive F, although the exact drive letter varies. If there are programs available on this drive, you can run them as if they were installed on your computer.

Formatting Floppies

(Initiating a disk)

If you buy formatted floppy disks, you don't need to read this section. If you didn't buy formatted floppies, read on. This section explains the why and how of formatting.

Why format? A floppy drive can't use a disk unless it is formatted. *Formatting* is a disk boot camp. DOS makes the disk do lots of pushups and chin-ups and run 25 or so miles. Really DOS does some complex stuff that you don't really need to understand. You just need to know that it has to be done.

Here's the procedure for formatting a disk:

1. Insert the unformatted disk into the drive.

2. Type the formatting command and press Enter.

If you're using drive A, type

FORMAT A:

Note that there's a space between FORMAT and A:; and don't forget the colon after A.

If you're using drive B, type

FORMAT B:

CAUTION

> If you see the message, WARNING: ALL DATA ON NON-REMOVABLE DISK DRIVE C WILL BE LOST, press N to cancel the operation! You're about to reformat your hard disk, which would cause endless grief. You should ONLY format floppy disks, and those go in drive A or B. Don't ever, ever, ever type **FORMAT C:**. Ever.

3. You are asked to press Enter before proceeding. Make sure that you've inserted the correct disk into the drive, and that it doesn't contain any valuable data. Then press Enter. The format process begins!

At the conclusion of the format, you are prompted for a volume label.

4. Type a name (called a *volume label*) of up to 11 characters. This volume label will appear when you use the DIR command. If you are crazy about names, type one. Otherwise, just press Enter to skip the volume label.

After the format is complete, you see a message telling you how many bytes (characters) of storage are available on the disk. The message looks something like this:

```
          1213952       bytes total disk space
          1213952       bytes available on disk

    512   bytes in each allocation unit
    2371  allocation units available on disk

  Volume Serial Number is 1D19-0FFD
```

5. After the message, you see a prompt informing you that you can format another disk. Press Y to format another one, or N to stop formatting and return to the DOS prompt. Then press Enter.

If you're using DOS 6, FORMAT checks to see whether the disk is already formatted. If so, FORMAT makes a backup copy of important information on the disk so that you can *unformat* the disk, should you later find that formatting the disk was a terrible mistake. (Say you happened to format a disk that contained information necessary to the known free world.) Grab a computer-savvy pal to help you unformat the disk.

Checklist

▼ If you're using the DOS Shell, you can access FORMAT by choosing [Disk Utilities] in the Main window, and then choosing Format. Then just type the drive name in the Format dialog box, and choose OK.

▼ If DOS reports that the disk has any bad sectors, discard this disk.

▼ There's no visual difference between an unformatted and a formatted floppy disk. So that you can tell which ones you've formatted, put blank labels on the formatted ones. To be really sure about which ones are formatted, write a little "f" in the upper-right corner of the label.

EXPERTS ONLY

Facts about formatting a formatted floppy

You can format a formatted floppy disk. Formatting a formatted disk provides a way of erasing *everything* on the disk. Of course, you could just type **DEL *.***, which would have the same effect. But you can use FORMAT instead. To make the process go faster, use the /q switch (the whole command is then **FORMAT /q**). The /q switch tells FORMAT to skip checking the integrity of the disk and get on with the job. To totally wipe out all the data on the disk, use the /u switch. This switch prevents you or anyone else from ever recovering the old data, so it's a good choice if you want to toss data for security reasons—sort of the electronic version of running paper documents through a shredder.

CAUTION

Sooner or later, a "helpful" colleague will tell you that you can "save money" by buying double-density disks and then formatting them for high-density storage. Don't do it; the disk won't be reliable.

Making an Exact Copy of a Floppy Disk

DOS offers a command called DISKCOPY that you can use to copy everything on one floppy disk to another floppy disk. When you use program disks, you might want to make a copy of the original and use the copy. This prevents anything dangerous from happening to your

original disks. ("Tech support." "Yes, I somehow formatted my program disk. Can you send me a new one? Hello? Hello?")

Unless you have two drives that are exactly the same (which is unlikely), you'll have to swap the first disk (the one you're copying from) and the second disk (the one you're copying to) in and out of the drive, but the result is an exact copy. Incidentally, the first disk is called the *source disk* because it contains what you want to copy. The second disk is called the *target disk* because it is where you want to put the copy.

To make an exact duplicate of a disk, place the disk you want to copy in the drive, and type the following (if you put the disk in drive A):

    DISKCOPY A: A:

If you put the disk in drive B, type this:

    DISKCOPY B: B:

Notice that there's a space after DISKCOPY and after the first drive letter (A: or B:). When you're sure you've typed the command correctly, press Enter. DOS prompts you when to insert and remove the source and target disks. Just don't mix them up!

Is the Disk Full?

Disks fill up faster than you can believe. To find out whether a disk is full, you can use the DIR command, which tells you how many bytes (characters) are free. You find this information at the end of the directory list. If there are fewer than 30,000 bytes free, consider the disk to be full.

If a floppy disk is full, just use a new disk. If your hard disk is crowded, you need to do some major housekeeping. Delete any files and programs that you don't need.

Is the Disk OK?

It's inevitable—disks go bad sometimes. It seems that no matter what you do, some disks eventually end up hanging out in pool halls and ditching important data. And consequently, they develop two kinds of problems: physical and logical.

Physical Problems

Physical problems have to do with the surface of the disk. If an area becomes damaged and DOS cannot reliably use it to store data, the area is known as a *bad sector*. No, that's not an area where there are a lot of bars and adult bookstores.

Are bad sectors bad news? It depends. A lot of hard disks have a few bad sectors, and that's OK. DOS recognizes bad sectors and locks them out so that they can't get back in and ruin the data party. Don't be alarmed to see bad sectors on a hard disk.

On the other hand, don't tolerate bad sectors on floppy disks. Floppies are cheap; your data isn't. If you've just formatted a floppy and DOS reports bad sectors, toss the disk.

Logical Problems

The second kind of disk problem is *logical*. This problem is much less serious than bad sectors and has to do with the way DOS stores files. The details aren't important, but sometimes when you delete files, little pieces of the files are left. DOS calls these bits of data flotsam *lost allocation units*. They're common on hard disks, and once in a while you should run the CHKDSK command to clean them up.

Top Ten Uses for Dead Disks

10. Use as office Frisbee

9. Affix to coworker's hat to make zany Mickey Mouse ears

8. Insert into toaster just for the heck of it

7. Beer coasters

6. Hide in clothing and pretend disk contains Top Secret Government Information

5. Smart-looking saucers for office tea party

4. Pile up 3.5-inch disks to level legs of sofa, ottoman

3. Fuel for space-age Databurner fireplace insert

2. Spray-paint with snowflake stencil for festive holiday decorations

1. Target for popular Data Dart game

CHAPTER 6

Hard Disk Housekeeping

IN A NUTSHELL

- ▼ Make sense of directory concepts
- ▼ View your hard disk's directory structure
- ▼ Change directories quickly
- ▼ Create directories
- ▼ Remove directories
- ▼ Organize your hard disk with directories

If you're reading this, chances are all that directory, CD, and path name stuff is giving you fits. Don't feel bad. It gives everyone fits. But you've come to the right place. This chapter supplies the key to organizing the information on your hard disk.

Why Directories, Anyway?

Suppose that you have one giant folder that holds all 6,000 of the letters you've typed in the last three years. Even if the letters are alphabetized, it would still be difficult to find the letter you need when you need it. Instead, you would be better off keeping the letters in various folders organized logically, perhaps by date or recipient or subject.

Storing data on a computer is the same way—it's much better to put your files in *separate* directories. For example, you can put all your recipes in a directory called \RECIPES, your poems in a directory called \POEMS, and your enemies list in a directory called \REVENGE. When you use DIR in one of these directories, you see only the names of the files in that particular directory, not the files in any other directories.

BUZZWORDS

DIRECTORY

A section of your hard disk that has been set apart for storing files of certain type (such as recipes or WordPerfect program files).

The Famous Directory Tree

In the fanciful imagination of DOS's creators, the directory structure of DOS is said to resemble a tree—an upside-down tree, with the root at the top and the branches at the bottom. The following illustration conveys this bizarre idea:

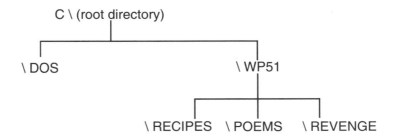

Checklist

▼ The root directory provides the "trunk" from which all the other directories branch out. The root directory, poor thing, doesn't get to have a name; it's indicated only by a solitary backslash (\ ).

▼ Every directory can have directories within it. In this tree, the root directory has two directories: \DOS and \WP51 (the WordPerfect directory). \WP51, in turn, contains three directories: \RECIPES, \POEMS, and \REVENGE.

▼ What are *subdirectories*? Basically the same as directories. Sometimes this term is used to talk about the relation between two directories. When a directory is placed within another directory, like \RECIPES within \WP51, the one that's *within* is called a subdirectory. Technically, all directories are subdirectories of the root directory. The bottom line is that the terms *subdirectory* and *directory* mean the same thing.

BUZZWORDS

PARENT/CHILD DIRECTORY

There's another way to describe the directory-subdirectory relationship. You'll run into references to the *parent* directory and its *children*, the subdirectories. The child directory is the subdirectory within the parent directory.

More on Path Names

You can type a file name in such a way that DOS knows exactly where the file is located. When typed this way, the file name is called a *filespec* (short for *file specification*). A complete filespec contains the path the computer has to follow to find the file. For example, suppose you type this command:

DEL C:\WP51\REVENGE\NBRS\JONES.TXT

DEL is the command name. The *path* is the remaining part. This command tells DOS, in English, to delete the file called JONES.TXT that's stored in the \NBRS directory of the \REVENGE directory, which in turn is stored in the \WP51 directory, which in turn is stored in the good old root directory on drive C.

Why are path names needed? Obviously, they're a pain to type. But remember that DOS always assumes that your commands affect the current directory only. Suppose the root directory (C:\) is the current directory, and you type the following:

DEL JONES.TXT

You'll get the endearing message, `File not found`. Why? The file is indeed on the disk. It just isn't in the current directory. This is like trying to find a love letter that you have stored in the Love Letters manilla folder, but you keep looking for it in the Insurance folder.

TIP

To avoid having to type a huge, horrible path name in a DOS command, and thus multiplying the possibility of error, change to the file's directory *before* typing the command. For example, suppose that you are trying to delete the file PIGEON.TXT, which is in the C:\WP51\POEMS\BIRDS directory. First type **CD \WP51\POEMS\BIRDS** to make the directory current. Then type **DEL PIGEONS.TXT**.

"I HATE THIS!"

Why can't I go directly to a directory?

You can't just type the name of the directory you want and go there. You have to go through the path. Think about a map. You can't drive from North Carolina to Georgia without going through South Carolina. Directories are the same way. You have to travel through the path.

Viewing the Tree Structure

If you're using DOS 5 or DOS 6, you can use the TREE command to see the tree structure of your disk on-screen.

To display the tree structure of your entire disk, switch to the root directory by typing **CD** and pressing Enter. Then type **TREE** and press Enter.

Here's how TREE displays a directory structure:

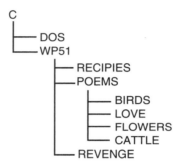

```
C
  ├── DOS
  └──WP51
         ├── RECIPIES
         ├──POEMS
         │       ├── BIRDS
         │       ├── LOVE
         │       ├── FLOWERS
         │       └── CATTLE
         └── REVENGE
```

TIP

Here's a way to deal with a lengthy tree, besides calling a lumberjack: display the tree by typing **TREE | MORE**. (You'll find the character above the backslash on your keyboard.)

EXPERTS ONLY

Printing a Tree

Use this neat trick to print your directory tree. You can then hang it by your system to help you remember how your disk is organized. To begin, turn on your printer. Then hold down the Ctrl key and press P to tell DOS to send its output both to the printer and to the screen. Now type **TREE** and press Enter. DOS prints the tree structure, just as you see it on-screen. Press Ctrl-P again to turn off printer output.

Top Ten Problems if the Enterprise Computer Ran DOS

10. Away team beamed to wrong planet due to typing error

9. Can't find file containing recipe for Romulan ale

8. `Load torpedo and press any key when ready` message takes thrill out of space battles

7. Captain's personal log accidentally rerouted to public address system

6. Dr. McCoy's computer recommends blood-letting for all ailments

5. Odd-sized floppy disks only available from Ferengi

4. Non-graphics display unable to show cool Star Fleet insignia

3. `Insufficient memory` message appears when trying to run ShieldsUp application and PHASER.EXE at same time

2. `File not found` message is only explanation when team fails to materialize on transporter pad

1. Accidentally reformatted disk containing navigation data

Timesaving Tricks for Changing Directories

When you start your computer, chances are good that the root directory will be the current directory. At the DOS prompt, you'll see `C:\`, which indicates drive C, root directory. The root directory prefers to remain nameless. It goes by the symbol \ (backslash).

To make another directory current, you use the CD command , as explained in the Chapter 1 section titled "You May Need to Change Directories." This section tells you some additional ways to make another directory current without having to type your brains out.

To change to a subdirectory of the current directory, just type the directory name without the backslash. For example, to change to C:\WP51\POEMS\CATTLE from the C:\WP51\POEMS directory, just type **CD CATTLE** and press Enter.

To get right back up to the parent directory, type **CD..** and press Enter. Those two little dots, incidentally, stand for "parent directory." That's why there are two. One stands for Mama, and the other stands for Papa.

To change to the root directory, type **CD** and press Enter.

Making Directories

With all this talk of directories, you're probably wondering how they are created. To create a directory, change to the directory where you want the new directory to be housed. For example, to create a directory called PIGEONS within the POEMS directory, you change to the POEMS directory.

Then type the command. Here's what you'd type to create the PIGEONS directory:

    MD PIGEONS

Note that there's a space between MD and the directory name.

TIP

To remember the command to use (MD), think of **Make Directory.**

Checklist

▼ You can also type **MKDIR** if typing unnecessary characters at the DOS prompt really turns you on.

▼ If you see the message `Bad command or file name`, check your typing. You probably forgot the space after MD.

▼ Directory names obey the same structure as DOS file names: 8-character first name, period, 3-character last name (extension). I wouldn't recommend adding extensions to directory names, however; it makes path names even more laborious to type. Also, when you use DIR, you'll have a tougher time telling the difference between files and directories.

Removing Directories If You Don't Have DOS 6

Before long, you'll accumulate unwanted directories—particularly as you decide to delete application programs.

"I HATE THIS!"

The directory that won't go away

To delete a directory, you must first delete all the files in that directory. And if the directory contains other directories, you first have to delete the files in those subdirectories and then the subdirectories themselves. Start at the bottom and work your way up. Remember that to delete all files, you type **DEL *.***.

Suppose that you want to delete the BIRDS directory, which is housed in the POEMS directory. To begin with, you change to the POEMS directory; then you type **RD PIGEONS**. Note that there's a space between RD and the directory name.

TIP

To remember the command to use (RD), think of **R**emove **D**irectory.

Checklist

▼ You can also type **RMDIR** if typing unnecessary characters at the DOS prompt gives you extra-big thrills.

▼ If you see the message `Invalid path, not directory, or directory not empty`, the problem could be any one of the following: you mistyped the directory name, you didn't change to the parent directory before using the RD command, or the directory isn't empty. Make sure that you are at the correct parent directory, check your typing, make sure that the directory is completely empty, and then try again.

▼ You can't delete the current directory. Keeping with the tree theme, it's like trying to saw off the branch you are standing on.

Removing Directories with DOS 6

DOS 6's new DELTREE command deletes a directory—even if the directory contains files and other directories. It also deletes all the files and directories inside the directory.

CAUTION

Warning! Danger! DELTREE is a very destructive command that can wipe out your work if you're not careful. Before using DELTREE, ask yourself whether there's anything in the directory you're going to delete—and anything in one of the directories it contains—that's of value. If so, move these files out of the directory before using DELTREE.

One instance where DELTREE might come in handy: You've given up using some big, fat program that's taking up 20MB of disk space. You've archived all your data files. There's nothing left in the directory except the program's hundreds of junky, stupid files. Nuke the whole thing with DELTREE.

To delete a directory with DELTREE, you type **DELTREE** followed by the directory name. Suppose that you want to delete the PIGEONS directory, including all the files and directories that it contains. Here's what you would type **DELTREE PIGEONS**.

Because this command is so drastic, DOS asks, `Delete directory 'pigeons' and all its subdirectories?` (You know that a command is a potential killer when DOS asks for confirmation.) To do so, press Y and then press Enter. To cancel this command and rethink the whole thing (a good idea if you're not sure), press N and then press Enter.

Tips on Hard Disk Organization

There are tons of theories on hard disk organization, but the following ideas usually meet with widespread agreement:

▼ When you install most programs, they create their own directories. For example, Microsoft Word for DOS creates its own WORD directory, and all the Word files go there. Don't reorganize.

▼ When you start creating documents with your application programs, you'll find that they probably get stuck in the same directory with all the program files. This mixes program and data files together and makes it hard to find files in directory listings and back up the data files.

▼ To simplify backup tasks, it's a good idea to put all your data files their own directories.

▼ When DOS was installed, the SETUP program automatically put all the DOS files in a directory called, appropriately enough, \DOS. Don't change this directory; it's where people and applications expect to find the DOS files.

▼ Don't create too many levels of directories. It makes typing path names even more of a pain.

▼ To remove all files from a directory, type **DEL**, a space, and the directory name—for example, **DEL PIGEON**. DOS asks you whether you are sure? Press Y, and then press Enter; all the files residing in the PIGEON directory are erased.

CHAPTER 7

On the Trail of the Missing File

IN A NUTSHELL

▼ Hunt for a file when you know the file's name

▼ Hunt for a file when you're not sure of its name

▼ Get the most out of DIR while you hunt for missing files

▼ Search for a file when all else fails

CHAPTER 7

I f there are computers in your office or home, you will sooner or later hear the keening wail of a user in distress: "My file! Heck, my file's gone! Oh, darn, where is my file?" (Note: The language here has been cleaned up for a family readership.) If this happens to you, you'll want help—fast. And here's where to get it.

Don't Panic—Yet

There are all kinds of reasons why you might have trouble finding a file. For most of them, there's a good chance the file still exists somewhere on your hard disk.

Checklist

▼ You might have saved the file to a directory other than the one you thought you saved it in.

▼ You might mistakenly think that you supplied an extension when you saved the file, when in fact you did not. Suppose that you typed **PIGEON** instead of **PIGEON.TXT**. If you tell your program to find PIGEON.TXT, it will tell you that the file doesn't exist, needlessly causing severe mental distress.

▼ You might have used a completely different file name than the one you remember. After all, with those sharp constraints on file name length, it's pretty easy to come up with a file name you'll have no chance of remembering, like MXPTLK.DOC.

If you can't find your file, take it easy—there's a very good chance you'll find it by using the tricks in this chapter.

Top Ten Destructive Acts Committed After File Loss
(followed by estimated average repair costs)

10. Revolver emptied into computer screen ($409, not including $175 fine and 30 days for possession of unregistered firearm)

9. Computer connected to high-voltage circuit in an attempt to "zap its brains out" ($1,487, not including loss of building due to fire)

8. Mouse thrown to ground and stomped to death ($72)

7. Computer system unit struck repeatedly with baseball bat ($1,219, plus $16 for a new bat)

6. Computer system unit thrown through plate glass window ($2,676)

5. Local DOS guru thrown through plate glass window ($2.8 million, assuming out-of-court settlement)

4. Foreign object thrust into floppy disk drive (dry object, $95; food or other moist objects, $387; explosives, $1,653)

3. Computer's chips immersed in Drano in an attempt to "teach them a lesson" ($211, not including charge for emergency room care)

2. Fist through monitor ($13,421, including medical care and disability)

1. Disk torn to pieces with bare hands and teeth ($0.62/disk)

Hunting for the File When You Know the Name

If you're sure you know the name of the missing file, the following commands are just the ticket. They tell DOS to hunt down every directory on your disk, looking for a file with the name you specify.

I'm Sure I Know the Name

To display the names of all the directories on drive C that have a file by the name of TEST.DOC, type this:

DIR C:\TEST.DOC /s /b

There's a space before C:\TEST.DOC, as well as one space before each switch (slash mark). To use this command, just plug your own file's name in place of TEST.DOC.

If DOS finds the file, it gives you a list of the directory or directories where that file is stored. For instance, if DOS finds the file TEST.DOC in three places, the list might look something like this:

```
C:\TEST.DOC
C:\WP51\POEMS\TEST.DOC
C:\WP51\ESSAYS\TEST.DOC
```

If there's no file by this name, you see the dreary message `File not found`. But don't give up yet.

I Thought I Knew the Name

You can use the DIR command with wild cards. Suppose that you're not sure you named the file PIGEON.TXT, PIGEON.DOC, or

PIGEON.YUK. Or maybe you didn't use an extension. Or maybe you named it PIGEON1.TXT, or something like that. But you know you started it with PIGEON! Here's the command:

DIR C:\PIGEON*.* /s /p /b

This command will find any of the following files, wherever they might reside on that big hard disk of yours:

```
PIGEON.TXT
PIGEON.DOC
PIGEON.YUK
PIGEON.FEA
PIGEON
PIGEON1
PIGEON1.TXT
```

Maybe I Don't Know the Name

Still haven't found it? Well, maybe you misspelled the file name. Try this:

DIR C:\PIG*.* /s /p /b

This will find PIGION.TXT, PIGIRON.NFL, PIGNEO, PIGOEN.YUK, and so on.

Decoding the Commands

If you don't really want to know *why* these commands work, skip this section. If you are truly curious, this section explains the cryptic commands.

▼ The /s switch tells DIR to look for the specified file name in the current directory *and* in every directory within that directory. That's why you indicate the root directory (C:\) before the file name—so that DOS searches your whole hard disk.

▼ The /b switch tells DIR to skip all the unnecessary header stuff like "Volume in Drive Z is Hot_Stuff." You're not interested in all that jazz right now. This switch also tells DIR not to display the size, date, and time.

Alphabetizing Directory Output

It's pretty hard to scan DIR's output on-screen when all those unsorted file names go zipping by. If you have DOS version 5 or later, you can alphabetize the directory list by using one of DIR's switches. Alphabetizing the list may help you find the file you want. For instance, if you know the files start with a B or C, you can look at all the B and C files.

To sort the output of DIR in alphabetical order, type this command and press Enter:

DIR /on /p

Note that there's a space before each of the slash marks. The /p switch, by the way, tells DIR to display just one screen of output at a time; you press any key to display the next screen.

EXPERTS ONLY

I just saved that file a second ago

Here's a very neat trick. If you're hunting for a lost file that you know you saved recently, you can sort DIR's output in reverse chronological order (the most recently saved files are listed first). Here's what you type:

DIR /o-d /p

The /o-d part contains a hyphen, which is probably next to the O above the alphabetical part of the keyboard. No spaces except before the slash marks!

The Ultimate DIR Command

The ultimate DIR command searches your entire hard disk for files that might be the one you're looking for. Not content with that, it also lists them in reverse chronological order, putting the most recent candidates first. Then, as if that were not enough, it routes the output to your printer, producing a printed version you can inspect at your leisure as you sip a mint julep. You are getting somewhere with this DOS stuff!

To use this command, turn on your printer first and then substitute your own file name for the one that's in this command. For example, you could type **ESSAY*.*** or **PIG*.TXT** rather than ***.DOC**. Type the filespec you think is most likely to retrieve your file.

DIR C:\ *.DOC /s /o-d > PRN

This command produces a printed list of all the files with the extension DOC on your whole hard disk, listed directory by directory, with the most recently created files listed first. Note that there's a space before C:*.DOC, before each of the switches, before the greater-than symbol (>), and before PRN.

Checklist

▼ The greater-than symbol is one of DOS's redirection symbols. This one tells DOS to send the output of the command (DIR, in this case) to the device to which the arrow points (the printer).

▼ If this command doesn't work, check your typing carefully. That's /o-d with a hyphen. Remember, backslashes are for directories, while forward-slanting slashes are for DOS switches. A space goes before and after the redirection symbol (>)!

When All Else Fails

Don't give up yet! Say you can't find the file by using any of the techniques discussed so far in this chapter. But you *know* you saved it. You must have used some radically different file name. However, you do have one clue to finding your file: you know that somewhere within the file, you typed the phrase "the same to you." If you particularly remember typing that phrase in your file, here's the command for you:

FOR %f IN (*.DOC) do find "same to you" %f

If you would like a complete explanation of how this command works and why it looks so funny, get one of those big, thick books on DOS and take two weeks off to read it. Or take it in faith.

▼ Before using this command, change to the directory you want to search. (You have to use it one directory at a time.)

▼ Substitute your own text for the text inside the quotation marks. And remember to type the quotation marks.

▼ Don't include any punctuation within the quotation marks, such as commas. Just try to think of one or two words that this document (but no other document) contains. Incidentally, one word is better, because DOS won't recognize a match if one word is at the end of a line and the second word is on the beginning of the next one.

▼ This command is case-sensitive, which means that you have to type the capitalization exactly the way you typed it in your file. If you put "Spleen" in your file but type **"spleen"** in your command, DOS won't find the file.

Assuming that you typed the command correctly, you see a lot of output. If a file name is listed with a line of dashes before it but nothing underneath, it doesn't contain the text you're looking for.

If DOS finds a hit, you see the dashes and the file name, and the text you're searching for is echoed on the next line. There it is!

Checklist

▼ If you see the message `syntax error` after pressing Enter, carefully check your typing and try again. There are spaces before the first %f, IN, (*.DOC), do, find, the text ("same to you"), and the last %f.

▼ This command searches only the current directory, not any of the directories within that directory.

CHAPTER 8

More Disk Space!
Faster Performance!

IN A NUTSHELL

- ▼ Double your hard disk's storage capacity
- ▼ Use a compressed hard disk
- ▼ Double a floppy disk's storage capacity
- ▼ Use a compressed floppy disk
- ▼ Get better performance from your hard disk

You can easily put together a list of stuff that there's never enough of: cash in your checking account, ice cream in the fridge, hours in a Saturday. And things that aren't fast enough: the checkout line at the grocery store, the person driving in front of you, and so on. Well, it's the same with computers. The commodities in chronic short supply for computers are hard disk space, speed, and memory. (Memory shortages are probed in Chapter 12.)

If you're lucky enough to be using DOS 6, you can use a utility called DBLSPACE that almost doubles the amount of hard disk space that's available for your programs and your data. You also can speed up your hard disk by using another DOS 6 utility, called DEFRAG.

If you don't have DOS 6, you can purchase utility programs such as Stacker or PC Tools that do the same things. But you'll spend less money if you upgrade to DOS 6. This chapter introduces the DOS 6 solutions to disk space and speed problems.

EXPERTS ONLY

You say you have 4MB of hard disk space and 120MB of memory? Huh?

One of the most basic mistakes a beginner (and even a not-so-beginner) makes is to confuse *memory* and *hard disk space*. But it's not the beginner's fault. Both are measured the same (by kilobytes or megabytes), but they serve different purposes.

Hard disk space is *permanent* storage. You use it to store programs and files when they're not in use. (Think of hard disk space as closet space.) Memory is not permanent. In fact, it's erased when you shut off or restart your computer. It's used to keep the programs and data you're using handy. (Think of memory as countertop space.)

EXPERTS ONLY

In other words, you have much more hard disk space than you will memory.

Squeezing More Space Out of Your Disk

It's inevitable that your hard disk will soon be crammed with programs, files, more programs, and more files. Files multiply at a furious pace. Sooner or later (probably sooner), you are going to run out of space on your hard disk.

You can free space by deleting the files and programs you no longer need. But there's an easier way if you have DOS 6.

Here's the pitch: How would you like to have an additional hard disk, almost as big as the one you've got? Sound too good to be true? Well, it's not. Read on—you're about to get one, and for free. No salesperson will call. And you may have already won a fabulous Winnebago camper or a two-week vacation to a Caribbean island paradise!

The key to this wonderful freebie is a utility called DoubleSpace, a disk compression program included free with DOS 6.

BUZZWORDS

DISK COMPRESSION PROGRAM

A disk compression program works by getting your disk into a full nelson and squeezing until the disk agrees to store your data more tightly than it normally does. Don't worry; it's safe.

Running DoubleSpace

There's only one bad thing about DoubleSpace—it takes a long time to set itself up, as much as an hour or more. You should therefore do these steps just before your lunch break, or maybe before you leave for the night:

1. Start your system, or if it's already running, quit any programs you are using.

2. Make sure that there's no floppy disk in drive A.

3. At the DOS prompt, type **DBLSPACE** and press Enter.

You'll see the Microsoft DoubleSpace Setup welcome screen. Don't worry about what it says on this setup screen. Basically, it's all good news.

4. Press Enter to see the next screen, and press Enter again to choose Express Setup. When you see the screen that tells you that DoubleSpace is ready to compress your drive, press C. DoubleSpace tells you how long this will take—probably an hour or more.

Many weird things will happen on-screen, but you can ignore them all. Go do something else.

Finally, the MS DoubleSpace Setup screen appears and reads `DoubleSpace has finished compressing drive C`. It also lists the space you had before and the space you have now and tells you how to reset your computer.

5. Press Enter to exit DoubleSpace and restart your system.

EXPERTS ONLY

A brief, unnecessary lecture on how DoubleSpace works

Believe it or not, there's lots of unused room in your files—like the air inside Cheetos. DoubleSpace takes all the "air" out of the files that are already on your disk, as well as any new ones you create or copy to the disk after installing DoubleSpace.

Of course, you're probably wondering whether this is safe. After all, if you smash a Cheeto to rid it of excess air, you'll never be able to restore that air, right? But DoubleSpace can reverse the trick it uses to squash the files. You can use DoubleSpace with confidence. In fact, after compressing your hard disk, you can forget about DoubleSpace. All you need to know is that you've got a lot more space.

Checklist

▼ If you see `Bad command or filename` when you type **DBLSPACE** and press Enter, you're not using DOS 6. Advice: get DOS 6.

▼ If your screen does not say `Microsoft DoubleSpace Setup` after step 3 and you see a dialog box in the middle of the screen titled `Compressed hard drive`, someone has already set up your computer with DoubleSpace. Just hold down the Alt key and press D followed by X to exit.

▼ DoubleSpace includes lots of options that allow you to tinker with the way it works. You don't need to worry about them now. The Express Setup uses the right options for most users.

▼ Don't worry about losing data, should DoubleSpace get interrupted while it's working. The program is designed to protect your data, even in the event of a sudden power loss.

Top Ten Rejected Names for the DoubleSpace Utility

10. Squisher

9. Squeeze-O-Matic

8. Smunch-Eze

7. RamIt

6. JamIt

5. CramIt

4. Stuff-'n-Run

3. FileStrangler

2. StowPro

1. Glut-Be-Gone

Using a Compressed Hard Disk

(The shortest section in this book)

Use a compressed hard disk just like you used it before you compressed it. The only difference is that now you have a lot more space.

Squeezing a Floppy

You can use DoubleSpace to increase the storage capacity of floppy disks, too. For example, you can compress a 1.2M floppy so that it can store a cool 2.3M. If you compress a 1.44M floppy, you get 2.8M of storage on it. (Disks and their related storage capacities are covered in Chapter 5.)

Does this mean that you should compress every floppy disk you use? No. As you'll see, compressed floppy disks aren't convenient to use the way compressed hard disks are. But compressing a floppy disk comes in very handy when you want to copy a lot of files to a single floppy disk.

To squeeze a floppy in drive A, type this command and press Enter:

    DBLSPACE /COM A:

Just substitute B: for A: to compress a floppy in drive B. This process doesn't take long—just a minute or two.

Checklist

▼ DoubleSpace compresses one disk at a time. It's OK if the disk has files on it; DoubleSpace will compress them. You can also compress a blank, formatted disk so that it's all ready to go. When you copy files to this disk, they'll be stored in compressed form.

▼ To use a compressed floppy, you must type a special DoubleSpace command that *mounts* (opens) the disk for use (the next section explains it).

continues

▼ If you want to use a compressed disk to give someone gobs of files, that someone must also have DOS 6.

▼ Be sure to label the disk "Compressed by DoubleSpace," since you'll need to take special steps to access the data you store on it. Read on.

Using a Compressed Floppy

To use a compressed floppy, you have to mount it. In the computer world, *mount* simply means to insert the disk and to use a command so that DOS can tell what the disk contains.

DoubleSpace automatically mounts the disk after you compress it, so if you've already compressed a disk, you can use it right away without having to do anything special. If you restart your computer, though, you'll need to mount the disk. Frankly, this is a bit of a hassle, so it's not worth compressing all the floppy disks in your office.

What happens if you try to use a compressed disk without mounting it first? If you try a DIR command, you discover that the disk has only one file (READTHIS.TXT) and that all the space is taken up. If you use TYPE to examine this file, you'll see this:

```
This disk has been compressed by MS-DOS 6 DoubleSpace.
```

To make this disk's contents accessible, change to the disk's drive, type **DBLSPACE /MOUNT**, and then press Enter.

The drive purrs and clicks happily, and you see the message
`DoubleSpace is mounting Drive A`. When DoubleSpace is finished,
you see the message `DoubleSpace has mounted Drive A`. Once the
disk is mounted, you can access the files.

▼ The drive stays mounted only as long as you use no other disk in
the drive. If you remove the disk and insert another one, even another compressed disk, you must use DBLSPACE /MOUNT again.

▼ If you restart your computer, you must use DBLSPACE /MOUNT
again to access this disk.

▼ All this is enough of a hassle to keep you from compressing a lot of
floppy disks. Use this technique only when you really want to cram
a lot of stuff on one floppy disk.

Spiffing Up Your Hard Disk's Performance

You won't like what you're about to read, but it's true: DOS is likely to
store your precious data here and there all over the hard disk, rather
than putting it all in one nice, continuous unit. This phenomenon is
called *file fragmentation* and makes your hard drive run more slowly.
When you tell DOS you want a file, it has to go around the hard disk
collecting all the pieces. This can take some time.

I HATE DOS!

EXPERTS ONLY

Curious about file fragmentation? Read this.

Why does file fragmentation occur? When you or a program delete a file, a gap is left on the disk. Later, when you use your program to save your data, DOS fills in the gaps whenever it can. Your file is broken up into pieces that are placed hither, thither, and yon. The result is file fragmentation.

There's nothing wrong with file fragmentation from the data security point of view—that is, your data is just as safe as it would be if it were all stored as a unit. But file fragmentation leads to sluggish hard disk performance, because the drive head (the part that copies the data from memory to disk and back again) has to go all over the disk as it works with your file.

The cure for file fragmentation is running a defragmentation utility, a program that rewrites all the data on your disk so that all the file parts are put back together. To keep your hard disk running at top speed, you should run a defragmentation utility about once a month.

VERSION 6

DOS 6 comes with its own defragmentation utility, called DEFRAG. If you don't have DOS 6, you can purchase a defragmentation utility program if you really want one, but it's better to upgrade to DOS 6 because you'll get lots of other useful things like the MSBACKUP utility, discussed in Chapter 9.

TIP

DEFRAG takes time to do its job—as much as 20 or 30 minutes. So start DEFRAG just before you're getting up for lunch or your Oprah break.

To run DEFRAG, type **DEFRAG** and press Enter.

You see a screen with lots of information you can ignore, as well as a dialog box asking you which drive you want to defragment. By default, DEFRAG targets your hard disk, so just press Enter. Next, DEFRAG analyzes your disk and shows you the Recommendation dialog box. This box recommends the best defragmentation method. Just press Enter.

As DEFRAG runs, you see a screen that shows a "map" of your disk. Initially, it's entertaining to watch this screen, which shows how DEFRAG moves your data around to defragment your files—but this gets old very quickly.

When DEFRAG finishes running, you hear three happy beeps; just press Enter. You then see a dialog box that lets you optimize another drive, if you want. To get back to DOS, press Tab twice to highlight Exit DEFRAG, and press Enter. If you have a mouse, you can just click Exit DEFRAG.

CAUTION

If you see a message informing you that you need to run CHKDSK before you can defragment your disk, get a DOS guru to help you. (Or check out Chapter 19, which tells you a little about the CHKDSK command.)

CHAPTER 9

Backing Up Is So Very Hard to Do

(But You'd Better)

IN A NUTSHELL

- ▼ Learn what you need to back up
- ▼ Find out what you need to back up to
- ▼ Back up your work by using older versions of DOS
- ▼ Back up your work by using DOS 6's MSBACKUP utility

F act 1: Very few people back up their work by copying it onto floppy disks or special backup tapes. Fact 2: All hard disks eventually die—and in many cases, you can't recover the files unless you have a backup. Fact 3: Many people fervently *wish* they had backed up when a nasty hard disk crash wipes out several months of work. Cheerful prospect, isn't it?

BUZZWORDS

BACK UP

To copy the data on your hard disk to a different disk (a set of floppies, another hard drive, or a backup tape—a storage device designed just for backups). If your hard disk fails, not to worry—you've got a backup copy.

In defense of people who don't back up, backup commands and programs are Not Fun. Still, you'll thank me if you follow the brief, to-the-point, no-frills backup procedures described in this chapter. Never mind that I haven't backed up *my* disk for about six months...

DOS version 6 includes a new backup program, MSBACKUP. If you have DOS 6, use MSBACKUP. Versions before 6.0 include a BACKUP command, which isn't as complete as MSBACKUP, but it's certainly better than nothing.

What to Back Up?

A lot of people back up everything on their hard disks, including programs. This type of full backup is quite an ordeal—you might need 50 or more floppy disks!

To save time (and make backups less of an ordeal), other people only back up their data files. Unless you really want to shovel 50 or 100 disks in and out of your computer, I'd recommend that you back up only data files. If your disk fails, you can reinstall your software using the original program disks and restore the data using your backup files.

If you keep your data in separate directories, backing up only the data files will be easy. If your data is mixed in with the program files, you'll have a harder time. Keep this in mind when setting up directories.

You might want to set up one main data directory with separate directories for different types of data, like the following:

C:\DOCS

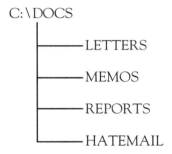

By the way, if you want to know even more about directories and organizing your hard disk, take a look at Chapter 6.

Top Ten Excuses for Not Backing Up (Famous Last Words)

10. Thought it was just another one of those scare tactics

9. Haven't heard that funny noise lately

8. Requires a truckload of floppies

7. Thought the good fairy was doing it

continues

6. Don't floss or exercise; why not be consistent?

5. Nobody else does it

4. I'm a risk-taker. I live on the edge.

3. *Probably* won't need these files again, anyway

2. My hard disk is brand new! What could go wrong?

1. I'll start next week. I promise.

Why Using COPY Just Isn't Good Enough

A lot of DOS users back up their work by copying their files to a floppy disk. If you have just a few files and they all fit on one disk, this procedure will work. But if you have lots of files, the disk fills up, COPY stops copying, and you get the `Insufficient disk space` message. Darn. You won't be able to tell which files were copied and which weren't. That's why backup commands were invented. Basically, they work like COPY, except that they prompt you when the next disk is needed.

Backing Up Using Older Versions of DOS

If you don't have DOS 6, you have to rely on the good old BACKUP command to back up your work.

To get ready to back up, get a bunch of formatted floppy disks. They don't have to be blank, but make sure that they don't contain any stuff that you need. BACKUP overwrites all the data on the disks. If the disks aren't formatted, BACKUP formats them for you.

How many floppies do you need? That depends on how much you're going to back up. If you insist on backing up your entire hard disk, you need dozens of them. If you back up your data files only, this number could be reduced to as few as two or three floppy disks. You'll need about one high-density disk for each megabyte of junk on your hard disk.

What to Back Up

If you have two floppy disk drives (3.5-inch and 5.25-inch), back up to the 3.5-inch drive. These smaller disks are more durable and less prone to finger smutches.

EXPERTS ONLY

A brief but optional lecture about the virtues of tape backup drives

If you're using your computer for business or professional purposes, safeguarding your data makes good cents (and dollars, too). As you'll discover, though, it's a hassle to back up with floppy disks—all that swapping disks in and out gets tedious.

A tape backup drive, on the other hand, makes the whole process much more pleasant. In fact, backup programs are available that back up your work every day at a set time (say, 4:30 a.m.) automatically! You can add a tape backup drive to your computer for less than $300, and it's money well spent.

Backing Up All Files on Your Whole Hard Disk

If you've decided to back up all the files on your disk, including program files, you'll need a lot of disks and a lot of patience. As a rule of thumb, you need about one high-density floppy disk for each 1MB of hard disk data. That works out to about 120 high-density disks for a 120MB hard drive that's stuffed with programs and data.

To back up your whole hard drive, type the following and press Enter:

BACKUP C:*.* A: /s

Note the spaces. There's one before C:*.*, one before A:, and one before /s. If you want to back up to drive B, type **B:** instead of **A:**.

BACKUP begins backing up the files to the first disk. When this disk is full, DOS prompts you to remove this disk and insert the next. Be sure that you label each disk in sequence—001, 002, 003, and so on. When BACKUP is finished, you see the DOS prompt again.

Backing Up Just Your Data Files

If you store all your data within one directory, you can back up just that directory. (This command also backs up directories within the directory.) To back up all the files in the C:\DOCS directory and all the directories it contains, type the following and press Enter:

BACKUP C:\DOCS*.* A: /s

Note the spaces: there's one before C:\DOCS*.*, one before A:, and one before /s. Don't type **DOCS**; type the name of the directory that you use to store your data files. If you want to back up to drive B, type **B:** instead of **A:**.

BACKUP begins backing up files to the first disk. When that disk is full, DOS prompts you to remove the first disk and insert another one. Be sure that you label each disk in sequence—001, 002, 003, and so on. This continues until everything has been backed up. When backup is complete, you see the DOS prompt.

TIP

What if your data files are in directories here and there all over your hard disk? If all your data files have the same extension (perhaps .DOC or .TXT), you can specify that extension in the BACKUP command. DOS will then ransack your entire disk for these files and back up only them. If you want to back up all files with the .DOC extension, type

```
BACKUP C:\*.DOC /s
```

When BACKUP is finished, put your backup disks away someplace safe—where they won't get coffee or YaHoo! spilled on them.

TIP

If you are really nervous about losing the data on the disks, you might want to store the disks at a different location. For instance, store a set of your work backup at home and a set of your home backup at work.

Checklist

▼ As you remove each disk, date it and label it in order (Disk 1, Disk 2, Disk 3, and so on). *This is important.* If you need to put these files back on your system after a disk failure, you need to know which disk to insert when.

continues

▼ You can vary this command in useful ways. To back up all the *.DOC files on your entire hard disk, for example, you type **BACKUP C:*.DOC A: /s**.

▼ The /s switch is an important key to the way this command works. It tells DOS, "Back up this directory and all the directories that it contains."

▼ If you're using DOS Version 4 or later, BACKUP will format disks, if they aren't already formatted. (This makes the backup process even slower, though, so start with formatted floppies.) To get an earlier version of DOS to format disks, use the /f switch. (You add the /f switch after the /s switch.)

▼ Chapter 19 tells you how to restore the data after a disk crash.

TIP

It's a good idea to write the command you used to back up the files on at least the first disk. This helps you when you want to restore the files (copy them back) or when you want to do a new backup (as described next).

Backing Up Only Files That Have Changed

OK, you've backed up your work. Very good. But then you make some changes to existing files. Or create new ones. What now? Do you have to repeat this whole, arduous process? Nope. A handy BACKUP switch, /m, tells BACKUP to back up only those files that have been changed or created since the last backup took place.

This process is called an *incremental backup*, a term that sounds like it involves something awful that happens to your septic tank.

INCREMENTAL BACKUP

In an *incremental backup*, you only back up the files that have changed, or that you've created, since the last backup occurred.

To back up the files that you have created or that have changed since the last backup, you need fewer disks than last time—maybe just one or two. You need *new* disks—don't use the disks you used for the original backup.

Use the same command you used for the last backup, except add the /m switch. For example, if you used the BACKUP C:\DOCS*.* A: /s command, type this and press Enter:

BACKUP C:\DOCS*.* A: /s /m

If you want to back up to drive B, type **B:** instead of **A:**. Don't forget the good old /s switch, which tells BACKUP to back up all the files and directories within the directory you specify.

DOS then backs up only changed or new files onto the disk. When the first disk is full, you're prompted for the next one. When backup is complete, you see the DOS prompt.

As before, carefully number and date each floppy disk as you remove it from the disk drive.

Starting Over Again

If you continue doing incremental backups, you get a confusing situation in which backup disks contain many different versions of files you have worked on. (The files are on the original disk and each incremental disk.) Sooner or later, you should do a full backup again, and start over from scratch. If you do an incremental backup every day (a good idea for "heavy users"), do a full backup once a week. If you do an incremental backup once a week, do a full backup once a month.

Use a new set of disks for the full backup. Put the old set away and use them for the *next* full backup.

Backing Up Using DOS 6

If you have DOS 6, you see the message `Bad command or file name` if you type **BACKUP** and press Enter. That's because DOS 6 comes with a new backup program called MSBACKUP. This is both good and bad. It's good because MSBACKUP does a lot more than the old BACKUP command did. It's bad because MSBACKUP is a very complex program with dozens and dozens of options. Rather than one command, you have to wade through more steps. But it looks good. And isn't that what's important?

In this section, you learn the minimum you need to work with MSBACKUP.

The Compatibility Test (Matchmaking)

The first time you run MSBACKUP, you have to go through an ordeal called a *compatibility test*. This test determines whether MSBACKUP can

get along with your computer. It's tempting to skip it. Don't. Only if you run the compatibility test can you be sure that MSBACKUP will work properly.

Before starting MSBACKUP, get two floppy disks that are the same capacity as the disk drive you're going to use for backups (but don't insert them into the drive yet). For example, if you have a high-density 5.25-inch drive, use high-density 5.25-inch disks.

To run MSBACKUP, remove any disks from your computer's disk drives, and type **MSBACKUP**. Then press Enter.

You see the MSBACKUP screen, but before you can get your bearings, a box pops up. This box accuses you of not having configured MSBACKUP. To do so, press Y or click Yes. You see another dialog box; make sure that there are no floppy disks in the drive, and then press S to start the configuration process.

If your computer has two floppy drives, MSBACKUP asks you which drive you want to use for backups. Press A or B to continue.

A lot of screens go by quickly. Ignore them. Just insert and remove disks as you're told.

If all goes well, you see a message informing you that your computer has passed the compatibility test. Just press Enter to see the main MSBACKUP menu (finally). Choose Quit to exit to the DOS prompt.

"I HATE THIS!"

We're not compatible!

You may see a horrible, depressing message telling you that your computer has failed to measure up to the compatibility test, and that you have to add something incomprehensible to a file you've never heard of. Don't despair; you can actually

"I HATE THIS!"

do this. Carefully write down exactly what you're supposed to type in which file, and choose OK to exit. Just flip to Chapter 18, which shows you how to use EDIT to add the missing line to CONFIG.SYS.

Backing Up All Files

MSBACKUP is loaded with options, fancy screens, menus, and hot mouse action. Ignore 98 percent of it. Why make backing up any harder?

Your first step in backing up your data is to perform a *full backup*. This doesn't necessarily mean backing up your whole hard disk. If you prefer, you can just back up your data files.

You need some blank floppy disks for this backup procedure. They don't have to be formatted. How many? Generally, about one high-density floppy disk for every 1MB of hard disk stuff you want to back up. If you back up just the directories containing your data, as I recommend, you may need only one, two, or three disks. If you insist on backing up your whole hard disk, you need a lot more—as many as 120 for a 120MB hard drive that is stuffed to the gills with data and programs. Date them and label them Full Backup Disk #1, Full Backup Disk #2, and so on. Here's what you do:

1. Start MSBACKUP by typing **MSBACKUP** and pressing Enter.

2. In the main Backup menu that appears after you start the program, press B or click the Backup button.

   You see the Backup screen. No files are selected for backup yet.

3. If you want to back up all the files on the disk, press the space bar. You see the message `All Files` next to drive C in the Backup From list.

4. If you want to back up only some files, press L or click on the Select Files button.

You see the Select Backup Files screen. You use this screen to tell MSBACKUP which files you want to back up.

5. To select a directory to back up, use the up- and down-arrow keys to highlight the directory; then press the space bar.

You see a triangle next to the directory name, indicating that it has been tagged for backup. In the File List, you see that all the files now have little check marks, indicating that they've been selected.

Note that directories that are contained in the highlighted directory are *not* selected—you have to press the space bar for *every* directory that you want to back up.

6. When you're finished choosing directories, just press Enter or click OK to return to the Backup screen.

7. Press S or click the Start Backup button to get things going.

You see a dialog box asking you to insert disk #1 into the disk drive.

8. Insert the first floppy disk into the disk drive and press C or click Continue. Insert additional disks when DOS prompts you.

When MSBACKUP is finished backing up your data, you see the Backup Complete dialog box—full of lots of statistics. Ignore them.

9. Just press Enter to return to the Backup screen, and press Q or click Quit to return to DOS. Done!

Put those disks away in a nice, safe place!

EXPERTS ONLY

Try this tricky backup, DOC

Here's another way to select files to back up. Some applications consistently assign a certain extension to your data files, such as .WK1 (Lotus) or .DOC (Microsoft Word). If you use a program that assigns an extension, you can tell MSBACKUP to back up files with that extension, wherever they might be found on your disk.

To do so, follow steps 1 and 2 in the preceding numbered list. Then choose the Select Files button in the Backup screen. When the Directory Tree and File List appear, use the arrow keys or the mouse to highlight the root directory (C:\). Then choose Include. When the Include Files dialog box appears, press Tab to highlight the File box, and press * and a period followed by your application's extension. For example, you might type ***.WK1** or ***.DOC**. Press Enter to confirm your choice, and proceed with the backup from step 5.

Backing Up the Files You've Created or Changed

VERSION 6

In an *incremental backup,* you back up only the files you've changed or created since the last full backup. Because far fewer files are backed up in an incremental backup, the whole process goes a lot faster. You can even do this at the end of every computing session without suffering too much pain or anguish. If that's too often, you can go a few days.

For this backup, you need a new set of blank disks (they don't have to be formatted). Don't use the disks you used to create your full backup. Date and label the disks Incremental Backup Disk #1, Incremental Backup Disk #2, and so on. Then follow these steps:

1. Start MSBACKUP by typing **MSBACKUP** and pressing Enter.

2. In the main Backup menu that appears after you start the program, press B or click the Backup button.

You see the Backup screen. Backup remembers which directories you selected from the last backup.

3. Press Y or click Backup Type.

You see the Backup Type dialog box.

4. Press I or click the little round thing next to `Incremental`. Then press Enter or click OK.

5. Press S or click the Start Backup button to get things going.

You see a dialog box asking you to insert Incremental Backup Disk #1 in the disk drive. (*Don't insert your Full Backup disk.*)

6. Insert the disk into the drive, and press C or click Continue. Insert additional disks when DOS prompts you.

When MSBACKUP is finished backing up your data, you see the Backup Complete dialog box—with lots of statistics. Ignore them.

7. Press Enter to return to the Backup screen, and press Q or click on Quit to return to DOS. Done!

Starting over Again (DOS 6)

One big problem with incremental backups is that you get a new incremental disk set every time you perform this procedure. Rather than letting the number of these disks increase indefinitely, perform another Full Backup.

TIP

> How often should you go through this backup cycle? It depends on how much you use your computer. To make sure you never lose a lot of your work to a hard disk failure, perform an Incremental Backup at the conclusion of any session where you've created or altered an important file. After seven or eight such sessions, you'll have seven or eight incremental backup disks, which is a lot, so you'll be ready for another Full Backup.

Remember that MSBACKUP always stores the options you choose, and that includes Incremental Backup. When you decide to perform another Full Backup, you need to choose Full Backup by clicking on the Backup Type button and selecting Full in the Backup Type box. Press Enter to return to the Backup window.

Using the Backup Disks

(I *hope* you can skip this!)

If your hard disk fails, you'll need to recover the information on your backup disks in an operation called a *restore*. The backed-up information isn't accessible any other way. Check out Chapter 19 for this and other disaster-recovery techniques.

CHAPTER 10

A Virus Ate My Computer!

IN A NUTSHELL

- ▼ Understand computer viruses
- ▼ Scan your system for viruses
- ▼ Protect yourself against "suspicious activities"

W hat's a virus? Basically, a *virus* is a program designed to do something unexpected to your computer. Sometimes the unexpected is something silly such as displaying a "Gotcha" message on-screen on a certain day at a certain time. Sometimes the surprise is vicious: the virus destroys your hard disk.

Viruses are created by *hackers* (computer enthusiasts who enjoy making unauthorized modifications to programs and breaking security systems). Viruses propagate by traveling unseen on floppy disks. If you insert an infected disk into your system and start an infected program, the virus immediately infects as many of your files as it can. After infecting your system, many viruses operate for a long time without your being aware of their presence.

Is there any defense against viruses? Thanks to Anti-Virus and VSafe, new features released with DOS 6, you can give yourself some protection against computer viruses. Anti-Virus scans your hard disk and memory for viruses and can even remove them from infected files. VSafe constantly monitors your system for signs of "suspicious" activity, which might indicate that a virus is at work.

Dealing with the Virus Scare

Don't let virus fear get to you. Almost all the little things that can go wrong with your system, such as forgetting to turn on the monitor, have nothing to do with computer viruses.

Your best defense against viruses is to run no program on your computer unless you've taken the program disks yourself from a fresh, shrink-wrapped package. Don't use programs from any other source.

If you've only used program disks and haven't exchanged disks with anyone else, you don't have to worry. And it's probably OK to exchange data files with coworkers and friends. You have to use an infected disk to get the virus.

Get a Checkup

(Before It's Too Late)

You can get a checkup to see whether your computer has any viruses. Type this command and then press Enter:

    MSAV

You see the Microsoft Anti-Virus screen. Press Enter to choose the Detect button.

Checklist

▼ Anti-Virus checks all the files on your hard disk. Although the program runs fast, it is very sensitive and examines each file minutely.

▼ If you hear a horrible, jarring, wrenching beep, Anti-Virus has found something. You may see the Virus Found dialog box, which isn't a fun thing to have happen. Choose Clean to remove the virus from your system.

▼ If you hear the dreaded beep and see the Verify Error dialog box, don't panic. It just means that a crucial system file, such as CONFIG.SYS, has been changed recently. You or a program might have done this for perfectly innocent reasons. If you have modified any system files (see Chapter 18) or installed a new program recently, relax. Just press Enter to update the change.

▼ When the checkup is over, you'll see the Viruses Detected and Cleaned dialog box. If your disk is clean, the dialog box indicates that no files were infected. Just press Enter to close this dialog box.

To exit the program, use the down-arrow key to highlight the Exit button, and press Enter (or click the Exit button or press X). When the Close Microsoft Anti-Virus dialog box appears, just press Enter. You're fine!

Be sure to come in for frequent checkups and eat lots of green and yellow vegetables. Drink plenty of fluids and stop smoking!

CAUTION

Anti-Virus can only *detect* and clean the viruses it knows about—1,234 of them, to be exact. Unfortunately, those clever hackers are constantly coming up with new ones, which Anti-Virus won't be able to detect. You'll be wise to get updated Anti-Virus disks from Microsoft, available for a nominal fee. There's a coupon in the back of your DOS manual for this purpose.

TIP

To make sure that your system remains free from viruses, run Anti-Virus every time you start your system. Even better, have it done automatically by adding a line to your computer's AUTOEXEC.BAT file, as explained in Chapter 18. Here's the line:

    MSAV /P

After you add this line to AUTOEXEC.BAT, Anti-Virus runs every time you start your computer. It takes time, though—as much as five minutes. But you may find that the peace of mind is worth the wait.

Top Ten Most Frightening Virus Names

10. Ha Ha Ha trojan horse

9. Terminator

8. Black Death

7. Dark Avenger

6. Anthrax Boot

5. Disk Killer

4. Kamikaze

3. Saddam

2. IB Demonic

1. Armageddon

Monitoring Your System for Suspicious Activity

Anti-Virus can't protect your system against viruses it doesn't know about. And that's too bad. You can bet your bottom dollar that hackers everywhere are examining Anti-Virus carefully. They are trying to create viruses that Anti-Virus can't detect.

But you have some defense against new viruses—VSafe. This utility runs even while you are using other programs. It constantly monitors your

system for signs of suspicious activity, like reformatting your whole hard disk without asking your permission first.

To load VSafe, type **VSAFE** and press Enter. DOS prompts you that VSafe was installed and tells you how much conventional memory the program will use.

VSAFE will be on the lookout for suspicious activities and will warn you if one is about to take place. If you see a VSafe dialog box, just choose Continue and keep working. But run Anti-Virus after you finish working.

Checklist

▼ VSafe has its downside: it uses up some of your computer's precious memory, of which there's seldom enough. You may want to run VSafe only when you've inserted "suspicious" disks in your system. In general, a suspicious disk is any disk that you get from a co-worker, colleague, stranger, friend, or (especially) college students. You don't have to worry about program disks that you yourself take from a hermetically sealed package.

▼ Don't run VSafe before installing new program disks. These programs legitimately make changes to your system files.

▼ To unload VSafe from your computer's memory without restarting your system, hold down the Alt key and press V. When the VSafe Warning Options dialog box appears, hold down the Alt key and press U.

PART III

The Bluffer's Guide to Hardware

Includes:

11: Handy Guide to Hardware Obsolescence

12: More Than You Ever Wanted to Know About Memory

13: Monitors

14: The Keyboard

15: The Printer

Handy Guide to Hardware Obsolescence

IN A NUTSHELL

- ▼ Brief, relatively pain-less introduction to the parts of a computer system
- ▼ Explanation of what a "clone" is
- ▼ Explanation of all that "80286, 80386" chatter
- ▼ Why faster isn't neces-sarily better
- ▼ Why your system has two or three disk drives
- ▼ What ports are and how to tell which is which

I HATE DOS!

CHAPTER 11

Computers keep getting cheaper—but at the same time, they keep getting better. You can't say that about many other products! For you, though, this amazing fact means frustration, which can come in three not-so-sweet flavors:

▼ Having to use an old system at the office, which might not have the capabilities of newer, snazzier systems.

▼ Getting your own newer, snazzier system, which is sure to be eclipsed by even newer, even snazzier (and, darn it, cheaper) systems in short order—say, six months. The system I paid $2000 for two years ago is now selling for $798.

▼ Getting suckered into buying a system that even six months ago was obsolete, and realizing, belatedly, that those nasty salespeople were snickering at you as you lugged all those boxes out the door.

All this adds up to a basic point: you only need to know just enough about computer hardware—just enough, that is, to figure out how "up-to-date" a particular system is. This might be a system you're thinking about buying or one you've been given to use at work.

To get this "just enough" knowledge, you don't have to be a computer genius or an electrical engineer. You just need this chapter, which covers the minimum stuff you should know to size up a computer system.

TIP

Since computers are getting cheaper and better at an amazing rate, should you wait before buying your own system? The short answer: no, not if you need the computer for something right now. But if you need the system for a job you're going to do six months from now, wait—you'll save money, and to top it off, you'll probably get a better computer.

What's "Hardware"?

Hardware is the physical part of the computer, all the drives, screens, boxes, chips, and wires. If it hurts when you drop it on yourself, it's hardware.

The other part of the computer is *software*, or programs. Different programs are designed for different tasks, such as designing Christmas cards, balancing your checkbook, or cruising bars as an obnoxious *Saturday Night Fever* leftover. (Yes, it's true; the program is called Leisure Suit Larry.) You'll take a closer look at programs in the next part of this book.

You Say I'm Using a Clone?

In the beginning (1981), IBM created the IBM Personal Computer—IBM PC for short. Soon it had lots of imitators, called *IBM compatibles* or, more derisively, *clones*. These machines weren't made by IBM, but they could run all the software created for the IBM PC. Pretty soon, clones became more numerous than genuine IBM computers, because the clones offered lower prices and good quality.

Chances are good that you're using an IBM-compatible computer or thinking about buying one. It's nothing to be embarrassed about. These can be great machines.

To try to get some of the market back from the clone makers, IBM has lowered its prices a lot and gained back some of its share of the market, which it once had all to itself. Today's IBM computers are called *Personal System/1* (for home computers) and *Personal System/2* (for business computers), or for short, *PS/1* and *PS/2*.

The acronym *PC*, incidentally, has become synonymous with IBM and IBM-compatible computers, the way *Coke* has with soft drinks.

You might hear someone say, "Oh, I'm running a Windows system." Here's what this person is really saying: "I'm using an IBM or IBM-compatible computer that is capable of running Microsoft Windows and Windows programs."

Checklist

▼ What's Windows? This topic is explored in Chapter 16, but essentially, it's a program that provides an easy-to-use screen appearance for other programs, including DOS.

▼ *Windows programs* are programs specifically designed to run with Microsoft Windows. DOS programs don't require Windows. Chapter 16 elaborates on this distinction in painstaking detail.

▼ Windows requires a fast, modern computer system with lots of memory and a huge hard disk. So when someone says, "My system is Windows compatible," he's bragging.

"I HATE THIS!"

This *$&% Macintosh disk won't work in my computer

There's another type of computer called a *Macintosh*, made by Apple. This is also a personal computer, but the IBM style and the Macintosh style differ. You can't run programs designed for IBM or IBM clones on a Macintosh, and vice versa. Disks you use on the Macintosh can't be used on an IBM or a clone, at least not without some special maneuvering and software.

"I HATE THIS!"

Macintosh users tend to have an attitude problem. They think their computers are superior. Ignore them.

The Parts of a Typical System

You can divide a typical IBM or IBM-compatible computer system into two parts, the ones you can see and the ones you can't. The system's capabilities, wouldn't you know it, are determined largely by the stuff you can't see. It's sort of like the fine print in that "Spend Four Days and Three Nights in Cancun for $19.95" brochure.

The Parts of the System You Can See

Name	Description
System unit	Big box with one or two slots in the front and lots of plugs in the back. The front panel probably has a Reset button, some lights, and a key, which you can lose so you won't be able to start your computer.
Ports	Plugs on the back that you connect computer accessories to, like monitors and printers
Floppy disk drive	One or two slots in the system unit. You insert disks into these slots.
Monitor	Television-type thing
Printer	Box that looks like a copier or a typewriter without a keyboard

Name	Description
Keyboard	Keyboard
Cord	Cords (lots)

Checklist

▼ This chapter discusses the system unit, ports, and disk drive, as well as some of the stuff you can't see.

▼ If you want to know more about monitors, take a look at Chapter 13.

▼ Chapter 12 discusses the painful details of memory.

▼ Chapter 14 goes over all the funny keys on computer keyboards.

▼ For a discussion of printers, turn to Chapter 15.

The Parts of the System You Can't See

Name	Description
Power supply	Converts electrical current into a form the computer can use. Tucked away inside the system unit.
Hard disk	Disk that stores DOS, your programs, and your data when you're not using them or when the computer is off. Stored inside the system unit. Can hold lots and lots of data.

Name	Description
Motherboard	The mother of all circuit boards inside your computer; contains microprocessor and memory (RAM). Again, inside the system unit.
Microprocessor	Tiny, complex plug-in module that contains the computer's processing circuitry. Also called *CPU*, short for *central processing unit*. The "brain" of the computer. Stored inside the system unit.
Memory (RAM)	Place where your programs and data are kept while the microprocessor is working on them. RAM can only be used when the computer is on, which is why the hard disk is necessary.
Expansion boards	Plug-in circuit boards (also called *adapters*) that add capabilities such as sound to your computer system.

The next chapter tells you all about RAM, in case you're curious.

A Quick Guide to All That "80286, 80386, 80486" Chatter

A computer's microprocessor determines its capabilities, such as how fast it works. Most microprocessors are made by a company called Intel. Intel gives each microprocessor a distinctive model number, the way Boeing numbers its airplanes. As time goes on, Intel Corporation, which makes

the microprocessors used in IBM and IBM-compatible computers, keeps making improvements. Basically, the larger the number, the greater the capabilities.

EXPERTS ONLY

"And how do you pronounce that, Sir?"

"Eight-oh-three-eight-six" is hard to say, so people just say "three-eight-six" or "four-eighty-six." The cool way to write this is '386 or '486. Nobody talks about 8088s or 8086s, though, out of respect for the dead. Incidentally, it is considered an extreme social faux pas to enter a computer store and loudly announce, "Please show me an eight-thousand-three-hundred-eighty-six, if you don't mind."

Here's a quick guide to the microprocessors that drive the machines you're likely to encounter. You'll notice that these microprocessors are evaluated in terms of how well they run Microsoft Windows, which is discussed in Chapter 16.

Windows (and Windows programs) are clearly the wave of the future, but millions of people are content to run DOS and DOS programs. For these people, these old, obsolete microprocessors are just fine, thank you.

Model Number	Nickname	Snap Assessment
8088	XT or Turbo XT	The original (circa 1981) microprocessor of the IBM PC. Still serviceable, but very slow by today's standards, and doesn't run Microsoft Windows programs.
8086	XT or Turbo XT	A slightly faster version of the 8088, but still woefully clunky by today's standards. Won't run Windows programs.

Model Number	Nickname	Snap Assessment
80286	286 or AT	Introduced in 1984, this micro-processor runs faster and can use more memory than its predeces-sors. However, it has technical limitations that prevent it from taking full advantage of Microsoft Windows and Windows programs.
80386DX	386DX	A technical knockout, this speedy, capable microprocessor is ideal for using Microsoft Windows and Windows programs.
80386SX	386SX	A junior version of the 386DX; sacrifices some speed so that it can use cheaper (but slower) components, such as disk drives. Runs Windows a bit sluggishly. Today this is considered the entry-level microprocessor.
80486DX	486DX	The top-of-the-line microproces-sor *right now* (technology grows at lightning speed, so this informa-tion could be outdated tomor-row). An awesome microprocessor that shows what Microsoft Corporation has in mind for Windows.
80486SX	486SX	A junior version of the 486DX, but almost as fast—except in the case of heavy-duty number crunching.

I HATE DOS!

TIP

Not all of the microprocessors found in IBM-compatible machines are actually made by Intel. Intel microprocessors perform better because they have certain features that other manufacturers couldn't imitate. Look for the "Intel Inside" logo if you're planning to buy a system.

BUZZWORDS

MATH COPROCESSOR

An additional circuit that helps the computer work with numbers more quickly. If you plan to do a lot of number-crunching, you might want to add a math coprocessor to your system. This can be done when you order your computer, or later. 486DX systems have a built-in math coprocessor.

Timing Clock Speed

(On your mark, get set, go)

"My 386 is running at 33 megahertz," your colleague says, proudly. But you're not sure whether that is good or bad. Well, rest assured—your colleague probably doesn't either. The speed at which a microprocessor runs, called *clock speed* and measured in megahertz (MHz), is one of the most misunderstood measurements of a computer's capabilities.

BUZZWORDS

MEGAHERTZ

The term *megahertz* (MHz) refers to "one million cycles per second," which seems like a lot, but computers have a lot of data to crunch. The faster, the better.

EXPERTS ONLY

Why is clock speed misunderstood?

Because these speeds aren't easily compared from one microprocessor to another. Here's why: A great, big power backhoe shoveling 20 shovel loads in 10 minutes will shovel a lot more dirt than a teeny hand shovel, even if the poor shoveler can shovel 200 shovel loads a minute. Likewise, a 486 running at 20 megahertz is faster than a 386 running at 33 megahertz. But most people do not know that.

Clock speeds aren't a reliable guide to system performance when you are comparing two different microprocessors. But when you're comparing two systems that use the same microprocessor, they are.

Here's a quick, no-details bluffer's guide to clock speeds:

Speed	Snap Assessment
4.77 MHz	Like walking through sand; a Game Boy is faster
8 MHz	Cold molasses
12 MHz	Lukewarm molasses
16 MHz	Barely tolerable

continues

Speed	Snap Assessment
20 MHz	Not bad
25 MHz	Better; there's a genuine zip to it
33 MHz	Very satisfyingly zippy
50 MHz	A screamer; wish mine did 50
60 MHz	A rocket; awesome

Checklist

▼ If you're planning to run DOS and only DOS programs, you don't need as much speed. 16MHz might be plenty in a 386DX.

▼ If you think you might run Microsoft Windows, you'll need all the speed you can get.

Disk Drives

What's a disk drive? A disk drive is like a cassette recorder that uses round cassettes (disks). Only rather than play and record music, the drive "reads" (puts in memory) and "writes" (puts back on disk) information. You insert floppy disks into the drive. Without a disk in the drive, the drive is useless—just like you can't play music from a cassette player without inserting a cassette. In a hard drive, though, the disk is built in.

Some computers have two disk drives: one hard and one floppy. Some have three drives: one hard and two floppy. A few computers even have two or more hard drives.

Checklist

▼ A floppy disk is small (either 3.5 or 5.25 inches) and portable. You can take it with you. The 5.25-inch disk is floppy (flexible). The 3.5-inch is encased in a hard plastic case, but it is still considered a floppy disk, even though it doesn't wiggle like the big ones do.

▼ Floppy disks and all their various statistics are covered in Chapter 5.

▼ A hard disk is a nonremovable drive; you can't take it with you. The hard disk usually isn't visible. It's inside the computer.

▼ Two things make up a floppy disk (the disk and the drive); for a hard disk they are the same thing. That's why you might hear the terms *hard disk*, *hard drive*, and *hard disk drive*. Some people just give up and call their hard disks Jerry or Nancy.

▼ Hard disks have lots more storage space, and they operate much faster than floppy drives.

TIP

If possible, try to get or use a system equipped with two disk drives, a little one (3.5 inches) and a big one (5.25 inches). That way you can put either kind of disk into your system. If you have just one type of drive, you're in for a hassle—sooner or later you'll need something that's on one type of disk, but you only have the other type of drive.

Ports o' Call

A port is a plug, on the back of your computer's case, through which you can connect the computer to accessory devices, such as printers. There are two types of ports: serial and parallel. You don't have to worry about these things, unless you're unfortunate enough to have to hook up something like a printer.

"I HATE THIS!"

We wouldn't want things to be too simple, would we?

If you look at the back of your computer, you'll see that the ports aren't labeled. Isn't that nice? This makes it impossible to tell which is which without getting some help. As you'll see in this section, you can tell the difference yourself if you're willing to inquire into the sensitive subject of whether the plug is "male" (has pins sticking out) or "female" (has holes for "male" pins).

Checklist

▼ The parallel port is designed for printers. It has 25 holes ready for the "male" end of the printer cable.

▼ You can use a serial port for printers, modems, scanners, and neat stuff like that. The serial port plug has either 25 or 9 "male" pins, all ready for a "female" cable.

▼ The monitor cable goes to a plug that looks deceptively like a 9-pin serial port, except that the plug has 9 "female" holes for a 9-pin "male" cable.

▼ Your mouse might be plugged into a 9-pin serial port, or into a special, round plug with 9 pins.

▼ Your keyboard is plugged into a round port with 5 pins.

Top Ten Things Overheard in a Hardware Design Lab

10. "Cool! They'll *never* figure this out!"

9. "So what if it takes up the whole desk? They're gonna do all their work with the computer now, anyway."

8. "The heck with that last test. 'The Simpsons' is starting."

7. "I keep forgetting—is the female connector the one with the holes or the one with the pins?"

6. "The money we save on all that radiation reduction stuff can go into marketing, you know."

5. "Why don't we put the power switch *under* the case? That way, there's no chance they could shut off the power by accident."

4. "Is it *still* crashing? Well, fudge the report. I'm sick of fooling with it."

3. "Oh, *that* specification? We just made it up."

2. "Hey, look what happens when I pour my Coke into this power supply."

1. "Sorry, we can't finish this job until you buy us the *really* big Erector set."

More Than You Ever Wanted to Know about Memory (RAM)

IN A NUTSHELL

▼ Understand why you need memory

▼ Measure memory

▼ Understand the "640K RAM barrier"

▼ Get around the 640K barrier

▼ Figure out how much memory you have

▼ Decide whether you need more memory

▼ Add more memory

▼ Make more memory available

L et's say you're going to whip up something delicious in the kitchen—mmm, how about a spicy seafood gumbo? From that neat set of Le Creuset, you pick just the stuff you're going to work with: the 10-inch skillet, the filet, the squid, the chilis. You put everything on the countertop. The rest—the stuff you don't need right now—stays in the cabinets.

You can think of memory as the countertop, and your hard disk as the cabinet storage space. Memory is where you put stuff that you're working with, while your hard disk is where you store all the rest. There's a lot more hard disk space than memory, just as there's a lot more cabinet than countertop space.

TIP

> Be sure to remember the distinction between memory (RAM) and disk space. A shortage in one doesn't necessarily mean there's a shortage in the other! "Oh, Dad, I was trying to run Word, and it said there wasn't enough memory. So I deleted a whole bunch of your files from the disk. You don't mind, do you?" If DOS says there isn't enough memory to run a program, you need more memory, not more disk space.

What's Memory For, Anyway?

Memory is a lot faster than your hard disk. And that's all to the good. When your computer is working with your programs and data, speed is the keynote. That's why your computer puts your programs and data in memory while you're working with them.

Checklist

▼ Technoid types like myself like to call memory *RAM*. You'll hear this term a lot—as in "How much RAM do *you* have?" *RAM* and *memory* are synonymous. Other terms for memory are *primary memory* and *internal memory*. They all mean the same thing.

▼ When you start a computer session, you start a program, such as WordPerfect. DOS transfers the program from your hard disk to RAM. Then you start working on something or retrieve a file from the hard disk. This work goes into RAM, too. Your program and data are both in RAM, together. They get to know each other very well while they're crammed in there.

▼ RAM has one very, very unfortunate drawback: it's volatile. No, this doesn't mean that it has a short-fuse personality. It means something far worse: you lose all your data if there's a sudden power loss. RAM needs power to keep the data stored in it.

▼ RAM's volatility explains why you have to save your work to disk, as computer people put it. (You don't, however, save to *the* disk. This terminology is considered uncool.) Disks don't need power to keep the data. After you save (that is, transfer your work from RAM to your disk), you can turn off your computer without wiping out your work.

EXPERTS ONLY

Tormenting twaddle about "random access"

Why *do* they call it *random access?* There's nothing random about it. Here's what this distinction is really all about. A cassette tape has sequential access—you have to wind through all the songs, in a sequence, before you get to hear Barry sing "Copacabana." A CD player, in contrast, has

I HATE DOS!

EXPERTS ONLY

random access—you just punch the number of the song you want, and the device goes right to it, with no further ado. In a random-access device, you can directly access what you want, without going through a sequence of stuff—and that's why it's a lot faster.

The Art and Lore of Measuring Memory

Memory is measured the same way as hard disk space. In fact, one of the most basic mistakes a beginner (and even a not-so-beginner) makes is to confuse memory and hard disk space. Remember that hard disk space is *permanent* storage (like cabinet space). There's a lot of disk space. Memory is not permanent; it keeps stuff you are working on (think of counter space). There's less space in memory.

EXPERTS ONLY

Fake your way to memory measurement knowledge

Term and Abbreviation	Approximately	Exactly
Byte	One character	8 bits
Kilobyte (K or KB)	One thousand characters	1,024 bytes
Megabyte (M or MB)	One million characters	1,048,576 bytes
Gigabyte (G or GB)	One billion characters	1,073,741,824 bytes

EXPERTS ONLY

Why the difference between "approximately" and "exactly?" It's because computers are like Noah—they count everything in twos. We humans count things in tens, which is just fine, thank you. You can forget about the "exactly" figure; the "approximately" figure is close enough. You'll see the difference, though, in some DOS commands, which stick the exact figure in your face.

Checklist

▼ Memory is another one of those expandable things—your computer comes with a certain amount, but you can add more. Memory upgrades (adding more memory) probably account for 75 percent of the upgrade business at your local computer shop.

▼ There is probably room in your computer for adding more memory. Most computers come with just enough memory to seem competitive. Inside the computer case, a lot of the places where you can press in additional memory chips are probably empty, just waiting for an upgrade.

▼ Why should you care about measuring memory? Some programs require more memory than others. Do you have enough? This is the burning question that motivates computer users to learn the art and lore of memory management.

▼ The amount of memory you have depends on the number of memory chips installed in your computer. (*Memory chips* are little electronic circuit things that each contribute a certain amount of storage, such as 256K or 1MB.)

continues

▼ If you have a 386 or 486, you have *at least* 1MB of RAM and maybe more. (Chapter 11 explains a bit more about the numbers 386 and 486.)

▼ You can only add so much memory to a given computer. Mine has room for 8MB. Technie types say that the memory is "fully populated" instead of the English, "the maximum amount of memory is installed." Your computer probably isn't "fully populated."

▼ Memory size, like disk space, is measured in characters . A character is a letter or number, like A or 8. This term is synonymous with bytes. The reason is that it takes one byte to swallow one character (pretty clever, huh?).

EXPERTS ONLY

Should you upgrade memory yourself?

If you browse through the back pages of computer magazines, you'll see plenty of adds for RAM (memory) chips, which supposedly come with "easy-to-follow" instructions for upgrading your system. If you're pretty clever with technical stuff, you might want to give it a try, but my advice is to let the computer shop do it for you. Two reasons: First, you need to figure out which memory chips to order, which isn't easy—there are dozens of different kinds of chips. Second, computer chips of all kinds are very vulnerable to damage from static electricity. If you tried to add the chips on a really dry day after petting your cat, you could wipe out your motherboard—a maneuver that would cost you hundreds of bucks to rectify.

How Much Memory Do You Need?

This one's pretty easy—you need enough to run your programs.

Checklist

▼ A program's memory requirements are usually listed right on the box. Look for a little area called "System Requirements." PC Tools Version 7.1, for example, requires 640K of RAM. To run PC Tools, you need 640K of RAM. Most DOS programs require 640K. You should have at least this amount. If you don't have 640K, upgrade your system to that level.

▼ It isn't very expensive to upgrade a 512K system to 640K—maybe $50 plus another $50 for labor. And its well worth the cost.

▼ DOS programs are usually content with 640K of RAM, and sometimes less. Windows programs, though, require *humongous* amounts of memory—at least 2MB, but 4MB is necessary to run some memory-hungry Windows programs. If you're planning to run Windows, my advice is to upgrade your system, if necessary, with at least 4MB of RAM—8MB, if your budget and your motherboard allow.

▼ Memory prices fluctuate according to market conditions, but you can usually get 1MB of RAM for about $75. Plan on spending another $50 or so for the installation.

"I HATE THIS!"

Another painful example of how something *could* be simple, but isn't

Ideally, a computer would have just three kinds of memory: the amount of memory you have, the amount your programs need, and the additional amount you have to add to run your programs. Unfortunately, DOS computers have several different kinds of memory, called horrible things like *conventional memory*, *upper memory*, *high memory*, *extended memory*, and more. The two most important terms to understand are *conventional memory* and *extended memory*. You need to understand these terms if you want or need to upgrade your memory.

Conventional Memory

The first part of your computer's memory is called *conventional memory*. This memory is also called lots of other things, such as *base memory*, *DOS memory*, or *that darned conventional memory*. Why the "darned" part? DOS can only use 640K of memory, even though your computer might be equipped with more memory than that.

When the first IBM PC was introduced, 640K seemed like a lot. After all, it *was* ten times the amount of memory other computers had back then. Now, however, this amount is barely enough for today's big, feature-filled programs. That's why 640K is also referred to as the "640K RAM barrier."

TIP

The most important memory upgrade you can make is to "bring your system up to 640K," as technoweenies like to say. This means, "upgrade your conventional memory to the 640K maximum." Some DOS programs won't run unless you have the full 640K of RAM installed.

How Much Conventional Memory Do You Have?

You can find out real quick with the CHKDSK command. At the DOS prompt, type **CHKDSK** and press Enter. You'll see lots of stuff about your disk, but at the end of the CHKDSK output, you see something like this:

```
655360 total bytes memory
613440 bytes free
```

"I HATE THIS!"

"It says I have 655,360 total bytes memory. Do I have 655K?"

Nope. 1K is 1,024 bytes. If you divide 655,360 by 1,024, you get 640. You certainly don't need to divide every memory figure you see by 1,024. An approximation is enough.

And Just What Is This "Extended Memory" Thing?

DOS and DOS programs are restricted to 640K of conventional memory. This was a limitation built into DOS and into the design of the original IBM Personal Computer. But the need for more memory is an insistent drumbeat throughout history. Before long, programmers and users were clamoring for bigger programs that would require megabytes of RAM instead of just 640K.

The 640K RAM barrier is tough to break, just like the sound barrier used to be. But those clever engineers found two ways to get beyond it. The first, and by far the most important for you if you're using a 386 or later computer, is *extended memory*.

The second, *expanded memory*, is important only if you're using an older computer. You learn about this type of memory later in this chapter.

Checklist

▼ Extended memory is any memory beyond 1MB. (The memory between the 640K conventional memory and 1MB adds up to 384K, but it's different—it's called *upper memory*. Upper memory is discussed later.)

▼ Extended memory can be added only to computers that have the 80286, 80386, and 80486 microprocessors. (See Chapter 11 for an explanation of microprocessor model numbers.)

▼ Today's 386 and PCs have lots of room for additional extended memory right on the motherboard.

▼ If you have a 386 or 486, your system probably has some extended memory—probably 1MB (for a total of 2MB, including conventional and upper memory).

▼ In general, DOS and DOS programs can't take advantage of extended memory. If you're just running DOS and DOS programs, you can have all the extended memory in the world, like 8MB, which will just sit there and not be used. There is, though, one exception. A few DOS applications, such as some versions of Lotus 1-2-3, can use extended memory.

▼ Extended memory comes into play when you use Microsoft Windows. Windows can use all the extended memory you can stuff into your computer.

▼ Extended memory is also called XMS memory.

Do You Have Any Extended Memory?

If you have DOS 5 or 6, you can use the MEM command to find out whether you have extended memory. Unlike CHKDSK (which only lists conventional memory), the MEM command lists all the types of memory you have in your system.

To use MEM, type **MEM** at the DOS prompt and press Enter. What you see on-screen depends on whether you have DOS 5 or DOS 6. Read on.

DOS 5 Memory Stats

With DOS 5, you see something like this (your screen will vary, depending on how the memory in your system is set up, how much memory is

actually installed in your system, and the current location of the planet Jupiter in the zodiac):

```
 656384   bytes total conventional memory
 655360   bytes available to MS-DOS
 608640   largest executable program size

3145728   bytes total contiguous extended memory
      0   bytes available contiguous extended memory

1027072   bytes available XMS memory
```

For our purposes (figuring out how much extended memory you have, if any), the only thing worth noticing here is the total contiguous extended memory figure—four lines down in the reading. This system has 3MB of extended memory.

"I HATE THIS!"

"It says I have 3MB of extended memory but 0 bytes are available! What gives?"

It's OK. That 0 bytes available contiguous extended memory line refers to an *unused extended memory configuration technique.* Just ignore this line. The one above it tells you how much extended memory is installed in your system.

DOS 6 Memory Stats

VERSION 6

The DOS 5 MEM command's output got a lot of criticism, justifiably, so DOS 6's MEM command produces output that's a lot easier to understand:

```
Memory Type       Total = Used + Free
----------------  ------  ------  ------
Conventional      640K    127K    513K
Upper             155K    88K     67K
Adapter RAM/ROM   229K    229K    0K
Extended (XMS)    4096K   1944K   2152K


----------------  ------  ------  ------
Total memory      5120K   2388K   2732K
Total under 1 MB  795K    215K    580K
```

This command's output is a lot easier to read. The system has 4M of extended memory (XMS memory).

What about Expanded Memory?

The second way you can get around the 640K RAM barrier is called *expanded memory*, which is different from *extended memory*. (I didn't make up these terms; don't get mad at me.)

Expanded memory is the only way to get beyond the 640K RAM barrier if you are using an older PC—one based on the 8088, 8086, or 80286 microprocessors. (Chapter 11 has the gruesome details on what these numbers mean.)

Checklist

▼ Unlike extended memory, *expanded memory* isn't added to the motherboard. It's added using one of those plug-in expansion boards that fit into the expansion slots inside your computer's case.

continues

▼ Expanded memory may be old-fashioned, but it's great for people who use DOS programs. Lots of DOS programs can use expanded memory. The expanded memory gives you room for larger documents, such as spreadsheets. Quattro Pro 4 is an example of a DOS application that can use expanded memory.

▼ Expanded memory is also called EMS memory.

EXPERTS ONLY

Just a bit more useless info about extended/expanded memory

If you're using a 386 or later computer with extended memory, you can use the EMM386.EXE program, included with DOS, to make this extended memory seem like expanded memory to your DOS programs. The details of using EMM386.EXE to do this are beyond this book's level. Get your local DOS guru to help you.

And What Is This "Upper Memory Area" Thing?

Conventional memory goes from 0 to 640K. Extended memory goes from 1MB up. Well, what about the memory between 640K and 1MB? There's 384K of unaccounted space in there. This is called *upper memory*. (It used to be called *reserved memory*.) In the original PC design, this area was set aside for various secret system purposes, but much

of it isn't used. An unused portion of the upper memory is called an *upper memory block*. (This is abbreviated UMB and pronounced like the *umb* in *numb*. Or *dumb*.)

One of the pet hobbies of DOS addicts is to move some DOS stuff into upper memory blocks. This leaves more room in conventional memory for your DOS programs, which is good. But it isn't something you should try doing yourself.

Yet Another Type of Memory

(High memory area)

There's *another* type of memory, believe it or not: the *high memory area (HMA)*. You may run into this term now and then, if someone's trying to ruin your day. Basically, the high memory area is the first 64K of extended memory. (That's the memory above 1MB. Remember?)

OK, OK, I'll Look at the Map

To get a picture of the various kinds of memory, you might find it helpful to look at the following memory map. This system has 640K of conventional memory, 384K or upper memory, and 2MB of extended memory, for a total of 3MB. This diagram *doesn't* include expanded memory. Expanded memory is off by itself on an expansion board; it isn't part of the memory on the computer's motherboard.

CHAPTER 12

A beautiful visual aid to help explain memory.

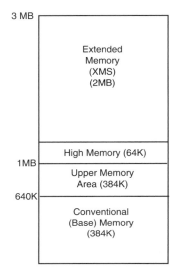

3 MB — Extended Memory (XMS) (2MB)

High Memory (64K)

1MB — Upper Memory Area (384K)

640K — Conventional (Base) Memory (384K)

Top Ten Recent Discoveries of Computer Science

10. Computer actually invented by ancient Egyptians but given up, according to recently discovered hieroglyphics, because it was "obviously such a stupid idea"

9. Fans inside PC system units can be used to power model aircraft

8. Keystrokes on notebook computer can be picked up and recorded by neighbors using portable phones

7. Annual loss of 2% of GNP attributed to time wasted trying to learn distinction between *conventional memory* and *extended memory*

6. First personal computers invented by former Vietnam-era student radicals in underhanded plot "to bring capitalism to its knees"

5. Large, flat area of computer cabinet handy for stacking papers, disks

182

4. DOS originally designed to control large remote bulldozer at hazardous waste facility near Seattle

3. Increase in computer orders followed by similar upswing in aspirin, Tylenol sales

2. Computer simulation of giant, digital chicken is actually alive

1. Large, cumbersome, boring computer books perfect for propping up short table leg

The *Angst* of Memory Configuration

If you check out the computer book section at the bookstore down at the mall, you'll find lots of books on configuring memory. To *configure* memory means to use *memory management programs* to set up your system's memory for your programs' use. The goal of memory configuration is to squeeze the last possible bit of space out of conventional memory and to make expanded or extended memory available for your applications.

BUZZWORDS

MEMORY MANAGEMENT PROGRAM
A program that helps you get the most out of your computer's memory.

DOS comes with two memory management programs, called HIMEM and EMM386. You can also buy other memory-management programs. The goal of these programs is to move some of DOS out of conventional memory into those unused upper memory blocks or to HMA.

The use of these programs for memory management is best left to your local DOS wizard or, if you're using DOS 6, to the new MEMMAKER program, which can configure your computer's memory automatically.

TIP

Memory configuration can really be a hassle—computer training firms are offering two-day courses on the subject! But DOS 6 comes with a very neat program called MEMMAKER, which is discussed in the next section. This program automatically configures the memory in your system, saving you from having to learn a lot of stuff that you'd use only once.

Memory Magic with DOS 6

VERSION 6

If you have a 386 or 486 computer with some extended memory, you can run a DOS 6 command called MEMMAKER that automatically optimizes the memory in your system. You'll get more memory to run your programs.

TIP

The only thing you need to know to run MEMMAKER is whether your programs want expanded or extended memory. Check the indexes of the programs' manuals under "expanded memory," "extended memory," "memory," or "RAM." If you're running DOS, chances are good that your programs want expanded memory. If you're planning to run Microsoft Windows, your Windows programs want *extended* memory.

Here's how to jazz up your system with MEMMAKER:

1. To run MEMMAKER, type **MEMMAKER** at the DOS prompt and press Enter.

2. At the welcome screen, press Enter.

You see a screen informing you that there are two ways to run MEMMAKER: Express or Custom setup.

3. Press Enter to choose Express.

4. The next question is, do you use any applications that require expanded memory (EMS)? If you're using DOS programs that can use expanded memory, press the space bar to change the answer to Yes, and then press Enter. Otherwise, just press Enter.

You see a screen telling you that MEMMAKER is going to restart your computer.

5. If you have a disk in drive A, remove it and press Enter to restart your system.

After your system restarts, MEMMAKER goes to work. You see lots of technobabble about what's going on. Just ignore the screens.

6. Press Enter to restart your computer with your new, optimized memory configuration.

After your system restarts, you see MEMMAKER again. You're asked whether your system is working. Well, if it weren't, you wouldn't see this screen, would you?

7. Press Enter.

You see another MEMMAKER screen that proudly describes all the wonderful things it has done to optimize memory in your system. Because most of this is incomprehensible, just press Enter to exit.

CHAPTER 13

Monitors
(Those Television Things)

IN A NUTSHELL

▼ Why you need *two* things—an adapter
and a monitor—to get a computer picture on-screen

▼ How to tell what's good and
what isn't so hot in the
adapter world

▼ What determines
how sharp the on-
screen image is

▼ How to protect yourself
from electromagnetic
radiation (EMR)

▼ How to adjust your
monitor for optimum
picture quality

▼ How to avoid the heartbreak
of phosphor burn-in

▼ How to clean the screen, and why you'd better

▼ What display modes are

"Monitor not included" is what you'll read in the fine print of computer ads, but that's about as ridiculous as selling an automobile without wheels. You and your monitor will spend a lot of time together. On the monitor's screen (also called the *display*), you see your own, wonderful input. And also on the screen, you see the horrifying things that the computer does to this wonderful input, such as scrambling it or displaying irritating error messages. Small wonder that the monitor is the first thing people attack when they get a little too angry at their computers.

The subject of monitors ought to be simple. Unfortunately, monitors surround themselves with a hefty armada of unpleasant terms, like *non-interlaced* and *multiscanning*. As with the computer system unit, you can cope with all this stuff by getting a degree in electrical engineering—or you can read this chapter.

This chapter provides just enough information to allow you to fake your way through the subject of monitors.

The Monitor and the Adapter

(It takes two)

Your computer requires two components to come up with a screen display: a monitor (the television-type thing) and a video adapter (an electrical thing inside the computer that you can't see).

BUZZWORDS

VIDEO ADAPTER

Electronic stuff inside the computer that generates the screen display. There are lots of different video adapters, and they vary in quality. It's called an *adapter* because, in most computers, its circuitry is on one of those plug-in adapter boards.

Checklist

▼ More than the monitor, the video adapter determines the quality of the text and graphics you see. Like your television, your monitor is just a *receiver*—something has to be a *transmitter*. That's where the adapter steps in; it does the job of creating the signal that the monitor displays.

▼ If you want a better display, you probably will have to upgrade your adapter as well as your monitor.

▼ Adapters fall into two general categories, color and monochrome (black and white).

▼ *Black and white* is a misnomer for early monochrome systems, which display green or amber characters on a black background. More recent monochrome systems display black text on a white background.

Adapters Demystified

Your computer's video adapter creates the signal that is then conveyed, via a cable, to your monitor. The older ones don't do such a hot job of this. The newer ones do better: they show sharper text, handle graphics better, and offer hundreds of colors or gray shades.

Adapter Type	Acronym	Faker's Guide
Color Graphics Adapter	CGA	The oldest color adapter, and pretty obsolete unless you just use the computer occasionally. Generates fuzzy text and just a few, garish colors. Not usually included with today's systems.
Monochrome Display Adapter	MDA	The oldest monochrome adapter. Great text quality, but one huge disadvantage: it can't display graphics. If you try to display a graph, for example, you just see a blank screen. Like the CGA, this adapter isn't often included with today's systems.
Hercules Graphics Adapter	HGA	Also called a *monographics* adapter, this adapter solved the MDA's no-graphics problem. Great text, good graphics. Often included in "budget" systems, and is OK if you just want to do word processing and number-crunching with DOS.

Adapter Type	Acronym	Faker's Guide
Enhanced Graphics Adapter	EGA	A much better color adapter than the CGA, this adapter produces great-looking text and graphics with lots of nice colors. But the VGA came soon afterward and offers even better performance for not much more money. You don't find too many systems with EGA adapters these days.
Video Graphics Array	VGA	This is the current standard adapter, which you'll find in almost all the 386SX budget systems being sold in places like Sears and K-Mart. Great text, lots of colors, and beautiful graphics. Good for DOS and Microsoft Windows alike.
Paper White	VGA	This is a monochrome VGA adapter that produces clear, sharp black text on a "paper white" background. People who produce black-and-white newsletters or brochures like this adapter because they can see what the final product will look like.
Gray Scale	VGA	This adapter is also mono-chrome, but it produces lots of intermediate gray shades that make pictures and drawings look really cool.

continues

Adapter Type	Acronym	Faker's Guide
Super Video Graphics Array	SVGA	The sharpest and latest color VGA adapter, with even more colors. Awesome. The "better" computers sold today usually include an SVGA adapter.

Monitors Demystified

The type of adapter you have pretty much determines what type of monitor you're using.

Checklist

▼ If you have a CGA adapter, you have a CGA monitor—also called an RGB monitor. RGB stands for *red, green, blue*, the colors that make up the color display.

▼ If you have an MDA adapter, you have a monochrome monitor. The text looks great, but you don't get graphics. This is a pain when you're using a program such as Lotus 1-2-3, which allows you to see graphs that are automatically generated from the numbers you're crunching. But read on for a quick, cheap fix!

▼ If you have an HGA adapter, you have a *monographics* monitor. This is just fine if you're planning to run nothing but DOS programs like WordPerfect, but it won't work with Windows.

▼ If you have a VGA adapter, guess what? You have a VGA monitor. It's probably color.

▼ If you have an SVGA adapter, you probably have a monitor designed to work with SVGA adapters. But you might have what's called a *multisynch* or *multiscanning* monitor, which automatically senses the type of signal your monitor is putting out and adjusts itself accordingly.

TIP

MDA users, incidentally, can replace their MDA adapter with a *monographics* adapter (HGA) for very little money—then you can see graphics on-screen without having to purchase a new monitor.

EXPERTS ONLY

Irritating technical verbiage about monitor quality

Two characteristics of VGA and SVGA monitors affect their quality: whether interlacing is used, and the monitor's dot pitch specification.

Interlacing is a method of faking a high-quality display by "painting" half the screen in one cycle, and then doing the other half in the second cycle. This produces a faintly detectable screen flicker that can be fatiguing to the eyes. The best monitors are non-interlacing monitors; they don't use this trick. But they cost more.

The *dot pitch* measurement tells you how fine-grained an image a monitor can display. The smaller the measurement, the better. For example, .28mm (millimeters) is very good; .43mm isn't so hot.

What Is This Resolution Number All About?

When I said earlier that adapters have been getting sharper as time goes on, I was talking about *resolution*. And just what is resolution?

BUZZWORDS

RESOLUTION

Resolution is a measurement of the amount of detail your monitor can show. It is measured by the number of dots (called *pixels*) that can be displayed on each line, as well as the number of lines that can be displayed on each screen. (Why use an unfamiliar word such as pixels? Well, it wouldn't be impressive to just say "dots.")

Checklist

▼ You'll see figures like 680 × 480 in advertisements and manuals. This figure means "680 dots per line and 480 lines per screen." 680 × 480 is the standard resolution for a VGA monitor, which is fine. SVGA resolutions are higher, such as 800 × 600 or 1,024 × 768.

▼ Your video adapter determines your monitor's display resolution. You can't improve the screen sharpness just by getting a better monitor: you have to get a better adapter, one that offers higher resolution.

Monitor Size

(Is bigger better?)

Adapters determine the overall quality of your computer's video display. But one thing the monitor determines is the size of the displayed image.

Checklist

▼ The bigger the monitor, the better. You can see more of what you're working on, which makes it easier to keep track of what you're doing. And the characters are bigger, making the system easier on your eyes.

▼ A lot of systems come with 12- or 13-inch monitors, measured diagonally. 14-inch monitors are better—one or two little inches can make a big difference.

Monochrome or Color?

PC displays fall into two broad categories: monochrome (black-and-white or green-and-black or orange-and-black—two colors, basically) and color. Which is better? The short answer: color, although monochrome still has its advocates.

Why color?

▼ Color is worth having even if you're planning to do nothing but word processing (text only). Most programs use color to highlight menu options and display messages. A message displayed in a bright, garish yellow is a lot easier to see than one that blends with the text.

▼ Most programs designed today assume that you're using a color system. Of course, you can still run a lot of programs on a monochrome system, but they don't look as nice.

▼ If you think you'll ever run Windows, color is a must. Windows makes great use of color.

▼ Take a break and play a computer game. But to do so, you'll need a color display.

Why not color?

▼ For the most part, color does not improve DOS. You still see that colorless DOS prompt regardless of the monitor you have.

▼ If you're using a monochrome adapter and display, do not despair. Many people feel that color is distracting and pointless, especially if you're using your computer for text processing. You print in black-and-white (mostly); why not see it in black-and-white?

EXPERTS ONLY

Will I glow in the dark after using my monitor?

Don't worry about X-rays, gamma rays, and all the rest of the really nasty stuff you may have heard about: today's computer monitors don't emit them in any measurable quantities. What may prove to be more dangerous to your health is a type of radiation that's emitted by just about every electrical device in homes and offices.

Many household devices, such as electric shavers, electric blankets, and computer monitors, emit extremely low-frequency (ELF) electromagnetic radiation (EMR). After years of denying that this radiation is dangerous, the scientific community is now coming up with some studies that suggest elevated rates of leukemia after prolonged exposure to such devices.

What about monitors? Here's the good news: Most of the EMR emitted by computer monitors goes out the sides and the back. And no matter which direction it goes, it falls off to undetectable levels at a distance of about 28 inches from the monitor.

To be ultra-safe, here are some tips:

▼ Work at a distance of at least 28 inches from your monitor.

▼ Don't sit at a desk where you're close to the back or sides of someone else's computer.

EXPERTS ONLY

> ▼ Those ever-cautious Scandinavians have worked out standards for EMR radiation. If you're really concerned about this, get yourself a low EMR radiation monitor that conforms to the Swedish standards.
>
> ▼ Don't waste money on a so-called radiation shield for your monitor. They don't block the type of EMR radiation that's been implicated in the health studies.

And What Adapter Do You Have?

Which video adapter is under the hood of the computer you're using? If you're using DOS 6, the MSD (Microsoft Diagnostics) program can tell you pronto. (If you don't have DOS 6, find out which adapter you have by asking the person who sold you the system or set it up for you.)

To find out which video adapter your system is using, type this command and press Enter:

    MSD

You'll see a screen with a lot of big buttons. Just look next to the one labeled Video. You'll see the acronym of your adapter (like VGA or SVGA) followed by the manufacturer's name. If you really want to know more, press V or click the Video button with your mouse. You see a screen full of information, some of which is useful—such as whether your system is capable of color.

DOS offers no clue as to whether or not you have a color monitor because the DOS prompt displays everything in monochrome even if you're using a color system.

Press Enter to exit the Computer dialog box, and then press F3 to quit MSD.

What Are Those Funny Knobs?

Monitors usually have two knobs in addition to the on/off switch, which is always carefully hidden. One knob controls brightness, while the other controls contrast. Very few monitors actually label these knobs Brightness and Contrast. Most use incomprehensible symbols. A little experimentation, however, will reveal which is which.

TIP

The best way to adjust your monitor, wouldn't you know it, is to display good ol' DOS stuff. Do a DIR or something like that, and then adjust the brightness just to the point that the background remains dark. (If you go too far, you start to get a sickly hue in the background.) Then adjust the contrast just to the point where the letters start to get kind of fuzzy. That's it!

Cleaning the Screen

Computer monitors attract dust like you wouldn't believe, thanks to the static charge that accumulates on the glass surface. Keep some glass cleaner and paper towels handy—you'll need them frequently. But don't spray the glass cleaner directly on the glass; some of the liquid might seep into the monitor's innards. Instead, spray the glass cleaner on the paper towel, and then clean the glass. You really ought to keep your screen clean.

The Heartbreak of Phosphor Burn-In

If you leave your monitor on for long periods, displaying the same thing all the while, the image can permanently impress itself onto the screen. Why? Doesn't matter. The point is that if you leave your monitor unattended for more than a few minutes, you should equip your system with a screen-saver program. This is a program that blanks your screen if your computer receives no input after a set period—say, 5 or 10 minutes. Screen savers even include sound to enhance the image. The current rage among Trekkies is a program called *Star Trek*, a screen saver for DOS that shows pictures of the Enterprise, Mr. Spock, and Captain Kirk. The $40 or so that it costs is well worth the price.

If you plan to run Windows, you don't need to go out and buy a screen-saver program—there's one built in. Unfortunately, it doesn't run with DOS or DOS programs.

TIP

If your screen goes blank, it probably means that somebody has helpfully installed a screen blanking program on your computer. Just press a key or move the mouse to see your screen again.

The Wacky World of Display Modes

Unless you're working with an ancient MDA adapter, your video adapter is capable of functioning in two or more display modes. They fall into two basic categories: text and graphics. This distinction is worth knowing about, because a lot of programs let you pick the mode you want to use.

▼ In *text mode*, also called *character mode*, the adapter can only use the two-hundred-something letters, numbers, punctuation marks, and funny graphics symbols built into your computer. Depending on which adapter you're using, you can probably display **bold** and even <u>underlining</u>, but you can't display *italic*. No pictures, either, unless they can be constructed out of the built-in graphics characters.

▼ In *graphics mode*, the adapter and monitor construct the picture freely by using all those itty-bitty dots that are on your screen. Your screen can show anything: Cindy Crawford, the Brooklyn Bridge, Sanskrit text, whatever. Windows requires that you use graphics mode and therefore selects it automatically.

▼ Is the text mode so horrible? No. It's fast. Is the graphics mode so great? No. It's slow. If you have a choice, you'll probably prefer to work in the text mode and switch to graphics mode only when you need to see how the graphics part will look.

▼ Your adapter might be able to display more than two modes. Standard VGA adapters, for example, can display several graphics modes that differ according to the number of lines displayed on one screen.

▼ Most programs set the video mode automatically, but many provide a command you can use to change the mode. This command is usually called Display Options or Display Preferences or something like that.

▼ The all-purpose, default graphics mode displays 25 lines on a screen, but your program may let you choose 43, 50, or even more lines. If you think that sounds great, take a look at the 50- or 60-line display—all the characters are so squished that they're hard to read.

EXPERTS ONLY

Try it!

You can experience the weird and wonderful effect of changing modes yourself. Type **DOSSHELL** to start MS-DOS Shell, which runs in the clunky old text mode by default. Press the Alt key, and then type **OD** to display the Screen Display Mode dialog box. Press the down-arrow key until you have highlighted Graphics 25 Lines Low Resolution; then press Enter. Look at the cool little pictures of the disk drives and everything.

TIP

Windows requires the graphics mode, which runs slowly. A whole new market has emerged for *graphics accelerator boards*. These are plug-in adapter boards that replace your computer's present video adapter. They include all the necessary video adapter circuitry, but they also have a little processing chip that can really zip up your computer's video performance. But you only need a graphics accelerator board if you're running Windows, which runs notoriously slow due to the complexity of its on-screen display.

CHAPTER 14

The Keyboard
(What Are Those Funny Keys, Anyway?)

IN A NUTSHELL

- ▼ Why the computer keyboard has more keys than a typewriter
- ▼ How to get keys to repeat
- ▼ How to disarm toggle keys
- ▼ What all those funny keys with arrows do
- ▼ What all those keys with weird names do
- ▼ How to use the keyboard with DOS
- ▼ What to do if you hear a beep while typing
- ▼ How to avoid repetitive strain injuries

I HATE DOS!

Thereafter the computer is definitely 20th century (maybe 21st), but the keyboard is 19th. To get information into the computer, we're still largely dependent on fingers and clickety-click. Maybe someday you'll be able to sit down and talk to your computer and see the words appear magically on-screen, but for right now, the attempts to get computers to listen haven't been much more successful than our attempts to get our friends, children, and spouses to listen. (Is this a pattern?) If you want to get it into the computer, chances are pretty good you'll have to type it.

Why the Funny Keys?

Those funny keys are there because this isn't a typewriter. A computer can do a lot more stuff. You don't just use it to enter data by typing; you also use it to control the computer. That's why the typewriter's Return key is called Enter on the computer. It's doesn't just start a new line, like the typewriter key does; it also sends a command to the computer.

The standard, 101-key extended keyboard has lots of keys that you won't find on a typewriter. Why is it called *extended*? Because it has more keys than the old, 88-key non-extended keyboard, which hardly anyone uses anymore.

The standard, 101-key extended keyboard.

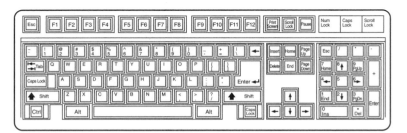

▼ The old part of the keyboard is laid out just like a standard type-writer keyboard. You press Shift to get capital letters or those punctuation marks above the numbers.

▼ The function keys (F1, F2, F3,...) appear along the top or to the left, or both, of the regular keys. These keys do different things, depending on which program you're running. In most programs, for example, F1 is the Help key.

▼ Your keyboard might not have an F11 or F12 key. Programs expect this and therefore give you substitutes.

▼ The cursor-movement keys move the cursor on the screen, but not in DOS, as you might have noticed. You can only move the cursor in programs.

▼ If you know how to do the fingering for super-fast number entry, like they do at the bank, use the numeric keypad.

▼ Note that the numeric keypad has some gray keys, which you can use to enter stuff like minus or plus signs when calculating. But some programs use these keys for different things, such as showing hidden headings in an outline. Remember that the gray plus, mi-nus, asterisk, slash, and Enter keys on the keypad aren't the same as the corresponding typing keys on the keyboard. If you are told to press the plus key on the numeric keypad, you can't just press the regular plus key.

Top Ten Reasons to Use a Typewriter Instead of a Computer

10. A lot cheaper

9. No snotty error messages, just that cute little *ding!*

8. Real writers do not use computers

7. Electricity optional

6. Combines keyboard, CPU, and printer in one compact, space-saving case

5. No agonizing decisions over which typeface to use

4. No software needed—load 8 1/2-by-11-inch paper for word processing, index cards for database management, and so on

3. Less clutter: no disks, no manuals, no nerds

2. You only have to learn a couple of terms, like *platen* and *carriage*

1. *Tap-tap-tap* clatter has promising potential to drive co-workers nuts

Those Highly Irritating Toggle Keys

The word *toggle* is familiar to anyone who spent his or her childhood building model railroads, ham radios, or those Lego structures. For the rest of us, toggle doesn't mean a whole lot—there's only the suggestive fact that it rhymes with *boggle*. But here's a tip: the word basically just means *switch*. When you toggle something, you switch it on or off.

The first time you press a toggle key, you turn on whatever it does. On most keyboards, a helpful little light comes on to let you know that you've engaged the key. The second time you press it, you turn it off. And right in synch, the light goes off.

Your keyboard has three toggle switches: Caps Lock, Num Lock, and Scroll Lock. Note them and beware. If you press them, the keyboard may do unexpected, funny things.

TIP

If your computer starts doing funny things, check the keyboard to see whether you've accidentally pressed one of the toggle keys.

That Cranky Caps Lock Key

By far the most irritating toggle key is the Caps Lock key. When you press it, you get uppercase letters, like on a typewriter. That's not so weird. What's weird is what happens when Caps Lock is on and you use the Shift key while you are typing. You get lowercase letters! lIKE tHIS. vERY iRRITATING. Of course you only notice this after typing half a page of text. Also irritating: Caps Lock shifts only the letter keys, not the numbers. This differs from the way a typewriter works.

The Numskull Num Lock Key

Very nearly as irritating is the Num Lock key, which controls the way the numeric keypad operates. When Num Lock is on, you get numbers when you press the number keys. When Num Lock is off, you can use the numeric keypad to move the cursor. So what's so bad about that?

Unlike the other toggle keys, Num Lock is set up on most computers so that it's on when the computer starts.

The Innocent Scroll Lock Key

In contrast to its two pesky counterparts, Scroll Lock isn't a trouble-maker. In fact, it doesn't do much of anything these days. The key actually does something interesting when you're running a spreadsheet program, but otherwise it doesn't do much more than turn the Scroll Lock light on or off.

Decoding Those Keys with the Funny Arrows

Some keyboards actually put the words Tab and Enter on the so-named keys, along with arrows. Some keyboards have only the arrows. Here's how to decode what the keys mean:

Arrow	Name	Purpose
←	Backspace	You press this key to rub out the character to the left of the cursor. It's a pretty neat key because it lets you correct mistakes right after you make them.
↵	Enter	In DOS, you press Enter to send a command to the computer.
⏐← →⏐	Tab	This key doesn't do much in DOS, but it works a lot like its typewriter counterpart in word processing programs.
↑	Shift	Press this key to type uppercase letters.

Arrow	Name	Purpose
→, ←, ↑, ↓	Cursor Movement Keys	Press these keys to move the cursor.

More and More Keys

In addition to the arrow keys, you'll notice some other unfamiliar keys on the keyboard. One look at these and you'll know you're not using a typewriter anymore.

Key	Purpose
Ctrl	Some programs use this key with another key to select a command. For instance, you might press Ctrl and B to select the bold command. The function of each key combination will vary, so just ignore this key in DOS.
Alt	You use this key, like the Ctrl key, for commands. It works the same way the Ctrl key does—you hold it down and press another key.
Esc	This key generally cancels the current operation or takes you back to what you were doing before.
Prt Scr or Print Screen	Use the Print Screen key to get a quick printout of what's on your screen.

continues

I HATE DOS!

Key	Purpose
Ins or Insert	For the most part, this key turns on a program's Insert mode, which lets you put characters within text you've already typed instead of typing over it.
Del or Delete	When you press this key in most programs, it erases the character that the cursor is on.
Pause/Break	You can press this key to stop a DOS command such as DIR from scrolling. When used in combination with the Ctrl key, this key cancels a DOS command.
PgUp	Programs usually use this key to scroll the screen up toward the beginning of your file.
PgDn	Programs usually use this key to scroll the screen down toward the end of your file.
F1, F2, F3...	These keys are called *function keys*, and different programs use them differently. Pressing F1, for instance, accesses help in a lot of programs.

TIP

If you get stuck in a program, try pressing Esc. It might just get you out of a jam!

Hot Keyboard Tricks with DOS

So! You've learned your way around the keyboard. And you've figured out that most of them aren't that useful in DOS. Well, *this* section explains the key DOS keys.

▼ Screen scrolling at a wild pace? Press Ctrl-S to pause the screen. Or press the helpfully named Pause key. Press any key to resume scrolling.

▼ DOS command doing disagreeable or incomprehensible things? Press Ctrl-C or Ctrl-Break to cancel. This command is great for stopping the display of a long DIR list.

▼ Turn on the printer by pressing Ctrl-P; after you do, the printer prints a copy of every DOS line you type (and every line that DOS responds with, including all those embarrassing error messages). To turn off the printer, use Ctrl-P again.

▼ You can reset your computer by pressing Ctrl-Alt-Del, but don't do it unless you're sure that your system has crashed and you've no other alternative.

The Madness and Mystery of DOS Editing Keys

Let's suppose that you've typed a nice, long DOS command, like

COPY C:\TIMELESS\PROSE\JUNK.DOC A:\JUNK.BAK

only to discover, after pressing Enter, that you typed the path name wrong or something. Wouldn't it be nice to be able to edit the command instead of typing it over again?

Well, you can—although the procedure you have to follow is so bizarre that only a very few DOS users employ it. That should be enough to send you merrily on to the next section, but if you're determined to learn this, it's your business. Read on.

Play It Again, Sam

To display a command again, press F3. If you want to use that command again, press Enter. If you want to make minor changes, press Backspace to erase everything back to the mistake. Then type the correct command.

One by One

To display a command, letter by letter, press F1 a few times. One by one, the letters from your previous command creep back on-screen. Is this useful in any way? Maybe. Suppose that you really wanted to type **POEMS** instead of **PROSE**. Press F1 until all of the following characters are back on-screen:

COPY C:\TIMELESS\

Then type **POEMS**. This wipes out the the word PROSE. Now you can press F1 until all the rest of the command is restored.

EXPERTS ONLY

Like those cool DOS editing keys?

Try this one! You can display a command up to a specific character by typing F2 followed by that character. For example, to enter COPY C:\TIMELESS\PROSE\J, you press F2 followed by J.

What to Do If You Hear a Beep while Typing Really Fast

The quick, easy answer: Slow down and let the computer catch up.

The boring technical explanation: Sometimes programs have to stop accepting keyboard input because they're busy doing something else, like saving your data to disk. You can keep typing for a little while, thanks to something called the *type-ahead buffer*, a temporary storage area that can store up to 16 keystrokes while your computer is busy. But once the type-ahead buffer is full, you hear a beep, which warns you that the characters you're typing at the moment will be lost. Wait until the program has finished doing what it's doing, and then resume typing.

Most programs can handle keyboard input as fast as you can dish it out.

What's That Funny Numb Feeling?

As rhythm guitarists have known for a long time, repeating the same hand action over and over and over can lead to health problems, which doctors call *repetitive strain injury* (RSI). This condition can cause a

really painful nerve disorder when scar tissue builds up in narrow areas of the hand and wrist. RSI can be serious and debilitating. A symptom of the injury is numbness in your fingers.

You can reduce your chances of contracting a repetitive strain injury by using the keyboard correctly.

Checklist

▼ Don't use a keyboard that's way up on the top of the desk. It should be positioned so that you can type with your elbows forming a right angle—and that usually means lowering the keyboard. If necessary, get a keyboard shelf that fits under your desk and slides out as needed.

▼ Be sure to rest your palms on something while typing. You can purchase a pad from your local computer store for this purpose.

CHAPTER 15

The Printer
(Tales of Dread and Woe)

IN A NUTSHELL

▼ What kind of printers there are, and how they differ

▼ How to get someone else to hook up your printer

▼ What fonts are, and how you can get more of them

▼ How to see if your printer is working

▼ Why you shouldn't bother printing from DOS

▼ How to deal with common printing problems

Printers ought to be easy to use. Ideally, you should just connect them, load the paper, and print. If that were true, this chapter wouldn't be necessary—and at least one life would have been saved. Yes, it's true: a printer (a serial printer, mind you) was implicated in the only known computer-related murder. In the late 1970s, an irate customer of a San Jose, CA computer store spent weeks trying, without success, to get a serial printer working, whereupon he returned to the store and opened fire on the unfortunate salesperson. This was the first serial murder of the computer age.

This chapter tells you what types of printers are available, such as the aforementioned serial printer, and what types of problems to expect, murderous ideas aside.

What this chapter doesn't tell you is how to print from DOS. For the most part, you print from a program. So you have to learn that program's dance routine for printing.

Types of Printers

Engineering geniuses the world over have invented dozens of ways to print computer output, but you'll find only four kinds of printers in widespread use today.

Printer	The Lowdown
Dot-Matrix Printers	The cheapest printers work by hammering a pattern (or matrix) of little wires against a ribbon, making an impression on paper. These printers tend to be noisy, and sometimes the dots don't connect very well. The best ones produce OK output, but they're slow because they have to go back over the printed text two or three times to connect all the little dots.

Printer	The Lowdown
Inkjet Printers	These printers are more expensive than dot-matrix printers, but less expensive than laser printers. They work by spraying the paper with ink. The output looks sort of like the print created by a laser printer, but not quite. Inkjet printers are slower than most laser printers.
Laser and LED Printers	These printers use parts from copying machines and work the same way, except that the image comes directly from the computer. Print quality is very good, and they print quickly (the best ones can print 8 or more pages per minute of double-spaced, plain text).
PostScript Laser Printers	These printers are much more expensive than any other type of printer because they have their own, built-in computer. The computer is needed to interpret printing instructions given in the printer's language (called *PostScript*). PostScript is needed only if you're doing professional desktop publishing.

You can also get color printers these days, and the quality's getting better. But they're still a lot more expensive to buy, and some of them require expensive, special paper.

Serial and Parallel Printers

Many printers are available in two models, serial and parallel. A serial printer is designed to be hooked up through one of your computer's serial

ports. A parallel printer is designed to be hooked up through one of your computer's parallel ports.

BUZZWORDS

PORT
A port is a connection in the back of your computer that lets you hook up accessory stuff, like printers and modems.

Hooking up a printer to a parallel port is easy. You just connect the cables. Because it's such a hassle to connect printers through the serial port, most of today's printers are parallel printers.

If you're using a system that's already set up, don't worry whether it has a serial printer—as long as it's working OK. Someone has made the system modifications that are necessary to get the darned thing to work.

Printer Names

Your computer is designed so that as many as three or four printers can be hooked up to it. Since you're probably just hooking up one printer, the whole process should be uncomplicated, no? Well, of course not. After all, DOS is involved.

To give you the ability to use more than one printer, DOS has a set of printer names, such as LPT1:, LPT2:, COM1:, COM2:, and so on. (The colons are part of the name. It makes the names easy to misspell.) The LPT ports are parallel ports, while the COM ports are serial ones. Chances are that your computer has just one parallel port, and if so, it's LPT1:.

If you need to hook up a printer to a parallel port and if you have the right cable (see the next section), all you do is connect the cables.

If you have a serial port, read the section "Connecting a Serial Printer."

Checklist

▼ If you've just bought a computer, don't take it out of the salesroom until the salesperson shows you which of those funny-looking plug-hole thingies is LPT1:.

▼ DOS, as well as your programs, assume by default that you're using LPT1: to connect your printer. Moral of the story: your life will be much easier if you connect your printer to LPT1:. You can't print to a printer connected in the other ports without making modifications to your programs or to DOS.

Making the Connection Physically

To connect your printer, you need a printer cable. This is one of the things that ought to be easy, but isn't—thanks to a lack of standards. There are lots of different kinds of connectors, and to top it off, you have to know the sex of the connectors (male or female). Obviously, this is a very distasteful and embarrasing subject, one that is best left to the salespeople at the store where you bought the computer. Just say, "I want a cable to connect my printer," and take the one they give you. Have them tell you where to plug it in, too, because some computers have two plugs that look exactly the same. And if the cable doesn't work, take it back and make them give you the right cable.

Connecting a Serial Printer

(You've been warned)

Don't try to hook up a serial printer! There are several reasons why serial printers are hard to hook up.

TIP

> If you have to hook up a serial printer, get someone who thrives on technical challenges to help you.

Checklist

▼ You need the right cable. There are lots of different serial cables for different purposes. Getting the right cable for your serial printer can be something of a trick. Unfortunately, many computer salespeople are not knowledgeable about this matter and can't figure out which cable to give you.

▼ You have to connect the cable to the right COM port. Your computer probably has only one parallel port, but it probably has two (or more) serial ports. Try to get the salespeople or technical support people to show you which COM port is which, among all those odd plug-in doohickeys in the back of your computer.

▼ You have to *configure* the serial port to meet your printer's characteristics. You do this by using a DOS command called MODE. If you don't enter this command at the beginning of every session, your printer won't work. (To have this process done automatically when you start up your computer, place the MODE command in the AUTOEXEC.BAT file, discussed in Chapter 18.)

▼ Just which MODE command you should type depends on your printer's needs, so check your printer's manual to find out. If you are setting up your printer for the COM1: port, the command would look something like this:

MODE COM1:9600,N,8,1

If you're setting up the printer for the COM2: port, it would look like this:

MODE COM2:9600,N,8,1

The exact stuff you're supposed to type in the "9600,N,8,1" area varies from printer to printer. Good luck! Have fun!

The Joy and Anguish of Printer Fonts

Today's printers usually come with two or more built-in *fonts*—that is, complete sets of letters and numbers in a distinctive typeface design. These designs have creative names that don't tell you a lot about them; you're just supposed to know. Here are some examples:

Bodoni

New Century Schoolbook

Avant Garde

Helvetica

Times Roman

Garamond Condensed

Courier

▼ Every printer has a default font, the one that it uses unless some clever program tells it otherwise. DOS isn't clever, so it always prints with the default font.

▼ Most laser printers proudly offer Courier as the default font. Courier is amazing: using a thousand-dollar computer printer, it produces output that looks as though it were typed on a $98 typewriter.

▼ With many printers, you can add additional fonts by using font cartridges. To use these fonts, you simply plug the cartridge into the printer's cartridge slot.

▼ If your printer has a lot of memory, it might be able to use *soft fonts*. Soft fonts are fonts stored on your computer's hard disk until needed, at which time they are sent (the term is *downloaded*) to your printer. Good word processing programs, such as WordPerfect, handle soft fonts automatically.

▼ To use your printer's fonts, your programs must be compatible with your printer. For more information on this bad news, read the section called "Program to Printer," near the end of this chapter.

Top Ten Rejected Font Names

10. IRS Tax Form Gothic

9. Bud Light

8. USDA "Choice" Block Letter Bold

222

7. Graffiti Dingbats

6. Mogadishu

5. Gang Territory SprayPaint Italic (outdoor use only; large-caliber automatic weapon strongly suggested)

4. Madonna

3. Publisher's Clearinghouse FormLetter Ultra (large font sizes only)

2. Ayatollah Calligraphic Death Threat Condensed (requires hostage)

1. NewEnquirer Roman (requires third-grade education only)

Test Your Printer

(And your ability to withstand stress)

To test whether your printer works, make sure that the power's on and, if necessary, load it up with paper.

To print, your printer must be *on line* or *selected* (ready to receive stuff from the computer). This is usually the case, but you should check to make sure. Look for a button called On Line or Select. This button probably has an indicator light. When it's on, the printer is ready to go. (If it's off, press the button to turn the light on.)

"I HATE THIS!"

On line, off line, out of line

Why would someone have turned off the On Line button? With most printers, you have to take the computer *off line* (a techie expression that means *break the connection*) to advance the paper. Most printers have Line Feed and Form Feed buttons that advance the paper one line or one page at a time, respectively. If the printer's off-line, it's probably because someone wanted to eject a page.

When your printer is on and selected, type this command at the DOS prompt:

        DIR > PRN

and press Enter. Be sure to leave a space before and after the greater-than sign (>), which tells DOS to send the command's output to the printer. This command prints the current directory.

"I HATE THIS!"

Didn't work?

Is the printer on? Is the printer selected (on line)? Is there a cable between the printer and the computer? Did you type the command correctly? Is there paper in the printer? Is there a user at the keyboard? Is the user reading a Harlequin romance again instead of typing these wonderfully cool DOS commands?

If you've checked all the obvious stuff and your printer still doesn't work, don't torture yourself—find someone who knows this system, and get help.

EXPERTS ONLY

Showing the printer who's boss

If you're using a laser printer or an inkjet printer, you might need to eject the page after DOS finishes printing the directory. To do so, you need this command: (but don't type it yet!)

    ECHO ^L > PRN

Why can't you just type it? It won't work, that's why. To enter the ^L part, you can't just type a caret followed by L. You have to hold down the Ctrl key and press L, so that DOS enters ^L for you. So here's how to do this: Type **ECHO**, followed by a space. Then hold down the Ctrl key and press L. Leave a space, and type the greater-than sign. Leave another space, and then type **PRN**. Then press Enter to make DOS spit out the rest of the final page.

Why You Shouldn't Bother Printing with DOS

You can press the Prt Scr (Print Screen) key to print whatever's on your screen; this is called a *screen dump*. You'll probably see a lot of garbage characters (the Greek alphabet, happy faces, card suits) surrounding bits and pieces of intelligible text. My advice: skip it.

TIP

If you accidentally press Prt Scr when your printer's turned off or off-line, DOS will wait forever for the printer to respond. You'll have to turn the printer on or press the On Line or Select button so that DOS can get the printing over with.

You also can print from DOS by using the PRINT command, but why? You should print from your programs, not from DOS. And the key to printing from your programs is uncovered next.

Program to Printer

(Can you hear me?)

Your programs talk (electronically, that is) to your printer. Why do your programs have to talk to your printer? To get your printer to do fancy stuff, like printing boldface or italic. Your program has to send a command (an instruction) to the printer to turn on these special features, and again to turn them off when they're no longer needed. The command set for a particular printer is called a *printer control language*. And when the printer and the program can converse, they are said to be *compatible*.

Checklist

▼ Each printer brand has its own, pet language. Commands written for one printer's language will do weird, unpredictable things if sent to another manufacter's printer.

▼ Because of the post-Tower of Babel situation among printer manufacturers, software publishers must keep abreast of all the popular printers, and they must include special files called *printer drivers* with their programs.

▼ If your printer is compatible with your programs, life will be easy. You'll be able to print without too much hassle, and you'll be able to take advantage of all your printer's features. If the printer is not compatible, contact the software company, which might have a special driver that will work with your printer.

▼ One way to make sure that your printer is compatible is to go with the herd: use a printer that just about everyone else is using. That means sticking with name brands, such as Hewlett-Packard or Epson.

BUZZWORDS

PRINTER DRIVER

A printer driver is a file that tells the program how to use a particular brand of printer, such as the Keen-O-Matic XL1568. Part of installing a program is telling it which printer you're using so that the installation utility can go fetch the correct printer driver.

So what's a *compatible printer?* It's a printer your program supports—and by that I mean that your program has a printer driver for the particular make and model of printer you're using.

The Pain and Heartbreak of Printing Problems

When you are printing, lots of things can go wrong. Most of them aren't serious.

Checklist

▼ The paper can jam. Laser printers are particularly prone to this mishap. You may have to open the cabinet and extricate the jammed pages from various rollers, clamps, and other sadistic devices. Be careful! One of those rollers is really hot.

continues

▼ Your printer can run out of paper. If so, your program will probably display a message informing you of this development. Load some more.

▼ If you have a laser printer, loading paper is easy. Just refill the tray. Loading paper is a feat unto itself with a dot-matrix printer. Sometimes you have to weave and bob and weave and clamp the paper through the printer. Ask someone to help you.

▼ You might see funny-looking garbage on your printout. If you're trying to print with DOS, this is pretty normal. If you're trying to print with a program, though, something's wrong. Maybe the program isn't set up for the printer you're using. There are so many programs in use that I can't really tell you how to do this here; get someone to help you, or—as a last resort—read the manual.

PART IV

The Bluffer's Guide to Software

Includes:

16: Software

17: Installing and Running Programs

18: Modifying Those Awful System Files

CHAPTER 16

Software

(Programs That Actually Do Things)

IN A NUTSHELL

- ▼ What an application is
- ▼ What a system utility program is
- ▼ How to tell the difference between a DOS and a Windows application program
- ▼ What the big three software applications are
- ▼ What shareware is and why it's so cheap

Y ou've set up your computer. You've learned DOS. You can print directories at will, and you can even force your printer to eject a page on demand. Why do you have this "all dressed up and nowhere to go" feeling? Simple: by itself, DOS is pretty worthless. Its only excuse is to help you run application programs. (That's good news!)

An application program turns your computer into a tool you can apply to a particular kind of task, such as writing, crunching numbers, or repelling alien invaders from space. This chapter provides a quick introduction to the world of application software. What's covered is intended to help you get oriented in the world of software.

Application? What's That?

Guess what! The point of using the computer isn't to refine your DOS skills to the maximum. It's to actually do something constructive. And to do something constructive you need an application.

BUZZWORDS

APPLICATION

An *application* is the use of the computer for some creative or productive purpose, such as printing mailing labels, composing prize-winning poetry, or designing a community newsletter. An *application program*, then, is a computer program that helps you do one of these things. In common use, any single or combination of these terms—application, program, software—works. Take your pick: application program, program, software program, software application, and so on.

System Software and Utilities

(The tool box)

System software refers to any and all programs that help you maintain or enhance your computer system. All the DOS programs are system programs. You have to have system software.

System utilities are programs that enhance the capabilities of the system software. For instance, you can use a screen-saver program to display cool pictures of the Enterprise and Mr. Spock when you aren't using the computer. System utilities are extras.

What the Heck Is a DOS Application Program?

If you buy a Nintendo cartridge, it won't work on your Sega Genesis system. The same goes for computer software. To use a program on your computer, the program must be compatible—that is, written for an IBM or IBM-compatible computer running DOS.

There are DOS applications, Windows applications, and Macintosh applications, plus some other, more obscure kinds.

Checklist

▼ A DOS application program isn't a Windows application program. See the next section to find out what a Windows application program is. But you can use a DOS program if you have Windows.

▼ It's pretty easy to tell whether a program is a DOS application program or not. It usually says "For DOS" on the package or in the advertisement. If it says something like "For Windows," it's a Windows application program; read the next section.

continues

▼ DOS application programs are still the hottest sellers. The best-selling DOS program of all time, WordPerfect for DOS, still tops the charts.

▼ Here's one reason people like DOS application programs: DOS programs run fast, even on fairly modest systems, like 286s and 386s. The Windows version of the same program probably requires a 486 running at 33MHz.

▼ A lot of people have gone through all the pain and turmoil of learning a DOS application program, and their attitude is, "The heck with learning anything new. This works just fine." That's why there are still so many DOS application programs in use, even though Windows is clearly the Next Big Thing.

What Is This Windows Thing?

Microsoft Windows is an optional program designed to run on IBM or IBM-compatible computers. Windows offers a lot of benefits.

Why Windows?

▼ Windows has something called a graphical user interface, or GUI (yes, it's true; it's pronounced "gooey"). The idea of a GUI is to depict commonly used computer operations in the form of cute little pictures, called *icons*. If you want to print, for example, you don't have to hunt for a print command—you just use the mouse to click a tiny picture of a printer. This makes Windows programs easier to use, at least in some peoples' opinion.

▼ Windows enables your computer to use more memory (if you have it). Chapter 12 gives you a fascinating look at memory.

▼ Most Windows programs work alike. If you learn one Windows program, you can pretty easily learn another one.

▼ One of the coolest things about Windows is that you can run two or three or more applications at once.

▼ The one catch here is that all these marvelous benefits are only available if you run Windows applications. A Windows application program is an application program specifically designed to run with Windows. To use such a program, you must have Windows installed on your system.

▼ Another down side of Windows is the demand it places on your system's performance. All those little icons, all that fancy on-screen stuff, and other assorted Windows virtues require a lot of computing power and memory. To run Windows at a brisk clip, you'll need something more powerful than the 386SX running at 16MHz, the machine that has become the standard, entry-level system these days. (To decode 386SX and 16MHz, see Chapter 11.)

The Windows and DOS Relationship (Friend or foe?)

Windows requires DOS. But when you start Windows, it "takes over" DOS. Actually, you can forget that DOS exists.

▼ Most Windows users set up their systems so that Windows starts automatically.

▼ From Windows, you can do all the stuff you do with DOS, like copying and deleting files, by using a Windows utility program called File Manager. If you really want to, though, you can quit Windows and see the good old DOS prompt.

▼ Windows runs DOS application programs. Of course, you don't get the benefits of Windows application programs—you just see your old, reliable DOS program, looking the same as ever. But at the press of a key, you can switch from the DOS program to a Windows program.

▼ A lot of people run both kinds of application programs, DOS and Windows, on their systems. There's nothing wrong with this at all. The two types of programs don't mind. They get along fine. They say, "After you" and "My warmest thanks, you fine, gracious fellow."

Do I Have Windows?

Most computers come with Windows these days. To find out whether your system has Windows installed, just type **WIN** at the DOS prompt and press Enter. You'll eventually see the Program Manager, a Windows utility that lets you start Windows applications. See the cute little icons? Know what to do next? If not, take a look at our sister book, *I Hate Windows*, published by Que.

I HATE DOS!

CHAPTER 16

TIP

If you're buying a machine, you'll probably get both Windows and DOS with it. If you just want to use DOS and DOS applications (also called "non-Windows applications"), you can forget about Windows for now. Later, if you want to learn Windows and use Windows applications, you'll find that your knowledge of DOS is really helpful.

TIP

Attention, shoppers: Windows is definitely the wave of the future. You'll probably use it someday, so you should get a system that's good enough to run Windows well. (Flip back to Chapter 11 if you're interested about what kind of system you need.)

The Big Three

The most common types of software are word processing programs, spreadsheet programs, and database programs. You can use each of these to create a variety of documents.

CAUTION

The biggest mistake people make with software is buying too many programs and getting overwhelmed. Most successful computer users run just two or three programs.

Word Processing Programs (The Village Wordsmith)

With word processing software, you can create, edit, format, and print all kinds of text documents. (*Formatting* refers to making the text look good on the page.) You can create memos, letters, resumes, newsletters, manuals, books. If text is your thing, get a word processing program.

Cool things about word processors

▼ Adding text with a word processor is easy. You just put the cursor where you want the text and type away. Deleting and moving text is just as easy. No more retyping!

▼ With a word processor program, you can jazz up a document. Add lines, make text bold, use two columns, and more.

▼ Are you a lousy speller? A lousy typist? Most word processors have a speller program that will check your spelling. Although a speller can't catch all your errors (it won't flag you if you use *their* when you mean *there*), it will point out most of them.

Popular DOS Word Processor Programs

The Program	The Scoop
WordPerfect	A great, full-featured, if somewhat quirky word processing program. Dynamite for just about every word processing application, including office stuff (it even does mailing lists and mailing labels), legal documents (it's a whiz at referencing legal citations), and university dissertations

The Program	The Scoop
	(great footnotes). A plus: in any organization, lots of people will know WordPerfect, so it's easy to get help. Available for Windows, too.
Microsoft Word	Another full-featured word processing program that a lot of people like, but for specific tasks such as legal, office, and scholarly word processing, it lacks WordPerfect's focus. Dearly beloved by scriptwriters because it handles those weird movie and TV script formats nicely. The Windows version is a lot better and is currently the hottest-selling Windows word processing program.
Ami Pro	A Windows-only word processing program. It's great if you do a lot of fancy formatting.

Spreadsheet Programs (I've got your number)

A close second in popularity is the electronic spreadsheet program. The term "spreadsheet" refers to the lined worksheet that accountants use, and spreadsheets deal with numbers. You can create budgets, financial plans, and profit and loss statements. Spreadsheets may sound as if they are only for businesses, but you can balance your checkbook and figure your taxes. If you need to fiddle with figures, you need a spreadsheet program.

Cool things about spreadsheets

▼ The beauty of a spreadsheet is that it can say something like, "Take all the sales figures for March, and add them up." The number that results from the formula appears. Boom. And if you change one of the March sales figures, the total is recalculated automatically.

▼ You can also say, "What if sales go up by 15 percent? What if sales go down?" You can make hypothetical changes and see the results to the big picture.

▼ Most spreadsheet programs can make cool-looking graphs of the numbers you enter so that you can see that your entertainment budget makes up 44 percent of your income this month. Too much fun!

Popular DOS Spreadsheet Programs

The Program	The Scoop
Lotus 1-2-3	The biggest-selling spreadsheet program—the standard. Like WordPerfect, a lot of people know Lotus, so it's easy to get help. Available for Windows.
Quattro Pro	A hot-selling rival to Lotus 1-2-3, this spreadsheet program sells for less—and claims to offer more—than 1-2-3. Also available for Windows.
Excel	The best-selling Windows spreadsheet program. This program is a powerhouse, and is also easy to use.

Database Programs

In third place, and not likely to zoom any further up the charts, are database management programs.

A *database management program* is essentially a computerized version of a library card catalog. In a library card catalog, each individual card is a data record—it holds one unit of information about one thing, a book. On the card are data fields, where certain types of information appear, such as the author's name and the title.

What's cool about databases?

▼ They make it really easy to maintain your data. Library card catalogs are a huge drag to maintain. They have to be sorted alphabetically. And when new cards come in, they have to be put in the right place. Basically, the big advantage of computer database management programs is that they provide help with such tasks. These programs let you enter new data with ease, and they sort automatically.

▼ You also can sort in all kinds of different ways. A library card catalog is sorted just one way, by author's last name. But a computerized version of the card catalog lets you sort in all kinds of ways—by call number, by subject, by publisher, whatever.

▼ Computerized database management also lets you do something that's next to impossible with card systems: you can group the information in all kinds of ways, called *querying*. You can say, "Show me a list of all the English poets who published between 1825 and 1838," or "Give me a printout of all the books we have on Latin American economic development after 1950."

Popular DOS Database Programs	
The Program	The Scoop
FoxPro	A powerful, but very quirky and difficult, database management program with many advanced features. Not really for people who aren't into computer programming.
dBASE	A big, complex database management program, but somewhat easier to use than FoxPro.
Paradox	Yet another big, complex database management program that tends to give nonprogrammers fits. Paradox is also available in a Windows version.

Beyond the Big Three

Besides the big three general applications—word processors, spreadsheets, and databases—there are hundreds and hundreds of other types of programs. This section gives you a sampling.

Other Popular Programs	
The Program	The Scoop
Turbo Tax (Chipsoft)	Walks you through the entire ordeal of doing your taxes, and prints the results on IRS-approved facsimiles of real tax forms.

The Program	The Scoop
BizPlanBuilder (JIAN Tools)	Take the entrepreneurial leap: put together a business plan that will catch your banker's eye.
Address Book and Label Maker (Power Up Software)	Keeps a mailing list and prints mailing labels in over 40 formats; includes soft fonts for attractive printouts.
Quicken (Intuit)	Get your checkbook, spending, and budget organized, finally. Track each check you write, and code it by category. Produce great reports and graphs that show just where your money's going. You can even write checks on-screen and print them on bank-approved computer checks; makes monthly bill-writing a breeze.
Publish It! (Timeworks)	Easy-to-use desktop publishing program that includes 150 ready-to-use templates for newsletters, flyers, brochures, and more. (A *desktop publishing program* is designed to help you lay out text on the page for special-purpose publications, such as newsletters or brochures.)
It's Legal (Parsons Technology)	Quickly generate binding legal documents such as wills, power of attorney letters, living trusts, and much more.
Typing Tutor (Que Software)	Quickly learn to type the ten-fingered way.

continues

Other Popular Programs Continued

The Program	The Scoop
WealthBuilder (Reality Software)	*Money Magazine's* comprehensive solution for tracking and optimizing your investments and personal finances.
Calendar Creator Plus (Power Up Software)	Create and print calendars with appointments, prioritized to-do lists, and personal scheduling.
Print Shop (Brøderbund)	Quickly print greeting cards, newsletters, posters, and more.
Harvard Graphics (Software Publishing Corporation)	Quickly print groovy-looking charts and graphs for your next winning presentation. You can save them to a special format that can be made into colorful 35mm slides, if you really want to wow 'em.

Top Ten Rejected Software Ideas

10. Generates numbers that "look right" for IRS Form 1040 and Schedule A

9. On-screen pop-up reminds you when Gilligan's Island is on

8. Tracks verified Elvis sightings; uses secret formula to predict location of his next appearance

7. Figures out all possible Mr. Potato Head configurations

6. Suggests the best way to sort your laundry (based on your own personal list of dirty clothes) and indicates prime water-temperature settings

5. Creates fictitious but plausible genealogy demonstrating roots back to the Mayflower

4. Reads Rod McKuen poems to you

3. For worriers: from user-supplied data, automatically constructs "worst case scenarios" for a variety of family, work, and health problems

2. Stores database of cheese product recipes

1. Adds scenic pictures from hazardous waste dumps to your document

What's This "Shareware" Stuff?

Programs for $4 a disk? It couldn't be worth bothering with, could it? Well, maybe. Shareware programs, also called *user-supported programs*, are distributed by mail order companies that sell them for this much, or even less. Here's the idea—you try the program on your computer, and if you like it, you send the program's author a registration fee. This might be as little as $10, although the typical fee ranges from $35 to $75. Don't expect miracles.

Why is shareware so cheap? Low expenses. There's probably a rudimentary manual, at best, and no telephone technical assistance. The author hasn't spent a dime on promotion, advertising, distribution, transportation, dealer incentives, or the like.

CHAPTER 17

Installing and Running Programs
(The Real Fun of Computers)

IN A NUTSHELL

▼ Determine whether a given program
will run on your computer
▼ A guide to all that stuff they
put in software boxes
▼ Install a new program
▼ Start a new program
▼ Learn a new program
▼ Decide whether to upgrade
to a new version
▼ Run more than one DOS
program at a time

T hat nice, new software package is sitting next to your computer, but there's one problem: the software's in the box, not in your computer. To use the program, you must install it—that is, copy the program from the floppy disks in the box to your computer's hard disk. Unfortunately, there's more. You will probably have to *configure* the program (which means telling it what kind of printer and video adapter you have), and other tedious stuff of that nature. This chapter covers the highlights.

"Will It Run on My Computer?"

A good question, and one worth answering before you tear open the package. Look on the program's box for a section called "System Requirements." (This is almost always printed on the *outside* of the box—often on the back of the box.)

"I HATE THIS!"

Oops! I opened the box and I can't run the program

Most computer stores and mail-order outfits will let you return the program if you haven't opened the box. But if you rip open everything, including the little envelope that contains the disks, some stores won't take the program back, out of fear that you ordered it with the dishonest intention of copying the disks and then getting a refund.

Also, before you tear the package open, make sure that you get a program that has the correct size of floppy disks for your computer. Most programs are available in two versions, one with 5.25-inch and the other with 3.5-inch disks. If you have both drive sizes, don't worry about which size comes with the program.

"I HATE THIS!"

If you only have one drive size, check the box to find out whether you purchased the right size; the box usually says something like, "Includes 3.5-inch disks." What if you didn't get the right size? Take it back and exchange it for the version that contains the correct disk size. Otherwise, you'll have to write to the software publisher to get the disks in the other size, and on top of having to wait, they'll probably hit you up for 10 or 20 bucks.

What I Have

Before you can know whether a program will run on your computer, you need to know what kind of computer and software you have. Use this handy checklist. (This information will also come in handy when you are installing the program.)

My system has...

▼ My computer has version _____ of DOS. (If you're not sure what version you have, type **VER** at the DOS prompt, and then press Enter.)

▼ My computer has a _____ microprocessor. (8088, 8086, 80286, 80386, 80486)

▼ My computer has _____K of conventional (base) memory, and _____MB of extended (XMS) memory. (If you're not sure how much memory you have and you're using DOS 5.0 or later, type **MEM** at the DOS prompt, and then press Enter.) **Hint:** All 386 and 486 computers come with at least 640K of conventional memory and 384K of extended memory.

continues

▼ My computer has a _____ floppy disk drive(s). (3.5-inch, 5.25-inch, both)

▼ My hard disk has _____MB of free disk space. (If you're not sure now much free disk space you have, type **DIR** at the DOS prompt, and then press Enter; look at the amount of free space remaining figure at the bottom of the directory list.)

▼ My computer has a _____ display adapter. (CGA, MDA, HGA, EGA, VGA, or SVGA) *Hint:* If you're using DOS Version 6.0, you can type **MSD** at the DOS prompt, and then press Enter. The text next to the Video button tells you the kind of display adapter you have.

▼ I have a color/monochrome monitor. (circle one)

▼ My printer is made by _____. Its model name or number is _____. (Be sure that you include all numbers or Roman numerals, like "DeskJet 500" or "LaserJet IIsi.")

TIP

For a definition of all these terms, read the chapters in Part III of this book.

What I Need

Now compare what you know you've got to what you need:

▼ If the system's requirement stuff reads "MS-DOS Version 2.11 or later," it is referring to the *DOS version number*. DOS 4 is later than DOS 3; DOS 6 is later than DOS 5. The requirement really should read, "MS-DOS Version 2.11 or any higher version number."

▼ The same goes with microprocessor numbers—you'll see something like "8088 or higher." 80286 is higher than 8088; 80386 is higher than 80286. If you're curious about these numbers and what they mean, flip back to Chapter 11.

▼ The system's requirement stuff might read, "5.25-inch or 3.5-inch low-density floppy disk drive." Don't let this one get to you. If you have high-density drives, they can read low-density disks just fine. If you're cloudy about the differences between a high-density and low-density floppy disk drive, take a look at Chapter 5, which explains a bit more about this subject.

▼ The memory requirement might read something like "512K of RAM required." This really means "512K *or more*." 512K is the absolute minimum you need to run this program. Chapter 12 explains more about the vexing and painful topic of memory.

▼ If you see a video adapter requirement such as "EGA color required," remember that this is another one of those *minimum* requirements. Here's an important point: All video adapters are *downwardly compatible* with earlier adapters. This means that a VGA adapter can run software designed for CGA, HGA, MDA, or EGA adapters just fine. (Whew! What a lot of horrifying acronyms; if you're completely in the dark and craving a little illumination, go to Chapter 13.)

continues

▼ Does the program require Microsoft Windows? (You might not yet grasp the difference between a Windows program and a DOS program. Have no fear, Chapter 16 will set you straight.) If the program *does* require Windows, you must have Windows installed on your system before you can even install this program, let alone run it.

TIP

If you're installing a Windows application, consider that the minimum system requirements are often wildly understated. If the requirement reads, "2MB extended memory required," for example, it means "This program will just barely run with 2MB." Double the figure if you want anything other than very sluggish performance.

What's in the Box?

OK, it will run on your system. So tear into that box (this is the fun part). Here's what you may find:

▼ **Program disks.** These live in an envelope, probably, that is securely taped shut. The tape probably has a frightening message printed on it, such as "Warning! By opening this package, you hereby submit and swear eternal obedience to all the stipulations, regulations, restrictions, and injunctions contained in the Software License. The Company's remedies for violation of these stipulations, etc., include but are not restricted to forfeiture of your home, family jewels, and Firesign Theatre album collection." This is a

rather coercive way of getting you to agree to the license terms, isn't it? Well, break open the package anyway—it's the only way you're going to be able to get the disks out.

▼ **Software license.** This might be in the manual, or printed separately. Basically, it probably says that you can use this program on one computer, and you can make backup disks for your own use. But you can't give or sell copies of the program to others without violating the law. It also denies that the publisher has any liability for anything, including lost data, lost time, chewed nails, or deteriorated personal relationships due to temper tantrums.

▼ **Documentation (manuals).** There might be one or more of these. Good programs include an "Installation" or "Setup" booklet, another booklet called "Getting Started," and one or more reference manuals that exhaustively detail every last aspect of the program.

▼ **Quick reference guide.** Hang onto this and keep it next to your computer. You'll need it. Through extensive product testing, the software publisher has determined all the stuff that people just can't remember when they're trying to use the program, and it's all listed here, in a concise look-up format.

▼ **Registration card.** Even if you never send in the registration card for lawnmowers or stuff like that, don't skip this one. Fill it out, and mail it immediately. Here's why. That nice, new program you just bought might contain a nice, big bug. To remedy this horrifying bug, the company may need to send out a *bug fix*—"correction" to the program that remedies a problem.

Another good reason to mail the registration card: the software publisher will notify you of program upgrades, which you can usually obtain at a small fraction of the new version's list price. (If you're not sure whether you should upgrade your programs—or you're not even sure what *upgrading* is—look at "Should You Upgrade?" later in this chapter.)

BUZZWORDS

BUG

A *bug* is a problem with the way a program runs. The term originated back when computers were the size of rooms. One computer went awry and the technical gurus traced the problem to a huge moth stuck in one of the parts. True story.

▼ **Keyboard Template.** Not all programs come with these, but they're cool things to have. They're plastic or cardboard cutouts that sit on your keyboard. Basically, these things are cheat sheets that help you remember all those funny key combinations, like what Shift-Alt-Ctrl-F11 does. Sometimes the template has a stickum that lets you affix it to your keyboard.

▼ **Junk advertisements.** You'll find ads for things like clip art, accessory programs, on-line computer information services, and more. Don't think for a minute that this stuff is the "best" stuff or that the software publisher "approved" it. These advertisements got in the box because two companies cut some sort of deal.

Installation

(Insert Disk #27 and press any key when ready)

Now you're ready. Note that the exact procedure varies from program to program, so be sure that you read the program's installation instructions. This is the general procedure that you follow to install a program:

1. Look for a disk labeled Setup or Install, and stick it into the floppy disk drive. If you can't find a Setup or Install disk, look for Disk #1, which probably contains the installation software.

2. Make the floppy drive current. To do so, type **A:** and press Enter to make drive A current.

Or type **B:** and press Enter to make drive B current.

3. Look at the installation sheet or manual to find out what to type to start the installation program. You probably type **INSTALL** or **SETUP**. If there's no installation sheet, look in the manual for a section titled "Installing Your Program," or something of that nature.

4. Type the installation command and press Enter. You'll probably type **INSTALL** or **SETUP**.

TIP

> If you see an option for a Quick, Express, Easy, or Handy-Dandy All-in-One installation, choose it!

5. You are now in your computer's hands. You must do what you are told to do. You must sit attentively, waiting for screen messages, and attempting to answer all questions to the best of your ability, and as truthfully as possible.

6. Eventually, you'll be told to remove and insert disks. Do so carefully, being sure the number on the disk you're inserting matches the number on the screen.

After a lengthy and grueling session of inserting and removing disks, you will finally see a message informing you that the installation is complete. You may be told to reboot (restart your system). If so, remove the disk from the drive, and press Ctrl-Alt-Del. Your computer restarts, and you see the good old DOS prompt again.

▼ You'll probably be asked where you want to install your software. The program wants to know *exactly* where to place the program—that is, in which directory. Probably, the installation software is proposing to make its own, new directory for the program. That's just fine. Let it.

▼ If the installation program doesn't propose a directory name, don't install the program in the root directory (C:\). You want to keep this directory uncluttered. When prompted to do so, type the name of a new directory. For instance, if you were installing WordPerfect, you might create a WP directory; you would type **C:\WP**. The installation program will probably create the directory for you.

▼ You may be subjected to a grueling list of questions, such as What printer are you using? What display adapter are you using? What was your mother's maiden name? Usually, you're shown a menu of options, from which you can choose your printer or display adapter. Use the arrow keys to scroll this list, if necessary. The installation program generally gives on-screen instructions for selecting printers and such, and often it is able to guess what kind of equipment you have.

▼ The installation program may ask you whether it's OK to modify your system configuration files (AUTOEXEC.BAT and CONFIG.SYS). Let it.

"I HATE THIS!"

There's no setup or install program!

If there isn't an automatic installation program, you'll have to wade into the manual to figure out how to install the program. Sometimes the installation requires you to create a directory (covered in Chapter 6) and then copy all the files on each disk to that directory (unveiled in Chapter 3). Check the manual for the exact instructions and try to get a computer-savvy friend to help.

Starting the Program

After you've installed your program successfully, give it a whirl. If the installation program is worth its salt, you should be able to start the program from any directory, just by typing its file name and pressing Enter. (Leave off the EXE or COM extension.) Look in the program's manual to find out what to type. For example, to start WordPerfect, you type **WP** and press Enter.

"I HATE THIS!"

"I just installed SnazzyCalc, but it says 'Bad command or filename' when I try to start it!"

There are a couple of possibilities here. What are you supposed to type? It could be SNAZZY, SNAZ, SC, or even SZCLC. Check the program's manual, and try again. If it still doesn't work, you need help from your local DOS wizard. Chances are that the installation program is dumber than a tree, and didn't add the necessary PATH statement to one of those weird DOS files in your root directory.

"I HATE THIS!"

> Ask your DOS wizard to add the necessary PATH command. In the meantime, you should be able to start your program by changing to the program's directory before typing the program's name.

Here are some common programs with the commands to start them:

Program	Command
WordPerfect	**WP**
Word	**WORD**
1-2-3	**123**
Quattro Pro	**Q**
Quicken	**Q**
dBASE	**DBASE**
Windows	**WIN**

Learning New Software

One look at those lengthy, thick manuals might make you break into a cold sweat. Take it easy. Chances are, you'll only use a tiny fraction of the program's commands and capabilities. Learn only what you really need to know.

▼ Learn the parts of the *main display screen*, the one you see after the program starts.

▼ Learn how to move the cursor around.

▼ If the program has menus and *dialog boxes* (those boxes that pop up with questions like "Print file?"), learn how to choose options from them. Also learn how to close them without choosing anything. (Pressing Esc generally works.)

▼ Find out whether you can undo or cancel commands. This knowledge can get you out of a whole heap of trouble.

▼ Learn the keyboard shortcuts, if they exist, for really common operations like saving your work, scrolling the screen, copying or moving text, and quitting.

▼ Above all else, learn how to save your work!

Should You Upgrade?

If you were a Good User and filled out your registration card, chances are you'll get a notice informing you of a grand and glorious new version of your program. These new versions, called *upgrades*, fall into two categories: maintenance upgrades and major revisions.

Maintenance upgrades fix something that was wrong with the program or add a feature that some people really want, like an additional printer driver. If the upgrade fixes a bug, order it. If it provides new features, order the upgrade only if you really need it. (What's the use of ordering an upgrade if it only offers a printer driver you don't need?)

Major revisions are new versions of the program, with major features added or drastically improved. These features are probably worth having; chances are they respond to the complaints users have been making, or offer features that competing programs already have. But it's up to you. No law dictates that you must upgrade.

"I HATE THIS!"

How can I tell whether I should upgrade?

Naturally, software publishers don't tell you whether an upgrade is a maintenance upgrade or a major upgrade. You're just supposed to know. How? By the version or release number.

If the upgrade is numbered with a decimal increase, like Version 2.0 going to Version 2.1 (or 2.01, or 2.0001), it's a maintenance upgrade.

If the upgrade is numbered with a whole number increase, like Version 2.1 going to Version 3.0, it's a major revision. Sometimes, though, you get a sort of "in-between" revision that's more than a maintenance upgrade, but less than a major revision. These are usually indicated by skipping a few tenths, like going from Version 5.1 to 5.5 (with no 5.2, 5.3, or 5.4 in between).

Running Two or More Programs at the Same Time

If you have Version 5 or 6 of DOS, you can run more than one DOS application at a time—and switch from one to the other at the touch of a key.

Let's paint a little scenario here. Suppose that you're writing a letter to the chairman of the board, informing her that profits have risen 38 percent this quarter since they finally let you run things your way. But a call comes from your broker, informing you that your stock has just zoomed up 250 percent, and asking you whether he should sell? At the touch of a key, you switch to Lotus 1-2-3 to see whether you've made enough to pay for that trip to Cancun—nay, to buy the whole resort! The technical part of this is called *task swapping*. The other part is called *wishful thinking*.

Task swapping isn't as hard as it sounds. Try it! Here's how:

1. Start the DOS Shell by typing **DOSSHELL** and pressing Enter.

2. From the Options menu, choose Enable Task Swapper.

   To do this, hold down the Alt key and press O, and then E. Alternatively, click **O**ptions, and when the **O**ptions menu appears, click **E**nable Task Swapper.

3. Use the Directory Tree and the File List to display the name of the first program you want start. (To learn more about using the File List and Directory Tree windows, flip back to Chapter 4.)

4. Highlight the name of the program you want to run and press Enter. You can also double-click the name of the program. (Program names always have the .COM or .EXE extensions.)

5. Hold down the Ctrl key and press Esc to switch back to the DOS Shell.

6. Repeat steps 3 through 5 to find and start another program.

7. To switch from one program to the next, just press Alt-Tab to move to the next program in the list of active programs, or Shift-Alt-Tab to move to the previous one.

Checklist

▼ You can run additional programs, if you want. Just press Ctrl-Esc to switch back to the DOS Shell, and then start the programs.

▼ You don't lose your work when you switch to another application, but to be on the safe side, always save your work before switching.

▼ What about quitting? Switch to each active program, and quit it, before quitting the DOS Shell. If you try to quit the DOS Shell before quitting all the active programs, you're told that one or more programs is still running, and you must quit them first. Don't ever quit the DOS Shell by just switching off the power.

CHAPTER 18

Modifying Those Awful System Files
(CONFIG.SYS and AUTOEXEC.BAT)

IN A NUTSHELL

▼ Understand what the system files are

▼ Start EDIT

▼ Open a system file

▼ Add a line to a system file

▼ Change an existing line in a system file

▼ Save your changes

▼ Quit EDIT

▼ Try making some cool changes

H ave to modify CONFIG.SYS or AUTOEXEC.BAT, do you? You must have been trying to track down the solution to a software problem—something minor like not being able to start the program. And the manual or the technical support person gave you this advice: "Add the statement BUFFERS=32 to CONFIG.SYS."

Of course, you got no direction about how to modify these files. Or where the files might be located. Or why this has had to happen to you. And, hey, if this has never happened to you, take my advice: stop reading right now. You're lucky. There's nothing in this chapter worth learning unless you're in this particular jam.

Ah, you're still reading. Well, you can do it.

CAUTION

Amendment: You can do it IF. If what? If you're *really careful*. You can really mess up your system by deleting some of the stuff in these files. You should only attempt the procedures in this chapter if: (1) You've been told to add a certain line to one of these files, and (2) You know exactly how to type what's on this line. Otherwise, get help!

CONFIG.SYS and AUTOEXEC.BAT in the Real World

When you wake up in the morning, you're brain's a blank, except for those last, few, fleeting memories of dreams you wish you could remember (or forget). Fortunately, several automatic programs kick in: WHERE_AM_I (checks out the room, remembers that, yes, it's your

bedroom), AM_I_LATE (checks out the clock, no, I'm not late), and IS_IT_SATURDAY (sadly, no). All this is followed promptly by WHERE'S_THE_COFFEE.

DOS is the same way—it's not too brilliant when it wakes up, and to get going, it benefits from the help of CONFIG.SYS and AUTOEXEC.BAT. Essentially, these are a couple of text files in your hard disk's root directory (C:\). They contain instructions that configure your system and tell DOS what to do. When you turn on the computer, the computer first looks for assistance on drive A. Finding nothing there, it starts scanning drive C. Lo! DOS finds CONFIG.SYS and AUTOEXEC.BAT.

Funny, illegible stuff then goes by on-screen. Why? DOS is "reading" the instructions in these files, and "echoing" (printing) them on-screen for your mystification and confusion. Isn't that nice? You've doubtless already learned that you can ignore all this babble.

Starting EDIT

If you have DOS 5 or 6, you can modify CONFIG.SYS and AUTOEXEC.BAT pretty easily, with the help of MS-EDIT (EDIT for short), a very nice text editor. (A *text editor* is a mini-word processing program that's designed to help you create or modify system files.) If you don't have DOS 5 or 6, though, you might as well stop reading. The instructions given here work only for DOS 5 or 6.

To start EDIT, type **EDIT** and press Enter. You see EDIT on-screen, and you may see a big, friendly dialog box that says, "Welcome to the MS-DOS Editor." Press Esc to clear this dialog box and get to work.

Opening the File

To open CONFIG.SYS or AUTOEXEC.BAT, you use the Open command. (The Open command is located on the File menu.) To choose the command, hold down the Alt key and press F; then press O. T+he Open dialog box pops up on-screen.

The cursor is positioned in the File Name box. If you want to open CONFIG.SYS, type **C:\CONFIG.SYS**. If you want to open AUTOEXEC.BAT, type **C:\AUTOEXEC.BAT**. Don't forget the colon or backslash. And remember—no spaces!

Check your spelling carefully. If you need to make corrections, press Backspace to erase whatever you typed incorrectly, and then retype it. When you're sure you've spelled everything correctly, press Enter. You'll see the horrifying insides of AUTOEXEC.BAT or CONFIG.SYS— whichever one you opened.

Checklist

▼ If you see a dialog box with the helpful message, `File not found`, either you misspelled the name of the file you're trying to retrieve, or the file doesn't exist. Press Enter to cancel this box. Then try again, checking your spelling very, very carefully.

▼ If you still see the `File not found` message, the CONFIG.SYS or AUTOEXEC.BAT file you're trying to find just doesn't exist. Not good. My advice: get your local DOS guru to take a look at your system and configure it properly.

Adding a Line

The easiest way to modify these files is to add a line. The trick here is to avoid disturbing anything in the meantime.

To add a line, just press the down-arrow key until the cursor is past all the on-screen junk and on a line by itself. (You can press Ctrl-End to quickly move the cursor down to this point.) Then type whatever you need to add. For example, suppose you've been told to add the line DOSSHELL to AUTOEXEC.BAT. (This does something rather cool: it starts the DOS Shell automatically whenever you start your system.)

To add this line to AUTOEXEC.BAT, press the down-arrow key until the cursor is on a blank line. Then type **DOSSHELL**. You don't need to press Enter, although nothing bad happens if you do.

You still need to save your work, as explained in the appropriately titled section "Saving Your Changes and Quitting EDIT" later in this chapter.

Editing an Existing Line

Let's say you've been told to add a statement to CONFIG.SYS that looks like this:

BUFFERS = 32

When you open CONFIG.SYS, you find to your dismay that there already is a line that contains the BUFFERS part and the equal sign. It just has a different number, though. It reads, BUFFERS = 16. You will have to *edit* this line.

To edit an existing line without messing up anything, follow these instructions carefully:

1. Check to see whether Num Lock is turned on. You'll be able to tell because the key's indicator light will be on. If the light's on, press Num Lock so that the light turns off.

2. Use the arrow keys to move the cursor to the first character you want to erase, and press Del. Do this again if you need to erase more than one character.

3. Carefully type the characters you need to add. Check your work carefully to make sure it exactly matches what you were told to type.

After you've finished editing, you still need to save, as explained in the next section.

Saving Your Changes and Quitting EDIT

You've made your changes. But, they exist only in the dream-like atmosphere of your computer's memory. They don't really become permanent unless you save them to disk.

To save your work, just choose Save from the File menu. (Press and hold down the Alt key, and then press F, followed by S.)

No sparks fly. No flags wave. In fact, nothing seems to happen. But it did! DOS saved your file so quickly you didn't even notice anything.

And now you can quit EDIT and be done with this anxiety-ridden adventure! From the File menu, choose Exit. (Press and hold down the Alt key, and then press F, followed by X.)

CAUTION

You might see a dialog box that scolds, `Loaded file is not saved, save it now.` This means you didn't save the file. Press Enter and DOS will save the file for you.

When Do the Changes Take Effect?

Can you start your program now? Will your troubles be over? Not quite. The changes you've made don't affect the current DOS configuration—you have to restart your system. To do so, press Ctrl-Alt-Del.

Checklist

▼ You can also reset your computer by pressing the Reset button, if your computer has one. You'll find the Reset button on the front panel of the computer.

▼ Watch the screen carefully when the computer restarts. If you see any funny error messages that you think weren't there before, repeat all the steps very, very carefully, making sure that what you typed exactly matches what you were supposed to type. If it does, and if the messages still appear after you restart your system, go beg for help from your local DOS wizard.

Some Cool Changes

Here's some stuff you might want to change:

▼ If you have a program that you use every day, you can tell DOS to load it automatically when you turn on your computer. At the end of the AUTOEXEC.BAT file, just type the command that you use to start the file. For example, if you start Microsoft Word by typing **WORD**, add WORD to a blank line at the end of the AUTOEXEC.BAT file.

▼ If you want to permanently change your prompt, add a PROMPT line to the AUTOEXEC.BAT file. The simplest prompt command, PROMPT pg, displays C:\> plus the current directory.

▼ For a really funky prompt, type a short phrase before you type PROMPT pg. If you type **PROMPT Hi, Handsome pg**, DOS will welcome you every morning with this ego-boosting greeting:

```
Hi, Handsome C:\>
```

PART V

Data Loss Anonymous

Includes:

19: Fear and Loathing at the DOS Prompt

20: Deciphering DOS Error Messages

CHAPTER 19

Fear and Loathing at the DOS Prompt
(It's Not Working!)

IN A NUTSHELL

▼ What to do if the computer won't start, the power shuts off, or the program won't start

▼ Fix the computer's time and date

▼ Deal with error messages

▼ Find a "missing" file

▼ Recover from accidentally reformatting a floppy or hard disk

▼ Remedy a crashed computer

▼ Make an obstinate printer print

▼ Determine whether hard disk is about to go bye-bye

▼ Restore your data if you reformat or replace your hard disk

▼ Determine when it's time to get help

I HATE DOS!

When you hear a computer user say, "Everything's fine—this system is really humming—why should I bother backing up my data?" take cover. Disaster is imminent. Computers are programmed to detect such remarks. And when they do, they arrange for a "little something" to go wrong—like a catastrophic hard disk crash here, a frozen screen there.

The fact that you're reading this chapter says that you're probably a believer in the computer's telepathic capabilities. In this chapter, you'll find the most common disasters, arranged in diabolical order. (*Diabolical order*, in case you haven't run into that term before, is like *chronological order* except that it starts with minor disasters and proceeds to the major ones. The concept wasn't necessary before people started using computers.) These disasters are organized by exclamation ("It won't start!" "My file's gone!"), so you can turn directly to your pet catastrophe. And just remember, we always save the Worst Case Scenario for last.

Cheer up. Most of the problems discussed in this chapter are minor ones. For the other 90 percent, you may need help from your local DOS guru, the store that sold you the computer, or your Higher Power.

"It Won't Start!"

It worked just fine yesterday, but today, you can't get your computer started. Chances are, you can solve the problem easily. Check the following:

▼ Is it plugged in? Is the power cord connected? Check the back of the computer. The power cord has two plugs, one on each end, and one of the ends has to be plugged into the back of the computer.

▼ If you're using a power supply center (one of those electrical things you can plug all your equipment into), make sure that the power switch is turned on. And make sure that the power supply center itself is plugged in.

▼ To make sure that the wall socket is working, plug something else into it, like a lamp, and see if it works. If there's no power, check the circuit supply box to see whether any of the circuit breakers have been thrown. Or, better yet, call an electrician.

▼ Is the computer turned on? Locate the switch, and make sure that it's switched to on.

▼ Do you hear something? If the hard drive is going, maybe you just forgot to turn on the monitor. Locate the switch, and make sure it's on. And press a key or move the mouse to be sure that the screen isn't being dimmed by a screen-saver program.

▼ Is the computer locked? Most computers these days have a funny round key that can be used to lock the system. To start the computer, you have to turn the key to the open position.

"It Started, But I See An Error Message"

If the computer starts, you're passed the first hurdle. But what if you see an error message? Check the following:

▼ Is the keyboard plugged in? (It should be plugged into the back of the computer.) If it isn't, your system won't start, and you'll see a weird message that says something like `Keyboard error`. Turn off the computer and plug in the keyboard cable. Then try again.

I HATE DOS!

▼ Do you see the message, `Non-system disk or disk error`? You left a floppy disk in drive A. Unlatch the drive, remove the disk, and press Ctrl-Alt-Del to restart your system.

▼ You start your system, and you see the message, `Starting MS-DOS...` but then, zip. Nada. Nothing. Zero. Chances are you've made some changes to your CONFIG.SYS or AUTOEXEC.BAT files—Did you change them yourself? Did you just install a program? Get your local DOS wizard to start your system by putting a floppy disk in drive A. Be sure to bring along some chocolate so that you can bribe this generous, wonderful person into taking a look at your system configuration files.

EXPERTS ONLY

Why drive A?

When your computer starts, it first tries to access drive A. This is because if your hard disk fails (horrors), you need some way to start your computer—so DOS lets you start from drive A and assumes that you'll be starting from this drive. Even with a bum hard drive, you can stick a disk into drive A, close the latch, restart your computer, and Lo! DOS loads from the floppy. You only need to do this if your hard disk fails, though. Under any other circumstances, make sure that drive A is unlatched when you start your computer.

TIP

DOS 6 contains a new feature that lets you bypass messed-up configuration files. To use this feature, press F5 when you see the message, `MS-DOS is starting`. This tells DOS to start your system with a *minimal configuration*. You can use the computer, although you may have to switch directories

TIP

manually to start programs, and some programs may not run. You'll still need your DOS wizard to help you check out those configuration files, but in the meantime, you'll at least be able to *do* something.

"I HATE THIS!"

Worst Case Scenario 1: Your memory has gone bad

The computer starts, and things happen on-screen, but then you see a message during the memory check. This message says something like, `Parity error checking RAM`, or `memory error`, or even just some stupid number. This is bad news— one of those little chips that makes up your computer's internal memory (RAM) has gone bad. Write down whatever error message you get—especially any numbers. Then call in an expert for service.

"I HATE THIS!"

Worst Case Scenario 2: Your hard disk has gone bad

When you try to start your computer, the memory test goes just fine, and there's no disk in drive A. But when your computer tries to access your hard disk, you see a truly horrifying message such as `Missing operating system` or `Invalid drive specification` or `Seek error reading Drive C`. This isn't good news. Something's wrong with your hard disk— probably something awful. See "I Can't Access My Hard Disk!" later in this chapter. Hope you backed up your work.

"The Power Just Went Off!"

You're working with your computer, and everything's just fine. Except you hear a little thunder in the background. Aren't you glad you're inside, all nice and warm? But then the lights go out. The screen goes dead. The realization slowly dawns on you: You've lost your data.

Checklist

▼ You've lost everything up to the time you last saved. Isn't that nice? That's why we computer book authors keep badgering you about saving repeatedly, preferably every 5 minutes. That way, you won't lose more than 5 minutes of work.

▼ When the power comes back on, your computer will restart, but you won't see your program. You'll see DOS.

▼ Restart your program. If you're lucky, it will have a very nice feature called Autosave that makes automatic backups of your work. If your program has this feature, you'll see a message asking you whether you want to restore the lost data. Answer Yes. Remember, however, that Autosave only saves work periodically—say, every 5 or 10 minutes. If it saved 3 minutes before the power went out, you have lost 3 minutes of work.

▼ Immediately try to reconstruct any work that you have lost—the longer you wait, the greater the chance that you'll forget. And make an immediate resolution to save your work more often.

"My Program Won't Start!"

For months, you've been typing **WP** to start WordPerfect. Today you type it and see the message, `Bad command or file name`. What gives?

Did you just install a program? Well, the installation utility messed up your AUTOEXEC.BAT file, and that's why you can't start your program. Get a DOS wizard to help you. You need a new PATH statement added to the AUTOEXEC.BAT file. (Your friendly local DOS wizard will know exactly what this is.)

In the meantime, you can start your program by changing to the program's directory. If you're using WordPerfect 5.1, for example, the program probably lives in a directory called C:\WP51. To change to this directory, type **CD \WP51** and press Enter. (Don't forget the space after CD.) For more information on changing directories, see Chapter 1 ("You May Need to Change Directories"), and Chapter 6 ("Timesaving Tricks for Changing Directories").

"I HATE THIS!"

Worst Case Scenario 3: You erased the program

Can't start the program after changing to its directory? Congratulations. You must have erased it. You'll need to reinstall the program. Chapter 17 covers this grueling process.

"The Time and Date Are Wrong!"

Almost all the computers sold these days have built-in clock/calendar circuits, which require a battery. The battery ensures that the circuits

won't "forget" the time and date when you switch off the power. When you make a change to a file, DOS notes the date and time the file was last changed. This information can be important if you need to figure out which file is more current.

On some older computers, you have to type the date and time each time you start the computer. These computers don't have a battery.

To make sure the date is correct, type **DATE** and press Enter. You'll see something like this:

```
Current date is Mon 02-01-1993
Enter new date (mm-dd-yy):
```

If the date's just off a little, reset it. Type the date in the MM-DD-YY format, like **6/30/93**, or **3/2/94**; then press Enter.

To make sure the time is correct, type **TIME** and press Enter. You'll see something like this:

```
Current time is 12:07:52.68p
Enter new time:
```

If the time is correct, just press Enter. If it isn't, type the time by typing the hour, a colon, the minutes, and **a** for AM or **p** for PM. For example, to set the time to 6:09 PM, type **6:09p** and press Enter.

"I HATE THIS!"

Worst Case Scenario 4: The battery is dead

If the date is January 1st, 1980, you've got a minor but irritating problem—your battery's dead. This minor inconvenience could become a major problem, however. Your computer's battery helps the computer remember what type of hard drive you have. If the battery goes completely dead,

"I HATE THIS!"

your computer "forgets" this information, and you may not be able to access your hard drive. Call for service; get that battery replaced immediately. Ask the service person to reset the date and time, too.

TIP

To avoid having your work interrupted by a trip to the repair shop, have your computer's battery replaced every other year. They're supposed to last longer than two years, but don't bet on it.

"It Won't Let Me Copy the File!"

This is pretty common, and easily solved. Check these possible solutions:

▼ If you see the message, `File cannot be copied onto itself`, you tried to make a copy of the file in the same directory, and with the same name. You can't do that. It's an impossibility. It's also unnecessary. Copy the file with a different name, or copy the file to a different directory.

▼ If you're trying to copy the file to a floppy disk and you see the message, `Insufficient disk space`, you've run out of room on the floppy disk. Get a floppy disk with more room on it, and try again.

▼ If you see the message `Write protect error Drive A` or `Write protect error Drive B` while trying to copy to a floppy disk, the disk has been *write-protected*, which means that you can't alter it. If you need to unprotect the disk, take a gander at Chapter 5, which explains how to accomplish this feat.

▼ If you see the message `File not found`, use DIR to make sure that the source file (the one you're trying to copy) is really in the directory. Also, check your typing.

▼ If you see the message, `Path not found`, DOS can't find the directory to which you want to copy the file. Check your typing.

▼ Chapter 3 tells you more about copying files. Chapter 6 tells you more about directory names.

"My File's Gone!"

At one time or another, this phrase has been heard echoing through the halls of every company whose employees use DOS. The cry is generally followed by a string of obsenities, although this latter is optional.

Relax. Your file's probably on your disk...somewhere. Chances are good that you saved it to some weird place, like your root directory. Chapter 7 can offer you some assistance if you've lost a file.

If you think you might have deleted the file by accident, immediately turn to the section "Recovering from an Accidental Deletion" in Chapter 3. Then run UNDELETE. (You must have DOS 5 or 6 to use UNDELETE. If you're using an earlier copy of DOS, stop what you're doing and go get a DOS wizard to help you.)

"Why Can't I Delete This File?"

If you're trying to delete a file and you see the message, `Access denied`, give up. Somebody evidently thinks that the file's important enough that the likes of you shouldn't remove it. Such a file is called a *read-only file*.

BUZZWORDS

READ-ONLY FILE

A read-only file is just what its name implies—a file that you can look at but that you can't erase or alter.

EXPERTS ONLY

I really, really, really want to delete the file

There might be a valid reason to remove a file that's protected from alteration. Suppose that you're no longer using a program, and you want to delete all the program files, and even the program's directory. You can delete everything except the file that produces an `Access denied` message. Unless you have DOS 6, you can't delete the program's directory, because it isn't empty. In such cases, you can use the ATTRIB command to change the file's setting (attribute) so that you can delete it. Here's what you'd type so that you could delete the file TEST.DOC:

    ATTRIB TEST.DOC -R

Note that there must be a space before the minus sign, but no space between the minus sign and the R. (R, incidentally, stands for Read-Only.) Now you can delete the file.

"I Just Reformatted My Floppy Disk!"

What did you do that for? If you're using DOS 5 or DOS 6, don't worry. These versions of DOS perform a *safe format*, which means that you can recover your data. The key to this wondrous capability is a DOS utility called UNFORMAT. But you must use UNFORMAT *immediately*, without doing anything else that would cause the disk to be changed in any way.

To unformat a floppy disk in drive A that you've just formatted accidentally, type

    UNFORMAT A:

and press Enter. You'll see a lot of messages, and finally a confirmation request. Press Y to unformat your floppy disk.

If you don't have DOS 5 or 6, don't do anything else with your computer. Go directly to your local DOS wizard and ask for help. Do not pass Go. Do not collect $200.

EXPERTS ONLY

The miracle of unformatting revealed

When DOS performs a safe format, it doesn't actually erase the information on the disk—if any. It just erases the *file allocation table* (FAT), a table stored on the disk that tells DOS where each file is located. To play it safe, though, DOS makes a hidden copy of this information. If you want it back, you can get it back. And once the table's restored, DOS can gain access to the files again—just as if you had never formatted the disk.

"I Just Reformatted My Hard Disk!"

This takes some real effort on your part—you had to ignore DOS's repeated warnings that this is probably a dumb thing to do. If you're using DOS 5 or 6, you can recover your data. Just use the UNFORMAT program. To unformat your hard drive, type the following and press Enter:

UNFORMAT C:

CAUTION

> Don't try this "just to see how it works." You could lose some or all of the data on your hard disk. Use UNFORMAT on your hard disk only if you've just accidentally formatted your hard disk.

If you're using a version of DOS earlier than 5.0, don't touch your computer; don't even turn it off. Just let it be and go get help. You'll need an unformat utility program.

"This Floppy Isn't Working!"

You can tell, because you're getting error messages such as `Data error reading (or writing) Drive A.`

Checklist

▼ If you see the message, `Drive not ready. Abort, Retry, Fail?`, you probably forgot to put the disk in the drive or to close the drive latch. Close the latch, and press R for retry.

continues

I HATE DOS!

Checklist Continued

▼ If you see the message `General failure reading (or writing)` `Drive A`, DOS can't access the drive, but it doesn't know why. (That's why you see the "general failure" message; it's the DOS equivalent of the "little technical problem" that the cockpit crew tells you about after explaining that they're going to make an unscheduled landing.) Probably, you put an unformatted disk into the drive. Try another disk, or format this one.

▼ If you see the message, `Data error reading (or writing)` `Drive A`, it's bad news—something's wrong with the surface of the disk. Immediately copy from this disk all the files that are still copiable, but don't use this disk again.

"I HATE THIS!"

Worst Case Scenario 5:
The File allocation table (what?) is bad

You may see the message `File allocation table bad Drive A`. This is really bad news—the table that keeps track of where files are located has been scrambled. Get your friendly local DOS guru to help.

"The Computer Won't Respond"

You type, you click, you swear, but there's no response—your program just stares at you, frozen on-screen. Is this a system crash? Hang? Freeze? Has it bombed? (Note that there are lots of picturesque synonyms for the same thing.)

Try pressing Esc. You might be in some weird mode of the program that you're not familiar with. Try pressing F1 to get help. Try pressing F10 or Alt to activate the menu bar, if there is one. Try clicking your heels and chanting "There's no place like home." If any of these methods produce results of any sort, your system's OK.

If you have a mouse, note that you might still be able to move the pointer around the screen even though the system is hung. Little parts of the computer are still alive—enough to move the pointer. If clicking the mouse does nothing, however, the system has crashed.

Look at the hard disk activity light (the little light on the front of the computer). Is it blinking on or off? If it's off, you've got another indication that the system is hung. If it's blinking on and off, the program is probably carrying out some really lengthy operation, so just wait. Chances are that control will return to the keyboard.

CAUTION

> Even if you *think* your system has crashed, don't reset right away. When you reset the computer, you lose any work you haven't saved. If there's still a chance you're just stuck somewhere in a program you don't know very well, try getting some help from somebody who's knowledgeable about the program.

If all else fails, press Ctrl-Alt-Del to restart your system. Unfortunately, you lose any work you haven't saved. (Reminder: Save your work, save your work, save your work.)

"My Printer Won't Print!"

Lots of likely causes here; most of them aren't serious.

▼ Is the printer plugged in? Is the power on?

▼ Is the cable connected at both ends (computer and printer)? Check both connections to make sure they're tight and secure.

▼ Is the printer selected or on-line? There's usually an indicator light with a little button. If it's off, press the button and try again.

▼ Is there paper? If not, load some.

▼ Is the paper jammed? Laser printers display a warning light when the paper's jammed. Clear the obstruction and try again.

"I HATE THIS!"

Worst Case Scenario 6: The printer isn't installed correctly

Is this the first time you've tried printing with a program? If so, maybe you didn't select the printer when you installed it. Get somebody to help you determine which printer is the current printer for this program. If it's listed incorrectly, change it. (You may have to reinstall the program to do so; Chapter 17 tells you all about this process.)

"I Can't Access My Hard Disk!"

Hard disks, unlike diamonds, are not forever. You'll be fortunate if you get three or four years of continuous use. And when the end is near, you

start getting little warning signs. Let's say you're trying to copy a file, and you get the message, `Read fault error reading Drive C`. You can't copy this file, but then again, other things work. But you start getting this, and other messages of the same sort, more often. These are pretty strong signs of impending disk death.

If you're using DOS 6, use MSBACKUP to back up all the data files on your disk. (Chapter 9 gives you the dirt on MSBACKUP.)

When you are sure you have successfully backed up all your data, have a DOS guru reformat your hard disk, and reinstall a program or two. Try using the computer. If it works smoothly (no error messages), the problem had to do with the surface of the hard disk. You might be able to continue using it. To restore your data, see the next section.

If the disk still acts funny after you reformat it, forget it—you need a new drive. Do yourself a favor and get a bigger one.

"I Have to Restore Data!"

If you've been forced to reformat or replace your hard disk, you can restore your data from the backup disks that you created using BACKUP. (Chapter 9 has the lowdown on BACKUP.) You did back up, didn't you?

To restore your data, place the first backup disk in drive A (or drive B). Then type the following and press Enter:

    RESTORE A: C:*.* /s

This command restores your files to their original directories.

"My Files Are Gone!"

If your hard disk suffers what is cheerfully known as a "catastrophic failure," you can restore the information from your backups. (You did make backups didn't you?)

CAUTION

Don't do this unless you are restoring your files after installing a brand new, blank disk. If you "experiment" by restoring files to a perfectly good disk that you backed up, you could wipe out all the work that you've done since the last backup.

If you're really serious about restoring, type **MSBACKUP** at the DOS prompt and press Enter.

The Microsoft Backup screen appears. Choose the Restore option, and when the Restore screen appears, highlight your hard drive in the Restore Files window; then press Enter to restore All Files. Now choose Start Restore. MSBACKUP tells you which disks to insert.

TIP

You can also restore selected files. This provides you with a way of recovering individual files that you may have deleted, or that may have become corrupted.

To restore individual files, choose the Select Files button in the Restore screen, and then select the files that you want to restore. (Selection works the same way it does in Backup; flip to Chapter 9 if you want to know more about Backup.) Choose OK, and then choose Start Restore.

EXPERTS ONLY

Cleaning up lost allocation units

Your hard disk will eventually accumulate lost allocation units (file pieces). They pose no threat to your data or programs, but you should clean them up occasionally. They're taking up disk space. And what's more, you can't run that cool DEFRAG utility until you get rid of them. (Chapter 6 gives you the lowdown on DEFRAG.)

To find out whether you have lost allocation units, type **CHKDSK** and press Enter. If there are any lost allocation units, you see the message `Errors found`, followed by the number of these irritating little things.

To get rid of lost allocation units, type **CHKDSK /f** and press Enter. Note that there's a space between CHKDSK and the /f switch. And don't forget to use a forward slash—not a backslash.

If CHKDSK finds any lost allocation units, you see a message like this:

```
117 lost allocation units found in 7 chains.
Convert lost chains to files (Y/N)?
```

There's no point in converting this stuff to files, so just press N and then press Enter.

You then see a message informing you how much total space is on your disk, and how much is taken up by files.

When to Throw in the Towel

If you get stuck and can't solve the problem, don't just sit there doing the same things over and over, trying to see whether "it might work this time." (I've seen people do this for hours.) Just leave your computer on, and get help.

Checklist

▼ Try to narrow down the problem so you can describe it to the person you're asking help from. Just *what* isn't working? Jot down any error messages that DOS shows you. The more specific the information you give, the better your chances of pinpointing the problem quickly. Especially important: Did you just install a program or modify the system configuration files (CONFIG.SYS or AUTOEXEC.BAT)?

▼ If the problem concerns one of the programs you're using, call the technical support hotline. (You do have a registered version of the program, don't you?)

▼ If your computer needs repair, tell the service person to *replace* the part rather than try to repair it. This is usually the best strategy; it's a lot easier to replace a part than to fix it. Plus, you get a brand-new component, which will probably last a lot longer than a patched-up old component.

▼ If your computer's no longer under warranty, shop around for repair costs, and don't be afraid to try freelance local repair people. Chain computer stores tend to be expensive. A computer store told me that it would cost $350 to repair my monitor. I got a television repair shop to do the job for $65.

Top Ten Sources of Data Loss

10. Threw entire system out of third-story window after fifteenth `Abort, retry, fail?` message

9. Jarred power cord loose while attempting to affix Garfield doll to monitor

8. Inserted Guns n' Roses CD into floppy drive just to see what happens

7. Told by "helpful" colleague that Ctrl-Alt-Delete is the Save Data key

6. Thought the manual was serious when it said to "give it a boot," and that the computer had it coming, anyway

5. Kept working during thunderstorm, having mistaken distant booming sounds for Honor Guard drum roll celebrating return of boss to building

4. Struck Reset button accidentally during flamboyant mouse maneuver

3. Sprayed floppy disk drive with WD-40 in attempt to reduce those irritating clanking noises

2. Reformatted hard disk to try to get a little more disk space freed up

1. Responded to `Drive not ready` message by shoving sandwich in drive door, and exclaiming, "Well, read this, pal!"

I HATE DOS!

CHAPTER 20

Deciphering DOS Error Messages

IN A NUTSHELL

▼ Learn what the error messages mean

▼ Learn what to do when you get an error message

DOS has its own, winning way of telling you that things aren't going so well: error messages like `Write protect error` or `Abort, Retry, Fail?` or `You again?` Doubtless, you're familiar with the old standby, `Bad command or file name`, and the intriguingly named `File cannot be copied to itself` message. And, if you're lucky, there are some you haven't seen yet, like `Disk boot failure` or `Bad or missing command interpreter`.

This chapter lists the most common DOS error messages, as well as the ones you're most likely to run into if your luck runs out. They're listed with the probable cause of the message and suggestions for solving the problem.

This chapter isn't really intended to be light, fun reading, unless you get your kicks reading stuff like *Your Guide to IRS Audit Notices.* Use this chapter as a reference when you get an error message and you're not sure what it means or what you're supposed to do.

Access denied

Cause: You tried to delete or rename a read-only file. A *read-only file* is one that has been coded with the ATTRIB command so that it cannot be deleted or renamed.

Solution: Let it be, let it be. The file was probably set to read-only status for a very good reason. Yours is not to question why.

Bad command or file name

Cause: DOS can't find a program with that name in the current directory. Perhaps you typed a file name incorrectly. Or maybe it's not in the current directory. Or maybe it just doesn't exist.

Solution: Try typing the command again, checking your spelling carefully. If necessary, change to the directory that contains the file.

If you still can't find the file, you might find some additional help in Chapter 7. Take a look-see.

Bad or missing command interpreter

Cause: An essential DOS file has been messed up on your hard disk, or there was a floppy disk in drive A when you restarted your computer.

Solution: If there's a floppy disk in drive A, unlatch the drive; then press Ctrl-Alt-Del (or press the Reset button) to restart your system. If there's no disk in drive A, call a local computer guru. You've got some kind of problem—minor or serious—with your hard disk.

Disk boot failure

Cause: Your computer could not access DOS on the hard disk.

Solution: This is very bad news—get help. Go get your local DOS wizard; it's possible that the problem can be repaired using a utility program such as PC Tools or Norton Utilities.

Disk error reading (or writing) Drive X

Cause: The hard disk drive couldn't read a section of the disk, or couldn't write (record) data.

Solution: Bad news. The file you're trying to access may not be readable, due to a surface defect on the disk. Try reading another file.

Checklist

▼ If you get this message while trying to access a floppy disk, copy all the files from the disk and discard it. Don't use a floppy disk that has bad areas. (These areas, incidentally, are called *bad sectors.*)

▼ If you get this message while trying to access a hard disk, the disk may soon fail completely. Back up all your work. Then flip back to the section "I Can't Access My Hard Disk!" in Chapter 19.

BUZZWORDS

BAD SECTOR

A defective area on the magnetic surface of the disk; the area has been damaged and the disk drive can't read the information that's stored on it.

Duplicate file name or file not found

Cause: You tried to rename a file, but the name is already used. Or you mistyped the file name and DOS couldn't find the file.

Solution: If you typed the name of the file correctly, rename it using a different name. If you misspelled the name of the file, check your spelling and try again.

TIP

> To see whether the file exists in the current directory, type **DIR** followed by the file name (as in **DIR JUNK.DOC**).

Error reading (or writing) fixed disk

See "Disk error reading (or writing) Drive X" earlier in this chapter.

File allocation table bad Drive X

Cause: The file allocation table has become corrupted.

Solution: Terrible news, dreadful. But don't give up yet. Get help from your local DOS wizard. He might be able to correct the problem with utility programs such as PC Tools or Norton Utilities.

BUZZWORDS

> **FILE ALLOCATION TABLE**
>
> The *file allocation table* (FAT) is a table kept on the disk that tells DOS exactly where the parts of each file are stored.

File cannot be copied onto itself

Cause: You're trying to copy a file, but you messed up typing the destination file name or location.

Solution: Type the **COPY** command again. If you're copying the file to the same directory, you must give the destination file a new name (for example, **COPY JUNK.DOC TRASH.DOC**). If you're copying the file to a different directory (but with the same name), you have to include path and/or drive information (for example, **COPY JUNK.DOC A:**).

File creation error

Cause: For some reason, DOS couldn't create. So it gave up.

Solution: Don't panic; the floppy disk might be full. Remove the disk from the drive, and try again with a disk that has more room available.

If you get this message while trying to access a hard disk, and if you're getting `Data error` or `Error reading (or writing)` messages, the disk may soon fail completely. Back up all your work and see "I Can't Access My Hard Disk!" in Chapter 19.

General failure reading (or writing) Drive X. Abort, Retry, Fail?

Cause: DOS can't access the disk, but it can't figure out why not.

Solution: Relax. Despite the terrifying connotations of "general failure," this probably isn't serious. You've probably just inserted an unformatted disk into the floppy disk drive. Press F to fail the command. Then type C: and press Enter to make drive C current.

If you want to format the disk, you can format it now. (Chapter 5 contains the dirt on formatting disks.)

Insufficient disk space

Cause: At last! A DOS message that's actually understandable. Simply put, you've run out of room on this disk.

Solution: If you're trying to copy something to a floppy disk, remove the disk and get another one that has more room.

If you get this message while using a hard disk, delete unwanted files (see Chapter 3). If you have DOS 6, you can run DoubleSpace to double your hard disk's storage capacity (see Chapter 8).

Invalid directory

Cause: You tried to change to a directory, but something went wrong. There are two possibilities. First, you may have mistyped the directory name, or left out some of those important backslashes. Second, the directory may not exist—maybe you deleted it or never created it.

Solution: Try typing the command again, and type the full path name including all those backslashes. If you haven't created the directory or you deleted it, create it again.

I HATE DOS!

TIP

The only time you can leave out the backslashes is when you're changing to a subdirectory of the current directory. For example, suppose you're in C:\DOCS. You can change to C:\DOCS\JUNK by typing **CD JUNK** and pressing Enter. But you can't change from C:\ to C:\WORK\BORING by typing **CD BORING**.

Invalid drive specification

Cause: You typed a drive letter in a DOS command, but DOS doesn't think there's any such drive. If you have drive A, B, and C, but refer to a drive D in a command, for example, you get this message.

Solution: Retype the command, using valid drive letters.

Invalid file name or file not found

Cause: Two possibilities here. First, you tried to rename a file, but you used illegal characters in the new file name. Second possibility: you used wild cards in a TYPE command; you can't do that.

Solution: If you're trying to rename the file, type a new name that uses legal characters (stick to the letters A through Z, and the numbers 0 through 9). If you're trying to display a file with TYPE, you must type a specific file name; TYPE doesn't work with wild cards.

Invalid media, track 0 bad or unusable

Cause: You're trying to format a disk, but the disk you inserted is no good for some reason. Perhaps you inserted a low-density disk in a high-density drive, or maybe the disk has been ruined.

Solution: If the disk is the same capacity as the drive (for example, you put a 1.2M disk in a 1.2M drive), the disk is no good. Discard it.

If you inserted a low-density disk into a high-density drive, see Chapter 5 for information on formatting the disk.

Invalid number of parameters, Invalid parameter

Cause: DOS can't understand the command you typed.

Solution: Look up the command again to make sure you're typing it correctly.

Invalid path, not directory, or dir not empty

Cause: You're trying to delete a directory. However, you mistyped the directory and/or path name, or the directory isn't empty. (With DOS 5 or earlier, you cannot delete a directory if it contains files or subdirectories.) Or you're trying to delete the current directory—which you can't do. (Remember: trying to delete the current directory is like trying to saw off a branch that you're standing on.)

I HATE DOS!

CHAPTER 20

Solution: Check your spelling and the path, and then try retyping the command. If you get this message again, switch to the directory to see whether it's empty. If it isn't, remove any files or subdirectories you find. Then change to the directory that is one level higher than the one you want to delete. (For example, if you want to delete C:\REVENGE\JONES, delete all the subdirectories and files in the JONES directory, and then change directories so that you are at the C:\REVENGE directory.) Then try again.

TIP

If you're using DOS 6, you can delete a directory, as well as all the files and subdirectories it contains, using the DELTREE command. Chapter 6 gives you the lowdown on this command.

Invalid switch

Cause: You included a switch in a command, but DOS doesn't recognize it. (A *switch* is a command option that you type with a slash mark and a letter, as in **DIR /p**.)

Solution: Look up the command again to make sure you're using the right switch. If you're not sure what switches are available for the command, at the DOS prompt type **HELP**, followed by a space and the command name (for example, **HELP DIR**). DOS will list the available switches for you.

Non-system disk or disk error

Cause: Stay calm. Don't panic. This problem is minor. A floppy disk was in drive A when you turned on or restarted your computer, and this disk does not contain DOS.

Solution: Remove the disk and press Ctrl-Alt-Del to restart the computer.

Not ready reading Drive X

Cause: The floppy disk drive doesn't contain a disk, or the drive door is unlatched.

Solution: Put a disk in the drive, latch the door, and press R for Retry.

Checklist

▼ If you get this message when trying to access a hard disk, it's very bad news. See "I Can't Access My Hard Disk!" in Chapter 19.

▼ Don't press F for Fail. If you do, you get the message `Current drive is no longer valid`, which sounds worse than it is. Press C, and then press Enter to make drive C the new current drive. (With older versions of DOS, you'd need to restart your computer before you could use the drive again.)

Read fault error reading (or writing) Drive X

Cause: The disk is probably damaged or corrupted.

Solution: Bad news, but there's some hope. The flaw is probably logical (as opposed to physical), so a DOS wizard, armed with a utilities package such as PC Tools or Norton Utilities, might be able to fix it.

Checklist

▼ If you get this message while trying to access a floppy disk, copy all the files from the disk, and then discard the floppy disk. *Don't* use a floppy disk that has spoiled areas (these areas are called *bad sectors*).

▼ If you get this message while trying to access a hard disk, the disk may fail completely soon. Back up all your work, and then see "I Can't Access My Hard Disk!" in Chapter 19.

Top Ten Least Popular DOS Error Messages

10. Invalid user, not competent, or brain empty

9. Random data error writing all over Drive C

8. Fatal user input error; file destroyed

7. Destroy another? (Y/N)

6. Qualified user not found

5. System tired of reading Drive C; drive no longer valid

4. Make my day? (Y/N)

3. /f parameter not specified; random dialog from Mary Worth comic strip written to all *.DOC files

2. Bad language or stupid file name

1. Get someone who knows what he's doing; press any key when ready

Sector not found error reading (or writing) Drive X or Seek error reading (or writing) Drive X

See "Disk error reading (or writing) Drive X" earlier in this chapter.

Syntax Error

Cause: You just typed a command, but you omitted something, put in too many spaces, used an incorrect switch, or included too much information.

Solution: Make sure you're typing the command correctly.

Too many parameters

Cause: You just typed a command, but you probably put one or more extra spaces in it.

Solution: Make sure you're typing the command correctly. And don't use extra spaces.

Unable to create directory

Cause: The disk is full. Or you're trying to create a subdirectory of a directory that doesn't exist. (For example, you're trying to create the directory \TRASH\JUNK, but \TRASH doesn't exist.)

Solution: Retype the command using a different directory name. If you see the command again, you need to move some files off this disk or delete unwanted files.

Write-protect error writing Drive *X;* Abort, Retry, Fail?

Cause: You tried to delete a file on a write-protected disk. Or you tried to copy a file to a write-protected disk.

Solution: If you're using a 3.5-inch disk, turn the disk over, and move the little write-protect tab down so that it covers the hole on the upper-left corner of the disk. If you're using a 5.25-inch disk, remove the tape that covers the write-protect notch. Then reinsert the disk and press R to retry the command.

TIP

Before you unprotect a disk, make sure that there isn't a compelling reason to keep the disk protected. One of your coworkers is going to be pretty miffed if you write over the only copy of an important file on a protected disk.

PART VI

Quick & Dirty Dozens

Includes:

12 Basic Facts about Computers That Everyone Assumes You Know

12 Minor But Embarrassing Beginner's Boo-Boos

12 Good Things You Should Always Do

12 Naughty Things You Should Never Do

12 Acronyms People Expect You to Know

12 Darned Good Reasons to Upgrade to DOS 6

I HATE DOS

Quick & Dirty Dozens

IN A NUTSHELL

▼ 12 Basic Facts about Computers That Everyone Assumes You Know

▼ 12 Minor But Embarrassing Beginner's Boo-Boos

▼ 12 Good Things You Should Always Do

▼ 12 Naughty Things You Should Never Do

▼ 12 Acronyms People Expect You to Know

▼ 12 Darned Good Reasons to Upgrade to DOS 6

12 Basic Facts about Computers That Everyone Assumes You Know

1. Files, programs, data, document...huh?

All the stuff stored on your disk is stored in files. A *file* is a collection of related stuff—like a program or your last letter to your boss pleading for a raise—that's stored on disk. The file has a name.

There are two kinds of files: program files and data files. *Program files* contain the instructions that make programs go. Programs are found in files with .EXE or .COM extensions, like DOSSHELL.EXE. But programs also require a lot of support files, with weird names and extensions (stuff like DOSSHELL.GRB or DOSSHELL.INI). Let these files be, because your programs need them to run correctly.

Data files contain your work. You create these files with your programs. For example, if you create a spreadsheet with Lotus 1-2-3, the program saves your work in a data file. You get to name your own data files, but it's a good idea to let the application supply the extension part, if it wants to.

Document refers to your work, such as a quarterly report or a chapter of the next Great American Novel, whether or not it has been saved. After you've saved your document, it's a data file. But it's still a document.

2. Is it a disk or a drive or what?

A floppy disk drive has two parts: the disk drive mechanism and the disk itself. The disk is removable, meaning you can take one out, and stick another one in. A hard disk drive has just one part because the disk is built-in; you can't remove it.

Floppy disk drive refers to the disk drive mechanism. *Floppy disk* refers to the disk part only. *Hard disk* and *Hard disk drive* mean the same thing.

3. **What's the difference between disk storage and that RAM memory thing?**

Think of your computer as a kitchen. When you're not cooking, you keep the Calphalon pots and pans, the Cuisinart, the pasta maker and the garlic press, and all the rest of that neat stuff in drawers and cabinets. When you're ready to make that delicious seafood pasta dish, you bring some of the stuff up to the countertop to work with—the sauté pan, the sun-dried tomatoes, the extra-virgin olive oil, the mussels, the shrimp, the mahi-mahi, the rice, the paprika, the Caesar salad, the Edna Valley Chardonnay.

OK, the disk storage is like the drawers and cabinets—that's where you store stuff when you're not using it. Memory (RAM) is like the countertop—you put stuff in memory while you're working with it.

4. **What do *input* and *output* really mean?**

Input refers to getting information into the computer. Normally, you do this by typing, but there are other input devices, like mice, scanners, and such. *Output* refers to the stuff produced by the computer. Screen output is the result of some processing operation that's displayed on-screen. For example, when you use the DIR command, you see its output on-screen. Printer output is another kind of output.

5. **What is *hard copy*?**

A printout of anything is *hard copy*. The printed chapters of your Great American Novel or the annual report are hard copy.

313

6. **Why do they say "Save to disk"?**

"Save to disk" just means "save your work."

7. **My memory is "volatile"? Will it blow up?**

Sooner or later, you'll be told, "You'd better save to disk. RAM, after all, is volatile." Doesn't *volatile* mean *explosive*? Should you panic and run?

In computer talk, *volatile* means maintainable only as long as the power's still on. When the power's cut off (or turned off), all the information goes bye-bye.

8. **It tells me to "Do a DIR" or "Invoke CHKDSK" or "Issue the MEM command"!**

Ignore the technospeak. These three expressions just mean "Use this command." To "invoke" CHKDSK, for instance, you type **CHKDSK** and press Enter.

9. **What does "Dumped at the DOS prompt" mean?**

This is an odd (but appropriate) expression. It means you've used a command that doesn't tell you it's done—it just returns you to the DOS prompt. That tells you it's finished.

You've probably noticed that some DOS commands tell you that they're done. COPY, for example, shows you the message 1 `file(s) copied` when it's finished copying a file. But other commands just dump you back at the DOS prompt. Don't worry, the command worked just fine. If something had gone wrong, you'd see an error message, such as `Bad command or file name`.

10. **Is an ASCII file the same thing as a text file?**

These terms are synonymous, for all practical purposes. A text file doesn't have anything in it but the standard ASCII characters. It contains no funny, special symbols that programs often insert in files to handle formatting and the like.

ASCII is a standard set of numbers and characters that correspond to the keys on the computer keyboard. An ASCII file doesn't have anything in it but the standard ASCII characters.

11. **What is this whole computer thing for, anyway?**

It's for working smarter and better. Ideally, the computer should help us accomplish tasks more efficiently than before, and to produce work of higher quality. Unfortunately, this ideal isn't reached by most computer users. According to a recent *Wall Street Journal* article, people in organizations spend an average of 5 1/2 hours per week just fiddling with their computers, trying to get something to work or struggling to recover lost data.

12. **What do you mean, I can't use this Atari program on my IBM-compatible computer?**

To use a program, it must be written with a particular computer in mind. A program written for an MS-DOS computer won't run on an Apple Macintosh (at least, not without equipping the Mac with special software and hardware). When you shop for programs, make sure they're compatible with your machine. A *compatible program* is designed to run on the type of machine you are using.

Programs for IBM PCs and compatibles fall into two categories: DOS programs and Windows programs. A DOS program requires DOS. A Windows program requires that you have Microsoft Windows *and* DOS installed and running on your system.

12 Minor But Embarrassing Beginner's Boo-Boos

1. Leaving a disk in drive A when you shut down the system.

When you start or reboot your computer, it goes a-hunting for DOS. First, it looks on drive A. And if it finds a floppy disk there, it tries to read DOS from the floppy disk. But, DOS isn't on this disk. And so you get that inspiring message, `Non-system disk or disk error`.

When you see this message, remove the disk and press the Reset button. If there isn't a Reset button, press Ctrl-Alt-Del.

2. tYPING wITH cAPS lOCK oN.

The Caps Lock key is one of those irritating toggle keys. When you press it once, you engage the Caps Lock mode. This is sort of like a typewriter's Caps Lock key, in that the letters you type are in uppercase. But just to be different, any letters you type with the Shift key depressed are in lowercase, resulting in a strange pattern of capitalization that is unique to the computer world. Press the key again to turn off Caps Lock.

3. Dumping your coffee into the keyboard.

Sooner or later, it will happen to you. Believe it or not, most keyboards can take an inundation of this sort—if you act immediately. Save your work, if you can, and turn off the computer. Disconnect the keyboard. Over a pile of newspapers, turn the keyboard upside down and burp it gently. Coffee will fall like rain from the keys.

Put the keyboard face down on a pile of tissues, and let it dry out. When it's dry, spray 409 or Windex onto a paper towel, and carefully clean off the coffee stains.

4. Inserting 5.25-inch disks the wrong way.

There are a total of eight possible ways you can insert a 5.25-inch disk into a disk drive, but as you've no doubt discovered, only one of them is correct.

To insert a 5.25-inch disk correctly, make sure that the disk's label is on the side of the disk that's facing up. Now rotate the disk (without flipping it upside down) until text on the label is upside down, from your perspective. The business end of the disk—the hole that shows the disk's surface—should be facing away from you. Put the disk into the drive. Close the latch on the floppy disk drive.

5. Inserting disks between the drives.

This happens more often than you'd think. To remove the disk, you may need tweezers. If you can't reach the disk, get your local DOS wizard to remove the computer's case.

6. Mispronouncing computer terms everyone else seems to know.

A quick pronunciation guide:

386	Three eighty six (not "Three hundred eighty six")
ASCII	Ask-ee
CPU	See-pea-you
DOS	Dauss, as in "floss" (not "dose")
GUI	Gooey
KHz	Kill-o-hurts

KB	Kay-bee, like that neat toy store at the mall. You ought to see the latest Lego Technic sets they have.
MB	Meh-guh bite
MS-DOS	Em-ess dahsss (not "Ms. DOS")
RAM	Ram, as in "Spam" (not "arr-ay-emm")
user	Rhymes with "loser." Is that an omen? Northeast of New Jersey, and intensifying in Boston, however, this is pronounced "use-ah," thus rhyming with "vigor" (vig-ah).
VGA	Vee-gee-ay
WYSIWYG	Whiz-eee-whig. Is this the dumbest acronym you've ever seen, or what?

7. Logging on to the wrong drive or directory.

When you change drives, you *log on* to the drive you indicated. From that point, DOS assumes that you want your commands carried out on that drive, unless you specifically tell it otherwise. Let's say you are logged on to drive A, and you want to delete the file JUNK.DOC. You type the following:

    DEL JUNK.DOC

but you get the message, `Bad command or file name`. Should you assume that JUNK.DOC doesn't exist? By no means! You're logged on to the wrong drive. JUNK.DOC is on drive C, in the directory called C:\DOCS\TRASH.

You've two options. You can override the default disk or directory by including all that nasty path information in the command, or you can switch to drive C, by typing **C:** and pressing Enter, and then change to the directory.

8. **Thinking your computer has crashed when it really hasn't.**

This is pretty common. Possibilities:

▼ You hit the Num Lock accidentally. Now you're trying to move the cursor but all you get are weird numbers. Just press the Num Lock key again.

▼ You forgot to turn on the computer or the monitor.

▼ You didn't close the latch on the drive door (5.25-inch disks only).

▼ You're using a new program and you've gotten into something you can't get out of. Try pressing Esc, Alt-F4, Ctrl-F4, Ctrl-C, Ctrl-Break, or F1.

▼ You're using DOS but you pressed the Esc key. The DOS prompt is gone and all you see is a funny little slash mark. This is OK; DOS is waiting for you to type another command.

▼ The mouse or keyboard cable came loose.

▼ The program you're using is taking its own sweet time to do something. Give it a chance.

9. **Buying software that turns out to be useless.**

There's only one kind of program worth buying—the one that's right for your needs. Unfortunately, it's not very easy to determine

your needs, and it's even harder to get salespeople to understand them. But give it a shot. If you need to print mailing labels, ask yourself questions like this: "Self, how many people are on my mailing list? Do I want the labels to look really cool, with neat fonts and stuff? Do I want to sort the mailing labels by zip code (so I can save money on postage)? Do I want to record other information besides name and address?" The better you're able to summarize your needs, the better the chance you'll buy a useful program.

Also, be sure that you get a program that your computer can run. Chapter 17 provides clues on decoding the requirement list you find on software boxes. Read the requirements *before* you tear off the cellophane.

10. **Not having enough floppy disks around.**

Computers have insatiable appetites for disks, so you'll need at least one or two boxes of them when the beast gets hungry. Otherwise, you'll have to go begging from coworkers, which annoys them, or you'll have to erase one of the disks you've already used—which could annoy *you* if it turns out the disk contained files you forgot were valuable.

11. **Using your computer with the monitor facing a big, bright window.**

You'll go blind pretty quickly. The glare from the window makes it close to impossible to see what's on-screen. You can get an accessory called a *non-glare filter*, but it's best to move your computer so that the glare goes away.

12. **Not backing up.**

OK, OK, I know, you've already had this lecture. But you can really get into trouble by not backing up. Right now, it's a minor booboo—but it could turn into a major catastrophe.

12 Good Things You Should Always Do

1. Save, save, and save some more.

When you are working with an application, your work is in the computer's memory. It's volatile. If the power goes to lunch, so does your work. To be on the safe side, save your work every five minutes.

2. Keep your UNINSTALL disk safe.

When you or someone else installed DOS 5 or 6 on your system, the DOS SETUP program created something called an UNINSTALL disk. This disk is really important. In the event of a serious hard disk problem, this disk could hold the key to regaining access to all the data on your hard disk. Keep it safe.

3. Keep your distance from the monitor.

The jury's still out about the health effects of the low-level electromagnetic radiation (EMR) produced by computer monitors, but why take chances? A careful study by *PC Magazine* indicates that the level of this radiation falls off to undetectable levels about 28 inches from the screen. If you keep your face and body that far away from the screen's surface, you've eliminated the risk.

4. Protect yourself from repetitive strain injury.

Repetitive strain injuries (RSI) represent one of the fastest-growing causes of occupational disability, and computers are clearly to blame. Sitting at the keyboard all day, performing the same hand and wrist movements over and over again, can contribute to RSI maladies such as carpal tunnel syndrome, an injury to the nerves of

the wrist caused by scar tissue forming in a narrow bone channel. RSI injuries can be extremely painful and disabling. To reduce your chance of injuring yourself while using the computer, follow these guidelines:

▼ Your keyboard should be positioned at the level of your elbows, so that you don't have to hold your forearms up to peck at those keys.

▼ Get a wrist rest. This is a pad that sits in front of your computer and takes the strain off your arms and wrist.

▼ Don't work more than two hours without taking a break.

5. Win prizes!

The registration cards that come packaged with software are valuable to you. When a new version of the program comes out, registered users can order the upgrade at a bargain-basement price, compared to what new buyers will have to fork over. You will also get notices of maintenance upgrades—minor revisions that fix annoying bugs or add certain new features—which may be of great value to you.

6. Do your housekeeping.

Spend some time organizing your hard disk, as suggested in Chapter 6; don't just add files and programs willy-nilly. Most important of all, create directories for your data files so that they're not mixed up with your program files. And periodically go through your files; delete the ones you're done with and don't need, and *archive* the ones you're done with but might be needed later.

7. Back up.

It's not a matter of *if*, it's a matter of *when*. All hard disks eventually die, and if you haven't backed up your work, you lose everything. Backups are your insurance policy.

8. Learn to archive.

There's another angle on backing up, called *archiving*. Here's the difference between backing up and archiving. When you back up your disk, you create an up-to-date backup copy of your disk as it is now, including all the files you're currently working with. If your disk fails, you can restore these files—that's why you back up. When you *archive* a file, you just move a finished file, one you're done with, off your hard disk to a floppy, and put it away. You're finished with it. You've printed it. You gave the report to your boss. Your boss turned it down. You don't need it on your hard disk. You probably wouldn't miss it if your disk failed. But who knows? Better archive it to make sure.

9. Out with the old! In with the new!

That big, behemoth program is taking up 12MB of disk space, and what are you getting out of it? Nada. Zip. Zero. If you don't use a program, archive any data files you created, and delete it. (If you later change your mind, you still have the original program disks, so you can reinstall it.)

10. Keep your root clean.

Your root directory (C:\) should contain nothing but the files DOS placed there when you installed the program, together with the names of the directories created by installation programs and by you. If you add too many files to the root directory, your hard disk's performance degrades.

11. **If at first you don't succeed, look it up.**

I've seen a lot of beginning users just sitting at the computer for hours trying to get something to work. Believe me, it's not worth it. Chances are pretty good that there's just one little thing you don't know, or you forgot, and no matter how you try, you're just not going to get anywhere. If you run into a wall like this, don't torture yourself. Get help. Look in this book. Get your local DOS wizard to stop by. Ask coworkers. Call technical support. Do *something*.

12. **Don't take any of this too seriously.**

Computers are nothing more than useful tools for our work and play. At their best, they are wonderful tools for creativity, expression, and professionalism. At their worst, they are so maddening that they can send us into an infantile rage. Whether fair or foul, though, computers are pretty near the bottom of any reasonable list of what's important in life. If the computer starts getting to you, take a break, take a walk, breathe some fresh air, take a look at the birds and the flowers. And then get someone to help you over whatever ridiculous roadblock the computer's thrown in your way.

12 Naughty Things You Should Never Do

1. **Don't erase or mess up the system configuration files.**

When you start your computer, DOS looks for files named CONFIG.SYS and AUTOEXEC.BAT, which are located in your hard disk's root directory (C:\). These files contain vital information. They tell DOS how to set up your system for your use. Should you erase them or modify them the wrong way, your programs may not start unless you switch to the directory in which they're stored. Or they may refuse to start period. Or some features may not be available.

Don't mess with CONFIG.SYS or AUTOEXEC.BAT unless you're sure you know what you're doing.

2. **Don't erase program support files.**

Most programs require more than one program file in order to run. For example, WordPerfect lives in a program file called WP.EXE, but it requires dozens of additional files (called *program support files*) before it can work its word processing magic. Some users say, "What's all this junk?" and start deleting willy-nilly. Surprise! The program won't run.

3. **Don't keep your data files and program files in the same directory.**

Some folks make the mistake of keeping their program and data files in the same directory, and when they're deleting unwanted data files, they accidentally delete a crucial program file.

Keep your program files and data files in separate directories. That way, there's little chance that you'll delete a necessary program support file while you're doing some housekeeping.

4. Don't take a disk out of the drive when the light's on.

The light is called a *disk activity light*. It indicates that the disk's magnetic part is in contact with the drive, and it's doing something. Should you try to remove the disk, you might drag this part across the surface of the disk, totally scrambling the data.

5. Don't remove a floppy while it's being used.

Let's say you're reading some data from a floppy disk in drive A. The data's on-screen, but then you remove the disk. DOS now goes looking for this disk, but it's not there. This could cause the computer to crash.

6. Don't keep all your data on floppies.

Some users are so mistrustful of hard disks that they keep all their data files on floppies. But this is a bad idea. Floppies, even the 3.5-inch type, are much more vulnerable than hard disks. Hard disks do fail, but not very often.

Even if you don't use your computer very often, you'll have tons of floppies around if you try to save all your work to floppies. Keeping them organized and safe will become a nightmare. You might forget what's on a disk, and erase something that turns out to be valuable.

Store your work on your hard disk, in nice, separate directories set aside for nothing but your data files. And back up to floppies.

7. Don't exit programs by shutting off or restarting the computer.

You've saved your work. You're done for the day. Why bother exiting to DOS? For many programs, there's a very good reason: as you work, you choose various program configuration options. These options modify the program so that it works the way you want.

However, these choices usually aren't saved until you quit. If you just switch off the power or reboot with the program still on-screen, you can lose these choices.

There's another reason to quit to DOS, even after you've saved your work. Many programs make temporary files while they're running, and don't get rid of them until you quit the program in an orderly way (for example, by choosing Quit from the File menu). If you switch off the power or reboot with the program still on-screen, the program will leave these unnecessary files on your disk. They take up room and you will eventually have to remove them manually.

8. **Don't format double-density disks to high-density capacity.**

Disks come in two capacities: double density and high density. Double-density disks are cheaper, so some people try to cheat by formatting these low-capacity disks with a high-capacity format. Sometimes you can actually get DOS to do this, but the resulting format is unstable and you could lose all the data you put on this disk.

9. **Don't use pirated software.**

Most people "experiment" with pirated software (illegal, unofficial copies of software), but there are several good reasons why you shouldn't:

▼ You'll put your organization at risk. The Software Publisher's Organization is a software industry group that's trying to stamp out software piracy in organizations. Disgruntled employees may tip them off that a single copy of Lotus has been copied in the hundreds and passed around. Chances are pretty good that your firm has better things to do than deal with this group's lawyers.

▼ You'll put yourself at risk. The software industry has been pushing to make software piracy a felony. It's unlikely that individuals would be prosecuted unless they were making and selling copies, but still, prudent persons don't put themselves or their dependents at risk by engaging in illegal behavior.

▼ It isn't fair to the people who create software. A computer program is an intellectual product, the result of the creative inspiration and toil of many bright and dedicated people. They deserve a slice of the rewards.

▼ You might introduce a virus into your system. Viruses mainly move from one system to the next on disks containing pirated software. Don't put an unknown disk containing "freebie" software into your system. Don't put any program into your system unless you yourself have torn open the package it came in.

10. **Don't use these dangerous DOS commands.**

You can really mess up your system by "experimenting" with high-end commands that should only be used by DOS wizards, computer store people who configure systems, and the like. These commands include CTTY, FDISK, FORMAT C:, JOIN, RECOVER, and SUBST.

11. **Don't ignore the need for system housekeeping.**

Spend some time periodically keeping your system in order.

I HATE DOS!

▼ Back up your work periodically.

▼ Run DEFRAG about once a month to keep your hard disk humming.

▼ Remove unwanted files and programs from your disk periodically.

▼ Run DoubleSpace, if you haven't already done so, to compress your hard disk. You need to do this only once.

▼ Run MEMMAKER, if you haven't already done so, to optimize your system's memory. You need to do this only once.

▼ Keep two or three boxes of formatted disks around, so you'll never run out.

▼ Keep your floppies well organized. Put those original program disks away, preferably in the box they came in, so you don't confuse them with your data disks. Label your disks clearly so you don't accidentally reformat over valuable data.

12. **Don't connect stuff while the computer's on.**

Some computers can handle this better than others, but you can sometimes cause the computer to crash by trying to plug a printer or mouse into those ports in the back of the computer. Only do this when the system has been shut off.

12 Acronyms People Expect You to Know

1. **ASCII**

   This is short for American Standard Code for Information Interchange. Basically, it's a set of numerical codes that correspond to the standard keys on a computer keyboard. An ASCII file is a file that contains nothing but the standard ASCII characters—no fancy extra stuff, like the junk that programs add to deal with extras like boldface or page numbers.

2. **DOS**

   Yes, DOS is itself an acronym; it stands for Disk Operating System. Back in the early days, DOS was only that—a program used to control these fancy new disk drives (which, believe it or not, were once a novelty). DOS is more than that now, but the name has stuck.

   Actually, the correct name for DOS is MS-DOS, as Microsoft likes to point out. There are other types of DOS for personal computers, like DR-DOS or PC-DOS. But for many people, "DOS" is practically synonymous with MS-DOS.

3. **GUI**

   Acronym for Graphical User Interface, and pronounced "gooey." An *interface* is the part of the program that communicates with the user. DOS, for example, uses a command-line interface, which means that you type commands and the computer fights back with error messages. This isn't considered very friendly, so computer designers came up with this GUI stuff.

   In a GUI interface, the screen is filled up with colorful boxes and little pictures of things called *icons*. The pictures represent

computer items or procedures, like disks or printers. You can use the mouse to move stuff around on-screen and to initiate computer operations by clicking the icons. Microsoft Windows insists that everything obeys GUI principles.

4. **KB (or just K)**

You'll frequently run into KB when people are talking about file sizes or disk capacities. It's short for Kilobyte. The *kilo* part means *one thousand*, and the *byte* part means *one character*, so the term means, basically, *one thousand characters*. Except not exactly, because computers measure everything in powers of twos rather than tens. But you can forget that part; just think of KB as 1,000 characters.

5. **MB (or just M)**

This stands for Megabyte, or about one million letters or numbers (characters). This measurement comes into play when people are talking about disk capacities and the amount of installed memory. For a hard disk, 40MB isn't actually very much, unless you just want to run one or two old DOS programs. 120MB is more like it, especially if you want to run Microsoft Windows.

If you're doing nothing but running DOS and DOS programs, the 1MB of memory that's probably installed in your system is OK, but Windows requires 4MB or more. (Remember memory and disk capacity are entirely different!)

6. **MHz**

This stands for Megahertz, a measurement of how fast the computer's microprocessor runs. A Hertz is one cycle per second, and since *mega* means *million*, we're talking about one million cycles per second here—a lot. But believe it or not, one million

cycles is an appallingly slow speed for a computer. The earliest IBM PC ran at 4.77MHz. Today's systems run at 20MHz or more, with the fastest widely available models running at 66MHz.

7. **MS-DOS**

The official name for Microsoft's disk operating system (DOS), the program you're reading about. Most people just shorten this to DOS.

8. **RAM**

Short for Random Access Memory. This is your computer's internal memory, which you can think of as being like the countertop in your kitchen. On the countertop, you place the items you're working with at the moment. The stuff you're not using stays down in the drawers and cabinets. In computers, RAM is like the countertop, while the drawers and cabinets are like the hard disk. RAM is measured the same way you measure disk capacity (KB and MB).

9. **ROM**

Short for Read-Only Memory. Every computer has some of this, and it helps the system get started when you turn it on or restart. It's pretty unimportant and you can forget about it.

10. **SVGA**

Refers to Super VGA. The VGA (Video Graphics Array) video standard has swept the PC world—almost all systems today are sold with VGA video adapters and monitors. Super VGA is an improvement on VGA that offers a sharper screen, more colors, and more detail.

11. TSR

Refers to Terminate-and-Stay-Resident, a type of program that isn't actually very good to use. When you quit most programs, they leave the memory and go back quietly and harmlessly to your hard disk. TSR programs, however, remain in memory, even if you quit them. The idea is that you can switch to these programs by using a special key combination called a *hot key*.

TSR programs sometimes conflict with each other, or with application programs, causing your computer to crash and wiping out your work. It's best to avoid them.

12. VGA

Short for Video Graphics Array. VGA is the standard for today's personal computer video adapters and monitors. If you're using a 386 or 486, chances are good that it has a VGA adapter and monitor. The best systems today come with Super VGA adapters and monitors. Super VGA technology offers sharper screen images and more colors, but it can cope with programs that expect you to have a VGA adapter and monitor.

12 Darned Good Reasons to Upgrade to DOS 6

1. DoubleSpace

Lots of people buy disk compression programs such as Stacker, which increase the amount of hard disk storage space by using a more efficient way of packing the data on disk. (Don't worry, it's safe.) But using these programs can be a hassle, because you have to configure your system manually. With DoubleSpace, the disk compression utility included with DOS 6, there's no hassle at all because DoubleSpace is part of DOS. It's easy to use and can double or even triple the amount of space available on your hard disk.

2. Automatic installation of weird but necessary system configuration files

If you take a look at the computer book section at your local bookstore, you'll probably find lots of books on configuring or optimizing your system with DOS and Windows. With previous versions of DOS, a good deal of mummery, chanting, and magic was needed to install a thing called SMARTDRV, which can really speed your hard disk when using big, bloated Windows programs. But all the pain is gone. DOS 6 automatically installs SMARTDRV when you run the DOS 6 SETUP program. All you know is that your system runs a heck of a lot faster (up to 20 or 30 percent) after installing SMARTDRV.

3. Automatic optimization of your memory

MEMMAKER, a nifty utility, automatically configures your system to use your system's memory in the optimum way. Again, this is one of those mysterious subjects that people write book-length treatises on. But DOS 6's MEMMAKER utility does it automatically, in a way that puts your data's safety foremost.

4. Disk defragmentation

As you create and delete files, your disk becomes *fragmented*, which isn't dangerous—it just means that DOS has to write your files in pieces here, there, and everywhere. The poor disk head (the thing that does the recording and playback, or *reading and writing* if you want to use technospeak), spends a lot of time going back and forth across the surface of the disk, hunting for these pieces. A defragmentation utility solves this problem by putting the files back together. People have forked over as much as $129 to get utility packages including defragmentation utilities, but a very good one comes free with DOS 6.

5. MSBACKUP

You really should back up. But backing up is a pain, largely because the DOS BACKUP command is about as friendly as all the rest of those DOS-prompt commands. But MSBACKUP, which is just as good as the backup utility programs available from other suppliers, comes free with DOS 6. In fact, MSBACKUP is based on what many experts feel is the best backup program around: Norton Backup (Symantec).

6. Anti-Virus

Those pesky viruses can really ruin your day. For this reason, a lot of people fork over as much as $79 to buy anti-virus programs, which can detect (and in many cases, remove) computer viruses that have infected your computer. But Microsoft Anti-Virus (MSAV), just as good as the utility programs available from other suppliers, comes free with DOS 6. MSAV examines your files and your memory for viruses, and if any are detected, attempts to re-move them. Included with DOS 6 are coupons for two free anti-virus updates per year.

7. Help

DOS 6 offers Help throughout every system feature, including the cranky old DOS prompt.

To get help with DOS commands, type **HELP**, followed by the command's name, and press Enter. You see a Help screen that explains the command's purpose, the command's syntax (the rules for typing the command), and any applicable switches. Use the PgUp and PgDn keys to display the text. By moving the cursor to the <Notes> or <Examples> buttons and pressing Enter, you can see additional information relevant to the command. (If you have a mouse, you can just click on these buttons.)

To see a table of contents, hold down the Alt key and press C. To see the next page of Help, use Alt-N. To see the previous page of Help, use Alt-B. With the menus, you can print the current topic, and even search throughout Help for a word or phrase. To exit Help, hold down the Alt key and press F followed by X.

8. Microsoft System Diagnostics

With DOS 6, you can just type **MSD** at the DOS prompt, and Microsoft System Diagnostics displays a screen telling you exactly how your system is configured, right down to who made the video adapter and which version of the mouse software you're using. This information is invaluable when you're talking with tech support or thinking of buying some new software.

9. Utility programs for Windows

This book discusses the versions of Undelete, MSBACKUP, and Microsoft Anti-Virus for DOS. But DOS 6 also comes with versions of these utilities that run with Microsoft Windows. If you

decide to run Windows and Windows applications, you will find that these utilities resemble their DOS counterparts so closely that you already know how to use them.

10. **Two new DOS commands**

DOS users have been clamoring for two commands for years: a way to move files without having to perform two steps (copy the files to the new destination and then delete the originals), and a way to delete directories without having to remove all the files and directories first. DOS 6 answers their pleas with two commands, MOVE and DELTREE.

11. **Cool new features for laptop and notebook computer users**

Lots of people have two computers: a big, clunky desktop one, and a sleek, little, notebook one. Problems arise, though, when you want to transfer programs or data from one computer to the other. You can use disks, to be sure, but this can be a hassle. With DOS 6's INTERLNK program and a cable connecting the two computers, you can use one of the computers to access data on the other. For your laptop or notebook, DOS 6 also has a POWER program that can conserve up to 25 percent of your computer's battery power.

12. **Automatic installation of latest mouse software**

Mouse users, rejoice! When you install DOS 6 on your system, the SETUP utility automatically transfers the latest, spiffiest version of the mouse software to your computer. This software contains information that helps your mouse cope with the latest versions of application programs, giving you one more very good reason—the twelfth—to upgrade.

I HATE

Index

Symbols

3.5-inch floppy disks, 79
   backups, 131
   drives, 163
   removing, 83
   versions of programs, 248
   write-protecting, 84
3M disks, 82
5.25-inch floppy disks, 79
   backups, 131
   drives, 163
   inserting, 317
   removing, 83
   versions of programs, 248
   write-protecting, 84
80286 microprocessors, 159, 176
80386 microprocessors, 172, 176, 180, 184
80386DX microprocessors, 159
80386SX microprocessors, 159
80486 microprocessors, 172, 176, 184
80486DX microprocessors, 159
80486SX microprocessors, 159
8086 microprocessors, 158
8088 microprocessors, 158

A

Access denied message, 283, 296
activity lights, 326

adapters
   video display, 188-192, 198, 250-251
      resolution, 194
adapters, *see also* circuit boards; expansion boards
Address Book program, 243
allocation units, lost on floppy disks, 92
alphabetizing list of files in directories, 110-111
Alt key, 209
Ami Pro program, 239
Anti-Virus program, 144-147
applications, *see* programs; software; utilities
archiving files, 54, 323
arrow keys, 208-209
ASCII files, 315, 330
ATTRIB command, 283
AUTOEXEC.BAT file, 146, 264-265, 276, 325
   adding lines, 267
   editing, 265-266
      lines, 267-268
   saving changes, 268-269

B

/b switch, 110
backing up
   changed data files with MSBACKUP program, 140-141

data files, 128-134
    changed, 134-135
    full backup, 136
    with BACKUP command,
        130-131
    with COPY command, 130
    with MSBACKUP program,
        136-142
    hard disk drives, 132
        with MSBACKUP program,
            138-140
    tapes, 131
backslash (\ ) character
Backspace key, 14, 39
BACKUP command, 130-136,
    289
backups, 320, 323, 335
    full, with MSBACKUP
        program, 142
    incremental, 135
        with MSBACKUP program,
            140-141
    restoring data, 142
Bad command or file name
    message, 119, 136, 279, 297
Bad or missing command
    interpreter message, 297
base memory, *see* conventional
    memory
.BAT file extension, 36
BizPlanBuilder (JIAN Tools)
    program, 243
black and white monitors, *see*
    monochrome monitors
blocks, upper memory, *see* UMBs

booting computers, 23-24
budget programs, Quicken, 243
buffers, type-ahead, 213
bugs, 254
business computers, 153
business plans, BizPlanBuilder
    (JIAN Tools) program, 243
bytes, 80

C

cables, printer, 219
    serial, 220-221
Calendar Creator Plus (Power Up
    Software) program, 244
calendar programs, Calendar
    Creator Plus (Power Up
    Software), 244
cancel (Ctrl-Break), 211
cancel (Ctrl-C), 211
canceling commands, 39
capacity, floppy disks, 80-82,
    90-91
Caps Lock key, 207, 316
cards,
    registration, 253
case-sensitive data, 113
CD command, 17, 100
CGA video adapter, 190
changing directories, 99-100
characters, file names, 36
charts and graphs program,
    Harvard Graphics (Software
    Publishing Corporation), 244

checkbook programs, Quicken, 243
checking
    for viruses, 145-148
    memory
        with CHKDSK command, 175
        with MEM command, 177-179
    spelling, 238
child directory, 96
chips, memory, 153, 171
CHKDSK command, 92, 291, 314
    checking conventional memory, 175
chronological order, 274
    list of files in directories, 111-112
circuit boards, 157
clearing screens, 30
clicking with mouse, 62
clock speed, microprocessors, 160-162
clones, *see* IBM-compatible computers
Close Microsoft Anti-Virus dialog box, 146
CLS command, 30
collapsing directories, 62
color monitors, 189, 195-198, 250
.COM file extension, 36
commands, 259
    ATTRIB, 283
    BACKUP, 130-136, 289

canceling, 39
CD, 17, 100
CHKDSK, 92, 291, 314
    checking conventional memory, 175
CLS, 30
COPY, 45, 50, 130
DEL, 45-47
DELTREE, 103, 337
DIR, 18-20, 87, 90-91, 108-109
    alphabetizing output, 110-111
    chronological order of hard drive files, 111-112
    wild cards, 38
DISKCOPY, 89-90
DOS, 32
    dangerous, 328
    displaying again, 212
    displaying letter by letter, 212
DOSSHELL, 202
FORMAT, 86-89
HELP, 33, 336
INSTALL, 255
MD, 100-101
MEM, checking all memory, 177-179
MEMMAKER, 184-186
MKDIR, *see* MD
MODE, 221
MORE, 43
MOVE, 52-54, 337
PATH, 258

PRINT, 226
PROMPT, 56
RD, 101
RENAME, 45, 55-56
repeating, 38
RMDIR, *see* RD
SETUP, 255
switches, 109-110
TREE, 97-99
TYPE, 42-43
UNDELETE, 48-49, 55
VER, 30
wild cards, 47-48
compatibility tests, MSBACKUP
  program, 136-138
compatibility of hardware and
  software, 315
compressing disks, 334
    floppy, 121-123
    hard, 117-120
computer viruses, *see* viruses
computers, 315
    connecting printers, 219-221
    IBM-compatible, 153-155
        Microsoft Windows,
            234-237
    laptop, 337
    logging on, 318-319
    Macintosh, 154
    notebook, 337
    peripherals, 329
    restarting, 23-24
    software compatibility,
        248-252

system requirements, 155-157,
  251-252
terminology, 317-318
troubleshooting
    crashing, 319
    error messages, 275-277
    freezing, 286-287
    power outage, 278
    program not starting, 279
    replacing, 292-293
    starting, 274-275
    time and date, 279-281
turning off, 22-23
turning on, 10-12
CONFIG.SYS file, 264-265, 276,
325
    adding lines, 267
    editing, 265-268
    saving changes, 268-269
configuring
    minimal, 276
    printer ports, 220-221
    programs, 248
connecting printers to computers,
219-221
contents of files, viewing, 42-43
conventional memory, 174-175,
249
coprocessors, math, 160
COPY command, 45, 130
copying
    files, 50
        groups, 52
        to different files or
            directories, 51

troubleshooting, 281-282
  with keyboards, 68-69
  with mouse, 71
 floppy disks, 89-90
cords, 156
CPUs (central processing
 units), *see* computers and
 microprocessors
crashing computers, 319
creating directories, 100-101
Ctrl key, 39, 209
cursor-movement keys, 205

D

dangerous DOS commands, 328
Data error reading (or writing)
 Drive A message, 285-286
data files, *see* files
database programs, 241
  FoxPro, 242
  Paradox, 242
DEFRAG program, 116, 124-125,
 291, 329
defragmentating
  disks, 335
    programs, DEFRAG, 124
DEL command, 45-47
Delete key, 210
deleting files, 45-47, 66-67
  groups, 47-48
  troubleshooting, 283
  undeleting, 48-49

DELTREE command, 103, 337
desktop publishing programs,
 Publish It! (Timeworks), 243
detecting viruses, programs, 335
diabolical order, 274
dialog boxes, 259
  Close Microsoft Anti-Virus,
   146
  Recommendation, 125
  Verify Error, 145
  Virus Found, 145
  Viruses Detected and Cleaned,
   145
  VSafe, 148
DIR command, 18-20, 87, 90-91,
 108-109
  alphabetizing output, 110-111
  list of files on hard drive,
   chronological order,
   111-112
  wild cards, 38
Dir not empty message, 303-304
directories, 16-18, 94
  backing up, 132-134
  changing, 99-100
  child, 96
  collapsing, 62
  creating, 100-101
  expanding, 62
  files, 325
    alphabetizing, 110-111
    copying to different drives,
     51
    deleting all, 47
    finding, 106-114

filespecs, 45
listing, DOS Shell, 61-62
nested, 62-63
parent, 96
path names, 44-45
removing
    with DOS 6, 103
    without DOS 6, 101-102
root, 19, 95, 323
subdirectories, 95
directory trees, 95-96
    printing, 98
    viewing, 97-99
Directory Tree window, 63
directory-subdirectory
  relationship, 96
disk activity light, 326
Disk boot failure message, 297
disk compression programs,
  DoubleSpace, 117, 121
disk drives, 85, 153, 162-163
    changing, 28-29
    copying files to different, 51
    double-sided, 79
    filespecs, 45
    floppy, 26-28
    hard, 26-28
    path names, 44-45
    purchasing floppy disks, 81-82
Disk error reading (or writing)
  Drive X message, 298
Disk Operating System, see DOS
disk storage space, 313
    free, 250

DISKCOPY command, 89-90
disks
    5.25-inch, inserting, 317
    backup, restoring data, 142
    compressing, 334
        floppy, 121-122
        hard, 117-120
    defragmenting, 335
    formatting, 80, 327
        troubleshooting, 284
    inserting, 26-28, 317
    program, 252
    source, 90
    target, 90
see also floppy disks; hard disk
  drives
display adapters, 250
display modes, 200-202
displaying files
    DOS Shell, 63
    floppy disks, 61
.DOC file extension, 35
documents, see files
DOS, 330
    commands, 32
        dangerous, 328
    editing keys, 211-213
    memory, see conventional
    memory
    Microsoft Windows, 235-237
    programs, 233-234
    prompt, 12-13
        WIN, 236-237

Version 5
  memory statistics, 177-178
  running two or more
    programs, 260-262
Version 6
  memory statistics, 178
  moving files, 53-54
  moving files without, 52-53
  MSBACKUP program,
    136-142
  removing directories, 103
  removing directories
    without, 101-102
  running two or more
    programs, 260-262
versions, 30, 249-251
DOS Shell, 13, 58-60
  directories, listing, 61-62
  files
    copying with keyboards,
      68-70
    copying with mouse, 70-72
    deleting, 66-67
    displaying, 61-63
    moving with keyboards,
      68-70
    moving with mouse, 70-72
    renaming, 73
    selecting, 64-65
    viewing, 65-66
  Files List, 60
  GUI, 60
  menus, 59

task swapping, 261-262
  windows, 59
DOSSHELL command, 202
dot-matrix printers, 216
dot pitch measurement, 193
double-density (DS) disks, 80
double-sided (DS) drives, 79
DoubleSpace disk compression
  program, 117, 121-125
DoubleSpace disk compression
  programs, 116, 329, 334
downloading fonts, soft, 222
drag and drop, mouse, 70-72
Drive not ready. Abort, Retry,
  Fail? message, 285
drivers, printer, 227
drives
  disk, 162-163
  floppy disk, 250-251, 312
  hard disk, 313
    file fragmentation, 123-125
    organizing, 104, 322
    tape backup, 131
dumped at DOS prompt, 314
Duplicate file name or file not
  found message, 298-299

E

EDIT text editor, 265-268
  exiting, 268-269
editing
  keys, DOS, 211-213

text with EDIT, 265-268
EGA video adapters, 191
electromagnetic radiation
  (EMR), 197, 321
EMM386 memory management
  program, 183-184
EMR (electromagnetic
  radiation), 321
EMS memory, *see* expanded
  memory
Enter key, 14, 208
entering data too fast, 213
error messages, *see* messages
Error reading (or writing) fixed
  disk message, 299
Esc key, 39, 209-210
Excel spreadsheet program, 240
.EXE file extension, 36
exiting
  programs, 21-22, 326
  system, 316
  text editor, EDIT, 268-269
expanded memory, 176, 179-180
expanding directories, 62
expansion boards, 157
  adding memory, 179
extended keyboards, 204
extended (XMS) memory,
  176-177, 249
extensions, *see* file extensions
extremely low-frequency (ELF)
  radiation, 197

F

/f switch, BACKUP command,
  134
FATs (file allocation tables), 284
File allocation table bad Drive A
  message, 286
File allocation table bad Drive X
  message, 299
File cannot be copied onto itself
  message, 281, 300
File creation error message, 300
file extensions
  .COM, 36
  .DOC, 35
  .EXE, 36
  .TXT, 36
file names, 33-36, 96
  characters, 36
  extensions, *see* file extensions
  filespecs, 45
  finding files
    name known, 108-110
    name unknown, 112-114
File not found message, 34, 43,
  97, 266, 282
file specifications, *see* filespecs
files, 18, 312
  alphabetizing list in directories,
    110-111
  archiving, 54, 323
  ASCII, 36, 315
    see also text files

AUTOEXEC.BAT, 146, 264-265, 276, 325
  adding lines, 267
  editing lines, 267-268
  editing with EDIT, 265-266
  opening, 266
  saving changes, 268-269
backing up, 128-134
  changed, 134-135, 140-141
  full backup, 136
  with BACKUP command, 130-131
  with COPY command, 130
  with MSBACKUP program, 136-142
CONFIG.SYS, 264-265, 276, 325
  editing lines, 267-268
  editing with EDIT, 265-266
  opening, 266
  saving changes, 268-269
contents, viewing, 42-43
copying, 50
  groups, 52
  to different drives or directories, 51
  troubleshooting, 281-282
  with keyboards, 68-69
  with mouse, 71
data, *see* data files
deleting, 45-47, 66-67
  groups, 47-48
  troubleshooting, 283
directories, 325

displaying
  DOS Shell, 63
  floppy disks, 61
  sets, 37
entering too fast, 213
finding, 106-107
  name known, 108-110
  name unknown, 112-114
fragmented, 123-125
lists from hard drive, chronological order, 111-112
missing, troubleshooting, 282
moving, 52
  with DOS 6, 53-54
  with keyboards, 69-70
  with mouse, 71-72
  without DOS 6, 52-54
printing hard copies, 313
program, 35, 312
program support, 325
read-only, 283, 296
renaming, 55-56
  DOS Shell, 73
restoring
  troubleshooting, 289-291
  with backup disks, 142
saving, 314, 321
selecting
  DOS Shell, 64-65
  with keyboards, 64-65
  with mouse, 64
single file name, 33-34
storing, 26, 326
  directories, 94
system, 264-265, 325

text, *see* ASCII files
troubleshooting, 290-291
undeleting, 48-49
viewing DOS Shell, 65-66
wild cards, 38
Files List, 60
window, 63
filespecs, 45, 96
finance programs, WealthBuider
(Reality Software), 244
finding files, 106-107
name known, 108-110
name unknown, 112-114
floppy disks, 78, 320
capacity, 80-82, 90-91
compressed space, 122-123
compressing with
DoubleSpace, 121-122
copying, 89-90
data files, backing up, 131
density, 80
drives, 26-28, 155, 163,
250-251, 312
files, displaying, 61
formatted, 82
formatting, 86-89
inserting, 82-84
Microsoft System Diagnostics
(MSD), 81-82
problems
logical, 92
physical, 91
purchasing, 79-82
removing, 82-84, 326

size, 79
storage capacity, 80
troubleshooting, 285-286
write-protected, 84-85
fonts
printers, 221-223
soft, downloading, 222
FORMAT command, 86-89
formatted disks, 82
formatting
disks, 80, 327
floppy, 86-89
hard, 285
troubleshooting, 284
FoxPro database program, 242
fragmented files, 123-125
free disk space, 250
MSBACKUP program,
138-140
with MSBACKUP program,
142
function keys, 205, 210

 G

gamma rays, 197
General failure reading (or
writing) Drive A message, 286
General failure reading (or writing) Drive X, Abort, Retry, Fail?
message, 29, 300-301
gigabyte (G), 170
graphical user interface, *see* GUI

graphics accelerator boards, 202
graphics mode, 200-202
greeting card programs, Print
  Shop (Broderbund), 244
groups of files
    copying, 52
    deleting, 47-48
GUI, 330-331
    DOS Shell, 60
    Microsoft Windows, 234

H

hackers, 144
hard copies, 313
hard disk drives, 26-28, 78, 156,
  313
    backing up, 128-132
       with MSBACKUP program,
       138-140
    compressing with
      DoubleSpace, 117-120
    crashing, 277
    files
       chronological list, 111-112
       finding, 106-114
       fragmentation, 123-125
    organizing, 104, 322
    reformatting, 285
    space, 116, 168-170
       compressed, 120
    troubleshooting, 288-289

hardware, 153
Harvard Graphics (Software Publishing Corporation), charts and
  graphs program, 244
HELP command, 33, 336
HGA video adapters, 190
hiding directories, *see* collapsing
  directories
high memory area (HMA), 181
high-density (HD) disks, 80
HIMEM memory management
  program, 183-184
home computers, 153
hot keys, 333

I

IBM computer systems, 155-157
IBM formatting standard, 82
IBM PCs, 153
IBM-compatible computer
  systems, 153-157
    Microsoft Windows, 234-237
incremental backups, 135
    with MSBACKUP program,
    140-141
initializing, *see* formatting
inkjet printers, 217
input, 313
Insert key, 210

inserting disks, 26-28, 317
    5.25-inch, 317
    floppy, 82-84
INSTALL command, 255
installing programs, 254-257
Insufficient disk space, 281
Insufficient disk space message, 281, 301
interlacing, 193
INTERLNK program, 337
internal memory, *see* memory (RAM)
Invalid directory message, 301-302
Invalid drive specification message, 302
Invalid file name or file not found message, 302
Invalid media, track 0 bad or unusable message, 303
Invalid number of parameters message, 303
Invalid parameter message, 303
Invalid path, not directory message, 303-304
Invalid switch message, 304
investment programs, WealthBuider (Reality Software), 244
invoking, *see* running
It's Legal (Parsons Technology), legal documents program, 243

K

keyboard shortcuts, 259
keyboards, 156, 165, 204-206
    damaging, 316
    DOS tricks, 211
    files
        copying, 68-69
        moving, 69-70
        selecting, 64-65
    repetitive strain injury (RSI), 213-214
    templates, 254
    toggle keys, 206-208
keys
    Alt, 209
    arrow, 208-209
    Backspace, 14, 39
    Caps Lock, 207, 316
    Ctrl, 39, 209
    cursor-movement, 205
    Delete, 210
    DOS editing, 211-213
    Enter, 14, 208
    Esc, 39, 209-210
    function, 205, 210
    Insert, 210
    Num Lock, 207-208
    Pause, 211
    Pause/Break, 210
    PgDn, 210
    PgUp, 210

Print Screen, 209
Prt Scr (Print Screen), 225
Scroll Lock, 208
Tab, 208
toggle, 206-208
kilobytes (K), 80, 170, 331

L

Label Maker program, 243
languages, printer control,
  226-227
laptop computers, 337
laser printers, 217
  PostScript, 217
launching, *see* running
learning programs, 258-259
LED printers, 217
legal documents programs, It's
  Legal (Parsons Technology),
  243
licenses, software, 253
lines, AUTOEXEC.BAT and
  CONFIG.SYS files
    adding, 267
    editing, 267-268
listing directories, DOS Shell,
  61-62
logging on to computers, 318-319
logical problems, floppy disks, 92
lost allocation units, 291
  floppy disks, 92
Lotus 1-2-3 spreadsheet program,
  240

M

/m switch, BACKUP command,
  134-135
Macintosh computers, 154
mailing labels programs, Label
  Maker, 243
mailing lists programs, Address
  Book, 243
main display screens, 259
maintenance upgrades, 259
major revision upgrades, 260
managing memory, 183-184
math coprocessors, 160
Maxell disks, 82
MD command, 100-101
MDA video adapters, 190
megabytes (MB), 80, 170, 331
megahertz (MHz), 161, 331
MEM command, checking all
  memory, 177-179
MEMMAKER program, 184-186,
  329, 334
Memorex disks, 82
memory, 157, 168-170, 251, 313
  conventional, 174-175, 249
  expanded, 176-180
  extended (XMS), 176-177,
    249
  hard disk space, 116
  map, 181-183
  optimizing, 184-186, 334
  requirements, 173-174
  upgrading, 172

upper, 176, 180-181
volatile, 314
memory chips, 171
Memory error message, 277
memory management programs,
183-184
menus, 259
messages, 291
  Access denied, 283, 296
  Bad command or file name,
    119, 136, 279, 297
  Bad or missing command
    interpreter, 297
  Data error reading (or writing)
    Drive A, 285-286
  Dir not empty, 303-304
  Disk boot failure, 297
  Disk error reading (or writing)
    Drive X, 298
  Drive not ready. Abort, Retry,
    Fail?, 285
  Duplicate file name or file not
    found, 298-299
  error, 16
  Error reading (or writing) fixed
    disk, 299
  File allocation table bad
    Drive A, 286
  File allocation table bad
    Drive X, 299
  File cannot be copied onto
    itself, 281, 300
  File creation error, 300

File not found, 34, 43, 97, 266,
  282
General failure reading (or
  writing) Drive A, 29, 286,
  300-301
Insufficient disk space, 281,
  301
Invalid directory, 301-302
Invalid drive specification, 302
Invalid file name or file not
  found, 302
Invalid media, track 0 bad or
  unusable, 303
Invalid number of parameters,
  303
Invalid parameter, 303
Invalid path, not directory,
  303-304
Invalid switch, 304
Memory error, 277
Non-system disk or disk, 276
Non-system disk or disk error,
  304-305
Not ready reading drive A,
  Abort, Retry, Fail? message,
  29, 305
Parity error checking RAM,
  277
Path not found, 282
Read fault error reading (or
  writing) Drive X, 289,
  305-306
Sector not found error reading
  (or writing) Drive, 307

Seek error reading (or writing) Drive X, 307
Syntax Error, 307
Too many parameters, 307
Unable to create directory, 308
Write protect error writing Drive X; Abort, Retry, 282, 308
Write-protect, 85
microprocessors, 157-160
    clock speeds, 160-162
    size, 249, 251
Microsoft Diagnostics (MSD), 198
Microsoft DoubleSpace Setup, 118-120
Microsoft System Diagnostics (MSD), 81-82
Microsoft Windows, 13, 154, 234-237, 252-354
    DOS, 235-237
Microsoft Word, 239
minimal configuration, 276
missing files, troubleshooting, 282
MKDIR command, *see* MD command
MODE command, 221
monitor cables, 164
monitors, 155, 188-193, 250, 333
    adjustment knobs, 199
    cleaning, 199
    color, 195-198, 250
    glare, 320
    monochrome, 195-198, 250

phosphor burns, 200
resolution, 194
size, 195
turning on, 11
monochrome monitors, 189, 192, 195-198, 250
MORE command, 43
motherboards, 157
    extended memory, 176
mounting floppy disks, 122-123
mouse, 165
    clicking, 62
    files
        copying, 71
        moving, 71-72
        selecting, 64
    software, 337
MOVE command, 52-54, 337
moving files, 52
    with DOS 6, 53-54
    with keyboards, 69-70
    with mouse, 71-72
    without DOS 6, 52-54
MS-DOS, 332
    Shell, starting, 202
MS-EDIT, *see* EDIT
MSAV for DOS program, 336
MSAV program, 335
MSBACKUP program, 124, 136, 289-290, 335-336
    compatibility test, 136-138
MSD, *see* Microsoft System Diagnostics
multiscanning monitor, 193
multisynch monitors, 193

N

naming printers, 218-219
nested directories, 62-63
networks, disk drives, 85
newsletter programs, Print Shop
  (Broderbund), 244
non-glare filters, monitors, 320
Non-system disk or disk error
  message, 276, 304-305
Norton Utilities WIPEOUT
  program, 48
Not ready reading drive A.
  Abort, Retry, Fail? message, 29,
  305
notebook computers, 337
Num Lock key, 207-208
numeric keypad, 205

O

off line printers, 224
on line printers, 223
opening
  directories, see expanding
    directories
  files
    AUTOEXEC.BAT, 266
    CONFIG.SYS, 266
optimizing memory, 334
order
  chronological, 274
  diabolical, 274

organizing
  hard disk drives, 104
  hard drives, 322
output, 313

P

Paradox database program, 242
parallel ports, 164
parallel printers, 217-218
parent directory, 96
Parity error checking RAM
  message, 277
PATH command, 258
path names, 44-45, 96-97
Path not found message, 282
Pause key, 211
Pause/Break key, 210
pausing screen (Ctrl-S), 211
PC Tools utility, 116
PCs, see computers; IBM
  computers
peripherals, 329
permanent storage, 116
Personal System/1 (PS1), 153
Personal System/2 (PS/2), 153
PgDn key, 210
PgUp key, 210
physical problems, floppy disks,
  91
pirated software, 327-328
pixels, 194

ports, 155, 164-165
    printers, 218
        configuring, 220-221
poster programs, Print Shop
    (Broderbund), 244
PostScript laser printers, 217
power outage, troubleshooting,
    278
power supply, 156
primary memory, *see* memory
    (RAM)
PRINT command, 226
Print Screen key, 209
Print Shop (Broderbund)
    graphics program, 244
printer control language, 226-227
printers, 155, 216-217, 250
    drivers, 227
    serial, 217-221
        cables, 219
        connecting to computers,
            219
    fonts, 221-223
    names, 218-219
    parallel, 217-218
    ports, configuring, 220-221
    testing, 223-225
    troubleshooting, 227-228, 288
printing, 211
    directory tree, 98
    files, hard copies, 313

problems, floppy disks
    logical, 92
    physical, 91
program disks, 252
program files, 35, 312, 325
programs, 232
    Anti-Virus, 144-147
    budgeting, Quicken (Intuit),
        243
    bugs, 254
    business plans, BizPlanBuilder
        (JIAN Tools), 243
    calendars, Calendar Creator
        Plus (Power Up Software),
        244
    charts and graphs, Harvard
        Graphics (Software Publish-
        ing Corporation), 244
    checkbook, Quicken, 243
    computers, compatibility,
        248-252
    configuring, 248
    database, 241
        FoxPro, 242
        Paradox, 242
    DEFRAG, 291, 329
    desktop publishing, Publish It!
        (Timeworks), 243
    disk compression,
        DoubleSpace, 117-122, 329,
        334
    DOS, 233-234
    exiting, 21-22, 326

finance and investment, WealthBuider (Reality Software), 244
installing, 254-257
INTERLNK, 337
learning, 258-259
legal documents, It's Legal (Parsons Technology), 243
mailing labels, Label Maker, 243
mailing lists, Address Book, 243
MEMMAKER, 184-186, 329, 334
memory management, 183-184
    HIMEM, 183-184
    EMM386, 183-184
Microsoft Windows, 154
MSAV, 335
MSAV for DOS, 336
MSBACKUP, 136, 289-290, 335-336
    compatibility test, 136-138
posters, greeting cards, newsletters, Print Shop (Broderbund), 244
purchasing, 319
registering, 322
running, 14-18
    two or more, 260-262
scheduling (personal), Calendar Creator Plus (Power Up Software), 244
see also applications; software; utilities

SETUP, 104, 337
shareware, 245
SMARTDRV, 334
spreadsheet, 239-240
    Excel, 240
    Lotus 1-2-3, 240
starting, 257-258
taxes, TurboTax (Chipsoft), 242
to-do lists, Calendar Creator Plus (Power Up Software), 244
UNDELETE, 282
Undelete, 336
UNINSTALL, 321
upgrading, 253, 259-260
VSafe, 144
WIPEOUT (Norton Utilities), 48
word processing, 238
    AmiPro, 239
    Microsoft Word, 239
    WordPerfect, 238
PROMPT command, 56
prompts
    DOS, 12-13
    WIN, 236-237
Prt Scr (Print Screen) key, 225
Publish It! (Timeworks) desktop publishing program, 243
purchasing
    floppy disks, 79-82
    programs, 319

Q-R

quick reference guides, 253
Quicken (Intuit) program, 243

RAM (random-access memory),
  see memory
RD command, 101
Read fault error reading (or
  writing) Drive X message, 289,
  305-306
read-only files, 283, 296
receivers, *see* monitors
Recommendation dialog box, 125
registration cards, 253, 322
removing
    directories
        with DOS 6, 103
        without DOS 6, 101-102
    floppy disks, 82-84, 326
RENAME command, 45, 55-56
renaming files, 55-56
    DOS Shell, 73
repeating commands, 38
repetitive strain injuries (RSI),
  213-214, 321-322
replacing computers,
  troubleshooting, 292-293
reserved memory, *see* upper
  memory
resetting (Ctrl-Alt-Del), 211
resolution, 194
restarting, *see* booting
restoring data files

troubleshooting, 289-291
    with backup disks, 142
RGB monitors, 192
RMDIR command, *see* RD
  command
ROM (read-only memory), 332
root directories, 19, 95, 323
RSI (repetitive strain injuries),
  321-322
running
    programs, 14-18
        DoubleSpace, 118-120
        two or more, 260-262

S

/s switch, 110
    BACKUP command, 134
saving files, 314, 321
scheduling (personal) programs,
  Calendar Creator Plus (Power
  Up Software), 244
screen dumps, 225
screens, 153
    clearing, 30
    DOS prompt, 12-13
    main display, 259
Scroll Lock key, 208
Sector not found error reading (or
  writing) Drive message, 307
sectors of disks, 91
Seek error reading (or writing)
  Drive X message, 307

selected printers, 223
selecting files
    DOS Shell, 64-65
    with keyboards, 64-65
    with mouse, 64
serial ports, 164
serial printers, 217-218
    connecting to computers,
        220-221
SETUP command, 255
SETUP program, 104, 337
shareware programs, 245
size
    floppy disks, 79
    monitors, 195
SMARTDRV program, 334
soft fonts, downloading, 222
software
    documentation, 253
    licenses, 253
    pirated, 327-328
    system, 233
    see also programs
Software Publisher's
    Organization, 327
source disks, 90
spelling, checking, 238
spreadsheet programs, 239-240
    Excel, 240
    Lotus 1-2-3, 240
Stacker utility, 116
starting
    computers, troubleshooting,
        274-275, 279

MS-DOS Shell, 202
    programs, 257-258
storage capacity, floppy disks, 80
storing files, 26, 326
    directories, 94
subdirectories, 16-18, 95
super VGA (SVGA), 332
support files, program, 325
SVGA adapters, 192
switches, 32
    /b, 110
    BACKUP command, 134
        /f, 134
        /m,134-135
        /s, 110
syntax, DOS, 31
Syntax Error message, 307
systems, exiting, 316
system
    files, 264-265, 325
    requirements, 251-252
    software, 233
    units, 155

T

Tab key, 208
tape backup drives, 131
target disks, 90
task swapping, 261-262
taxes, programs, TurboTax
    (Chipsoft), 242
templates, keyboards, 254

testing printers, 223-225
text, editing with EDIT,
   265-269
text files, *see* ASCII files
text mode, 200-202
times and dates, troubleshooting,
   279-281
to-do list programs, Calendar
   Creator Plus (Power Up
   Software), 244
toggle keys, 206-208
Too many parameters messages,
   307
transmitters, *see* video adapters
TREE command, 97-99
troubleshooting
   computers
      freezing, 286-287
      hard disks, formatting, 285
      power outage, 278
      replacing, 292-293
      starting, 274-275, 279
      time and date, 279-281
   disks
      floppy, 285-286
      formatting, 284
      hard, 288-289
   error messages, 275-277
   files, 290-291
      copying, 281-282
      data, restoring, 289-291
      deleting, 283
      missing, 282
   printers, 288

TSRs, 333
TurboTax (Chipsoft) program,
   242
turning off computers, 22-23
turning on computers, 10-12
.TXT file extension, 36
TYPE command, 42-43
type-ahead buffer, 213

U

UMBs (upper memory blocks),
   176, 180-181
Unable to create directory
   message, 308
UNDELETE command, 48-49, 55
UNDELETE program, 282, 336
undeleting files,
undeleting, *see* deleting
unformatting, *see* formatting
UNINSTALL program, 321
upgrading
   memory (RAM), 172
   programs, 253, 259-260
upper memory blocks, *see* UMBs
user-supported programs, 245
utilities
   defragmentation, DEFRAG,
      116, 124-125
   DoubleSpace, 116
   MSBACKUP, 124
   PC Tools, 116

Stacker, 116
VSafe, 147-148
see also programs; software

V

VER command, 30
Verbatim disks, 82
Verify Error dialog box, 145
versions
    DOS, 30, 249-251
    programs, 260
VGA (Video Graphics Array)
  video adapters, 191, 333
video adapters, 188-192, 198,
  251,
    resolution, 194
viewing
    contents of files, 42-43
    directory tree, 97-99
    files, DOS Shell, 65-66
Virus Found dialog box, 145
viruses, 144
    checking for, 145-148
    detecting programs, 335
Viruses Detected and Cleaned
  dialog box, 145
volatile memory, 314
volume labels, 87
VSafe
    dialog box, 148
    utility, 144, 147-148

W

WealthBuilder (Reality Software)
  investment and finance
  program, 244
wild cards, 37, 47-48
    commands, DIR, 38, 108-109
windows, 59
    Directory Tree, 63
    Files List, 63
Windows, *see* Microsoft Windows
WIPEOUT program (Norton
  Utilities), 48
wires, 153
word processing programs, 238
    Ami Pro, 239
    Microsoft Word, 239
    WordPerfect, 238
Word, *see* Microsoft Word
WordPerfect, 238
 Write protect error writing
  Drive X; Abort, Retry, message,
  282, 308
Write-protect error message, 85
write-protected floppy disks,
  84-85

X-Z

X-rays, 197
XMS memory, *see* extended
  memory

Count on Que for the Latest in DOS Information!

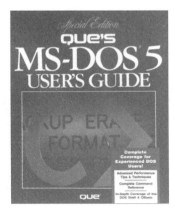

Using MS-DOS 5

Que Development Group
Version 3.X, 4.X, & 5.0

$24.95 USA
0-88022-668-4, 700 pp., 7³/₈ x 9¹/₄

Easy DOS

Shelley O'Hara
Through Version 5

$19.95 USA
0-88022-854-7, 200 pp., 8 x 10

Que's MS-DOS 5 User's Guide, Special Edition

Que Development Group
Versions 3.X, 4.X, & 5.0

$29.95 USA
0-88022-671-4, 1,000 pp., 7³/₈ x 9¹/₄

More DOS Titles from Que

Hands-on MS-DOS 5, Learning by Doing

Que Development Group
Through Version 5

$29.95 USA
0-88022-683-8, 400 pp., 7³/₈ x 9¹/₄

MS-DOS 5 QuickStart

Que Development Group
Version 5

$19.95 USA
0-88022-681-1, 420 pp., 7³/₈ x 9¹/₄

MS-DOS 5 Quick Reference

Que Development Group
Version 5.0

$9.95 USA
0-88022-646-3, 160 pp., 4³/₄ x 8

To Order, Call:(800) 428-5331 OR (317) 573-2500

Teach Yourself
with QuickStarts from Que!

The ideal tutorials for beginners, Que's QuickStart Books use graphic illustrations and step-by-step instructions to get you up and running fast. Packed with examples, QuickStarts are the perfect beginner's guides to your favorite software applications.

MS-DOS 5 QuickStart

Que Development Group

This is the easy-to-use graphic approach to learning MS-DOS 5. The combination of step-by-step instruction, examples, and graphics make this book ideal for all DOS beginners.

DOS 5

$19.95 USA
0-88022-681-1, 420 pp., 7³/₈ x 9¹/₄

Windows 3.1 QuickStart

Ron Person & Karen Rose

This graphics-based text teaches Windows beginners how to use the feature-packed Windows environment. Emphasizes such software applications as Excel, Word, and PageMaker, and shows how to master Windows' mouse, menus, and screen elements.

Through Version 3.1

$21.95 USA
0-88022-730-3, 500 pp., 7³/₈ x 9¹/₄

1-2-3 Release 2.4 QuickStart

Release 2.4

$21.95
0-88022-986-1, 500 pp., 7³/₈ x 9¹/₄

1-2-3 for DOS Release 3.4 QuickStart

Releases 3.4

$21.95 USA
1-56529-007-0, 550 pp., 7³/₈ x 9¹/₄

1-2-3 for Windows QuickStart

1-2-3 for Windows

$19.95 USA
0-88022-723-0, 500 pp., 7³/₈ x 9¹/₄

Excel 4 for Windows QuickStart

Version 4 for Windows

$21.95 USA
0-88022-925-X, 400 pp., 7³/₈ x 9¹/₄

MS-DOS QuickStart, 2nd Edition

Version 3.X & 4.X

$19.95 USA
0-88022-611-0, 420 pp., 7³/₈ x 9¹/₄

Q&A 4 QuickStart

Versions 3 & 4

$19.95 USA
0-88022-653-6, 450 pp., 7³/₈ x 9¹/₄

Quattro Pro 4 QuickStart

Through Version 4.0

$21.95 USA
0-88022-938-1, 450 pp., 7³/₈ x 9¹/₄

Windows 3.1 QuickStart

Version 3.1

$21.95 USA
0-88022-730-3, 440 pp., 7³/₈ x 9¹/₄

WordPerfect 5.1 QuickStart

WordPerfect 5.1

$21.95 USA
0-88022-558-0, 427 pp., 7³/₈ x 9¹/₄

WordPerfect for Windows QuickStart

WordPerfect 5.1 for Windows

$19.95 USA
0-88022-712-5, 400 pp., 7³/₈ x 9¹/₄

Word for Windows 2 QuickStart

Version 2

$21.95 USA
0-88022-920-9, 400 pp., 7³/₈ x 9¹/₄

**To Order, Call:
(800) 428-5331
OR
(317) 573-2500**

Using WordPerfect Is Easy When You're Using Que

Using WordPerfect 5.1, Special Edition

Que Development Group

The classic, #1 best-selling word processing book—only from Que! Includes tear-out command map, icons, margin notes, and cautions.
WordPerfect 5.1

$27.95 USA
0-88022-554-8, 900pp., 7³/₈ x 9¹/₄

WordPerfect 5.1 QuickStart

Que Development Group

A graphics-based, fast-paced introduction to 5.1 essentials! Numerous illustrations demonstrate document production, table design, equation editing, and more.
WordPerfect 5.1

$21.95 USA
0-88022-558-0, 427 pp., 7³/₈ x 9¹/₄,

WordPerfect 5.1 Quick Reference

Que Development Group

Instant reference for the operations of WordPerfect 5.1. Alphabetical listings make information easy to find!
WordPerfect 5.1

$9.95 USA
0-88022-576-9, 160 pp., 4³/₄ x 8

Check Out These Other Great Titles!

Easy WordPerfect

Shelley O'Hara
WordPerfect 5.1

$19.95 USA
0-88022-797-4, 200 pp., 8 x 10

Using WordPerfect 5

Charles O. Stewart III, et. al.
WordPerfect 5

$27.95 USA
0-88022-351-0, 867 pp., 7³/₈ x 9¹/₄

Using WordPerfect 5.2 for Windows, Special Edition

Que Development Group
WordPerfect 5.1 for Windows

$29.95 USA
1-56529-166-2, 850 pp., 7³/₈ x 9¹/₄

WordPerfect Power Pack

Ralph Blodgett
WordPerfect 5.1

$39.95 USA
0-88022-520-3, 593 pp., 7³/₈ x 9¹/₄

Look Your Best with WordPerfect for Windows

George Beinhom
Version 5.1 for Windows

$24.95 USA
0-88022-815-8, 500 pp., 7³/₈ x 9¹/₄

WordPerfect 5.1 Tips, Tricks, and Traps

Charles O. Stewart III, Daniel J. Rosenbaum, & Joel Shore
WordPerfect 5.1

$24.95 USA
0-88022-557-2, 743 pp., 7³/₈ x 9¹/₄

Easy WordPerfect for Windows

Shelly O'Hara
Version 5.1 for Windows

$19.95 USA
0-88022-899-7, 208 pp., 8 x 10

WordPerfect for Windows Quick Reference

Que Development Group
Version 5.1 for Windows

$9.95 USA
0-88022-785-0, 160 pp., 4³/₄ x 8

WordPerfect for Windows Quick Start

Greg Harvey
Version 5.1 for Windows

$19.95 USA
0-88022-712-5, 400 pp., 7³/₈ x 9¹/₄

WordPerfect 5.1 Office Solutions

Ralph Blodgett
Version 5.1

$49.95 USA
0-88022-838-5, 850 pp., 8 x 10

To Order, Call: (800) 428-5331
OR
(317) 573-2500

Learning is Easy with Easy Books from Que!

Que's Easy Series offers a revolutionary concept in computer training. The friendly, 4-color interior, easy format, and simple explanations guarantee success for even the most intimidated computer user!

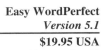

Easy WordPerfect
Version 5.1

$19.95 USA
0-88022-797-4, 200 pp., 8 x 10

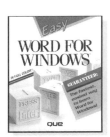

Easy DOS
Through Version 5

$19.95 USA
0-88022-854-7, 200 pp., 8 x 10

Easy 1-2-3, 2nd Edition
Releases 2.4

$19.95 USA
1-56529-022-4, 224 pp., 8 x 10

Easy Macintosh
All Macintosh Computers

$19.95 USA
0-88022-819-9, 200 pp., 8 x 10

Easy Quattro Pro
Version 4

$19.95 USA
0-88022-798-2, 200 pp., 8 x 10

Easy Word for Windows
Versions 1 & 2

$19.95 USA
0-88022-922-5, 224 pp., 8 x 10

Easy Quattro Pro for Windows
Version 5.1 for Windows

$19.95 USA
0-88022-993-4, 224 pp., 8 x 10

Easy Windows
Version 3.1

$19.95 USA
0-88022-985-3, 200 pp., 8 x 10

Easy WordPerfect for Windows
Version 5.1 for Windows

$19.95 USA
0-88022-899-7, 208 pp., 8 x 10

 To Order, Call: (800) 428-5331 OR (317) 573-2500